D1615427

C016018034

# Battle Beneath the Trenches

# Battle Beneath the Trenches

*The Cornish Miners of*
*251 Tunnelling Company RE*

Robert K. Johns

Pen & Sword
**MILITARY**

First published in Great Britain by
**PEN AND SWORD MILITARY**
*an imprint of*
Pen and Sword Books Ltd
47 Church Street
Barnsley
South Yorkshire S70 2AS

ISBN 978 1 47382 700 4

A CIP record for this book is available from the British Library.

Printed and bound in England by
CPI Group (UK) Ltd, Croydon, CR0 4YY

Typeset in Times by CHIC GRAPHICS

*Pen & Sword Books Ltd incorporates the imprints of*
Archaeology, Atlas, Aviation, Battleground, Discovery,
Family History,  History, Maritime, Military, Naval, Politics,
Railways, Select, Social History, Transport, True Crime,
Claymore Press, Frontline Books, Leo Cooper, Praetorian Press,
Remember When, Seaforth Publishing and Wharncliffe.

*For a complete list of Pen and Sword titles please contact*
Pen and Sword Books Limited
47 Church Street, Barnsley, South Yorkshire, S70 2AS, England
E-mail: enquiries@pen-and-sword.co.uk
Website: www.pen-and-sword.co.uk

# Contents

# List of Sketch Maps

(all northerly headings and distances approximate)

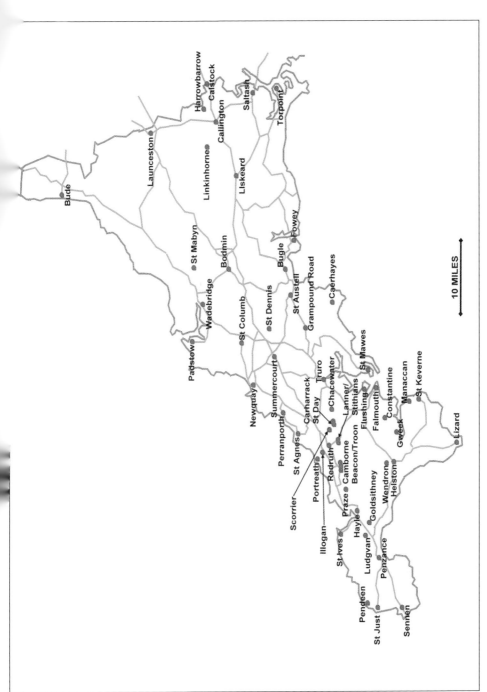

*Map 1: General Map of Cornwall.*

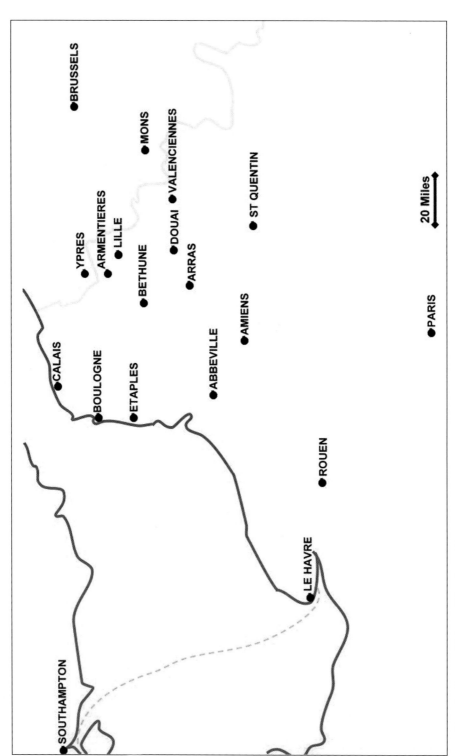

*Map 2: General Map of Northern France.*

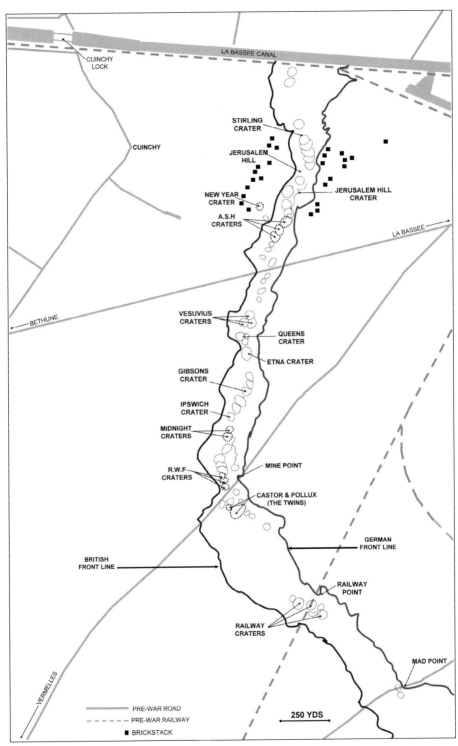

*Map 3: The craters from the Brickstacks to Mad Point.*

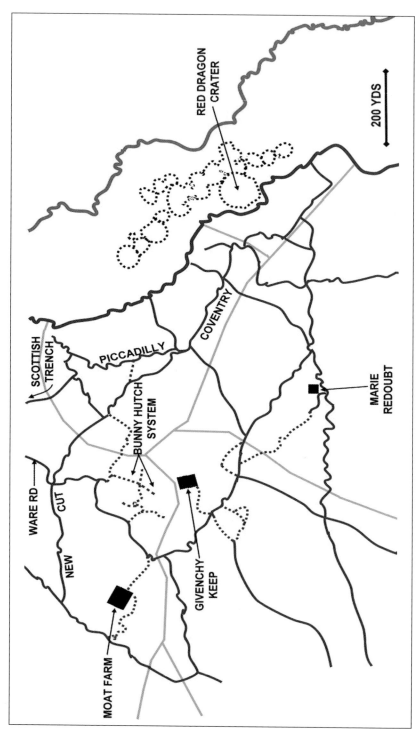

*Map 4: The Bunny Hutch System at Givenchy.*

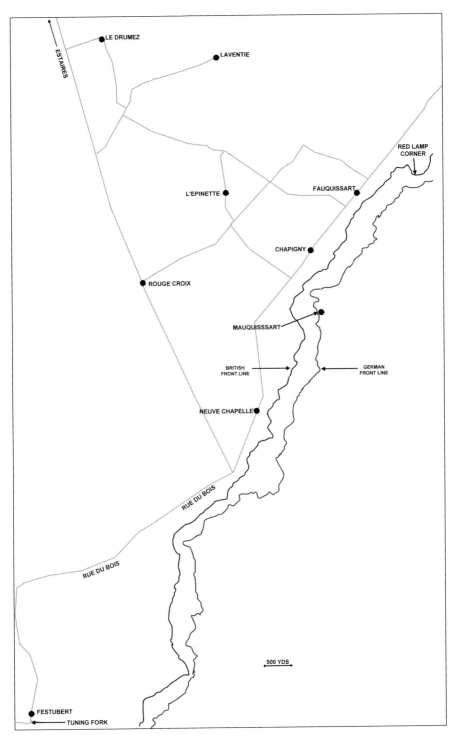

*Map 5: The Red Lamp Sector.*

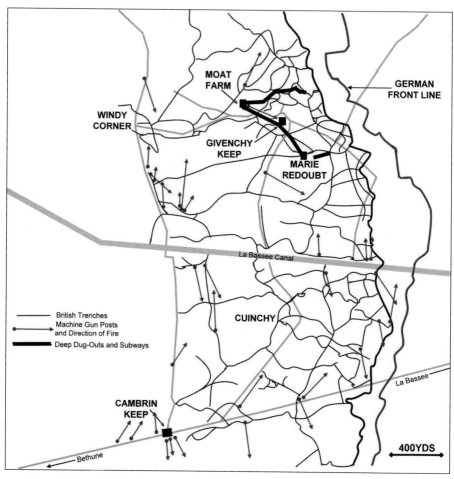

*Map 6: Givenchy Defences 1918: Battle of the Lys.*

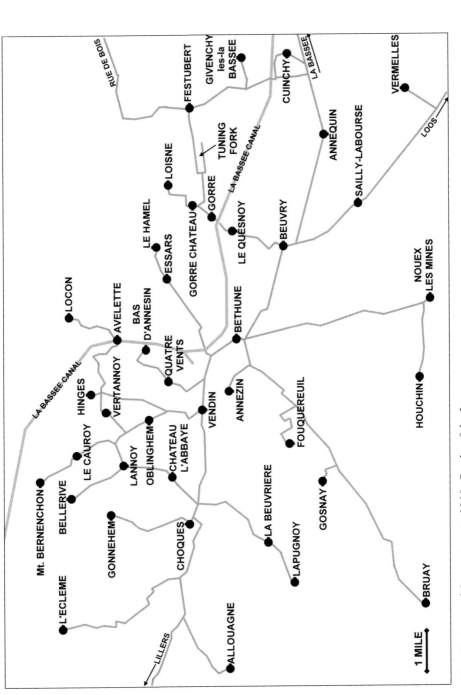

Map 7: *Areas of Operations in 1918: Battle of the Lys.*

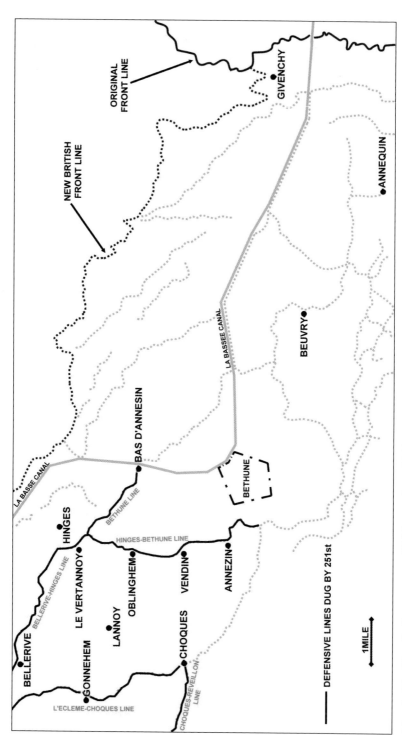

Map 8: *The New Defences around Béthune: June 1918.*

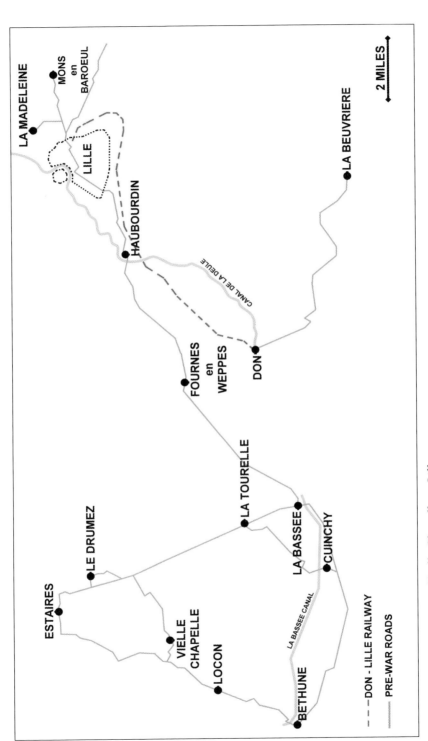

Map 9: *Advance to Victory: Vieille Chapelle to Lille.*

LA MADELEINE

MONS en BAROEUL

LILLE

LA BEUVRIERE

HAUBOURDIN

CANAL DE LA DEULE

FOURNES en WEPPES

DON

LA TOURELLE

LE DRUMEZ

ESTAIRES

VIELLE CHAPELLE

LOCON

LA BASSEE

CUINCHY

LA BASSEE CANAL

BETHUNE

2 MILES

– – – DON - LILLE RAILWAY

———— PRE-WAR ROADS

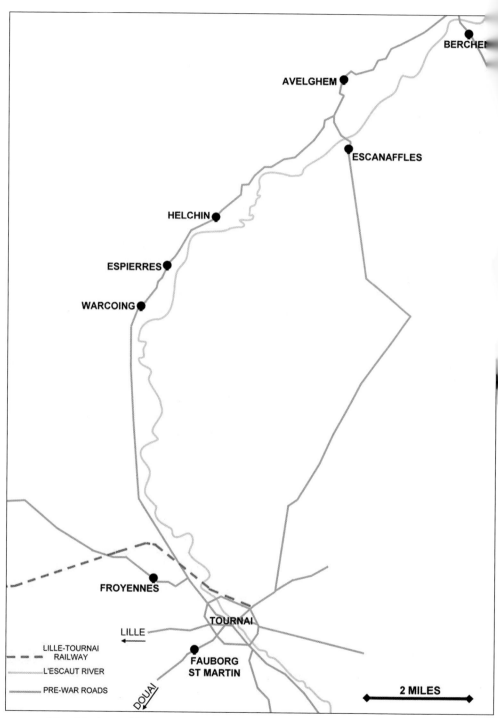

BERCHEM

AVELGHEM

ESCANAFFLES

HELCHIN

ESPIERRES

WARCOING

FROYENNES

TOURNAI

LILLE ←

FAUBORG
ST MARTIN

DOUAI

LILLE-TOURNAI
RAILWAY

L'ESCAUT RIVER

PRE-WAR ROADS

2 MILES

*Map 10: Around Tournai after the Armistice.*

# Acknowledgements

Many people have helped in providing the information required to complete this book, but my first thanks must go to Simon Jones and Peter Barton of the La Boisselle Study Group, following my visit to the archaeological dig and tunnels at the site near Albert. This proved to be a very emotional experience and was certainly one of the stimuli which spurred me on to write this account; my research led me to contact and meet many other people who made undertaking this work a pleasure. Some came from larger organisations, such as Cornwall's Regimental Museum in Bodmin, the original home of the DCLI, or others such as the excellent Memorial Museum Passchendaele at Zonebeke, whilst others were relatives of tunnellers who had served on the Western Front. I would also like to thank all of those who have allowed their pictures to be published. Credit has been given to them on the captions to the individual photographs.

However, most thanks must go to Liz, my wife, who has spent many hours not only in helping me with the research and in deciphering the *War Diary*, but who has also accompanied me on my travels around England and France whilst gathering information.

The writing of a book depends very much on having good advice on continuity and structure, and in this I was fortunate to have the help of Janey Fisher. What started as a few notes about my grandfather's life became a story about Cornishmen, especially those who served in 251 Tunnelling Company. At times it would have been very easy to drift away from the main story and set off on tangents; Janey has been very supportive and has gently refocused my attention when necessary since, as an author herself, she understood the need for me to be free to tell the story in my own way, whilst keeping the narrative on track when I was tempted to digress.

My final thanks must go to my excellent editor, the historian Nigel Cave whose knowledge, advice and clarification of various aspects of the conflict have been invaluable.

Writing this book has been a very enjoyable experience and I am particularly grateful to and proud of my grandfather and his fellow Cornishmen, without whom there would have been no story. To everyone who helped put this book together, I thank you.

Robert K. Johns

# Introduction

Visiting the now green fields of what were once the battlefields of the First World War, one tries to imagine what it must have been like for the soldiers who fought there, but I think it is almost impossible to comprehend just how difficult their existence was. Without question, for those who survived, their experiences must have had a major impact upon their lives and those of their families, and one asks whether there were any who did not arrive home emotionally or physically scarred, or both.

There have been many stories of the magnificent job our infantry did under such arduous circumstances and all due credit must be given to them; but the remarkable work the miners did during the First World War has only recently been recognised and brought to public notice, thanks to the research undertaken by military historians such as Nigel Cave, Simon Jones and Peter Barton, all of whom have written several books on the topic of underground warfare. The imagination of the general public has been fired by Sebastian Faulkes' novel *Birdsong* and the ensuing film, whilst with the centenary of the Great War upon us the television channels have screened documentaries about the tunnellers and their contribution to the winning of the war. The underground skills of those miners, coupled with their ability to undertake any engineering task, from making roads to building bridges, from constructing dugouts to mine clearance and, on more than one occasion, having to stand shoulder to shoulder with the infantry, rifle in hand, demonstrates that the tunnelling companies have to have been amongst the most multiskilled and flexible units of the First World War.

At the unveiling of the War Memorial at the Institution of Mining and Metallurgy in London, on 24 November 1921, Field Marshal Earl Haig had this to say:

> *You have afforded me an opportunity to say a few words of special thanks to a body of men whose work in France seldom drew upon itself much notice or glory at the time, but was*

*surpassed by none in the demands it made upon the skill, the courage and the resolution of the individuals concerned, or in the service it rendered to the Army as a whole.*

*One thinks naturally of the Battle of Messines, and of the mighty series of explosions that tore great gaps in the German line, on the 7th June, 1917, and gave the signal for one of the most successful of our attacks. That was the work of the Special Services to which you sent so many gallant men, and it was indeed a signal triumph of British mining in war. Yet few, I think, outside those who took part in the work and benefited by its results realise the immense amount of steady, persistent toil in every circumstance of peril, surrounded by danger in a form that might well appal the stoutest-hearted, that went to the preparation of that triumph. Few, I know, realise how vast, how important to the safety, comfort, and success of our troops was the work of our miners, work that was little commented upon in the Press, but yet went on steadily and continuously, day after day, and year after year, along the whole of the British Front. Every offensive undertaken by us, right up to the days of the last great series of advances, meant a fresh call upon the energy, the industry, and the courage of those Special Services upon whom the due preparation of these offensives so largely depended.*

*Tunnelled approaches had to be constructed from great distances, dugouts built for headquarters, dressing stations and shelters generally. Every big offensive made demand of that kind....*

*Then later, when the day of the elaborately mounted attack was over, the tunnelling companies found new work, hardly less arduous or dangerous, in the discovery and the removal of many thousands of German mines....*

*I am glad to thank, not for myself only, but on behalf of the whole Army, this gallant body of men.*

As a Cornishman who can trace his ancestry back to 1724, it is only in recent years that I realised that my grandfather had been one of those tunnellers, and it was whilst researching his life that I found some interesting links to his fellow Cornishmen who had also served in tunnelling companies on the Western Front. There were twenty five such tunnelling companies in the British Army, but the majority of these

Cornishmen joined 251 Tunnelling Company, Royal Engineers, as did my grandfather. I had never before heard of 251 Tunnelling Company or the magnificent work that they performed during the Great War, and it is this previously untold story upon which the book is focused. The Company was formed in Cornwall in 1915 with 221 Cornishmen as its core.

My insights into my grandfather's life brought a personal and individual element to this story – it was varied and interesting but at the same time, typical of a generation in Cornwall who started work in the mines at the age of twelve, were underground by fifteen, and who were to find themselves with no work or economic opportunities at the end of the First World War.

My research has been based in the main on information from primary sources; on the occasions where secondary sources have been used the accuracy of the source has been ascertained as far as possible. Part of the information in the book, the key detail, comes directly from the *War Diary* of 251 Tunnelling Company; unless they add interesting or sometimes quirky details about the life of the Company, day to day routine matters have not generally been included.

*In Memory of John Albert James Johns (1895–1962)*
*('Pop')*

*Chapter 1*

# Cornwall: Land of Tin

The idea for this book was born when, sorting through a collection of family papers, I happened to stumble across my grandfather's old 'box' which held the normal plethora of bits and pieces that get passed down through families. Amongst the usual old photographs were his war medals and another object which caught my eye: a silver cigarette case engraved with the Royal Engineers' crest and the words:

> *185ᵗʰ (Tunn) Coy R.E.*
> *France*
> *1915-16-17-18*
>
> *25 Dec 1918*

Despite on many occasions as a child asking my grandfather, or 'Pop' as he was called, to tell me some war stories, he would never talk about his experiences in the First World War, carefully changing the subject to something else that he knew would attract and hold my interest. I only discovered after he died in 1962 that he had never discussed the war with my grandmother, or indeed even with my father who volunteered for the Royal Artillery (RA) at the start of the Second World War.

With a growing curiosity, therefore, and with the modern advantage of the resources of the World Wide Web, I started researching 185 Tunnelling Company to try to establish just what the significance of the cigarette case was and how it had come into the family.

*The silver cigarette case that started it all.*

*Dolcoath, Camborne was the deepest mine in Cornwall, with its principal shaft, known as New Sump Shaft, eventually reaching a depth of 3,300 feet below the surface. It opened around 1738, but mining had taken place in Cornwall since 1800BC.*

This led to me buying a copy of Captain HW Graham's book *The Life of a Tunnelling Company*, which documents his time with the 185th. I subsequently discovered that cigarette cases and tobacco boxes had been purchased with surplus accumulated canteen funds to provide a suitable memento at the end of the war for all officers and men of the Company. Having read this, I was now filled with an even greater desire to establish just how this very well used and seemingly cherished cigarette case had come into my grandfather's possession. Had he been in the 185th? Was he a tunneller? Descended from a long line of miners, before the war he had worked as an underground miner at Dolcoath Mine in Camborne, at over 3,000 feet the deepest tin and the largest copper mine in Cornwall, and for many years the deepest mine in the world. That much I knew; but how did he get from there to the Western Front, as he would have been just nineteen years old when war was declared?

As luck would have it, it was about this time that I found out about an archaeological dig taking place at La Boisselle, in France, a village that had been on the front line of the July 1916 Somme offensive. I knew from Captain Graham's book that 185 Tunnelling Company operated in this location for part of the war, so I took up the invitation to meet Simon Jones on site and also had the pleasure of meeting Peter Barton, another keen supporter and member of the La Boisselle Study Group.

La Boisselle is a village near Albert in France and was a notorious sector for mining operations on the Western Front, with tunnels being dug at depths of over one hundred feet, whilst above ground the infantry occupied trenches some forty five yards apart from those of the enemy. The land above one part of this mining system was called the Glory Hole and this land had remained largely untouched since the end of the war. Permission was granted for the group to conduct an archaeological dig exploring both the mines and the farmstead that once stood on the site. At the time of our visit, some tunnels had been discovered and again, as luck would have it, a shaft connecting the upper gallery to the lower levels had only just been found a few days before our arrival. Whilst I was later to find my grandfather had not worked at this particular site, to enter tunnels similar to those he had worked in, together with the sight of items such as helmets and petrol cans discarded where they lay and left untouched and unseen for so many years was just amazing. As we moved deeper into the tunnels to view the shaft itself, to see the scorch marks left on the chalk face by candles, and to see the graffiti scribbled in pencil on the chalk by some long dead tunneller, all of which had lain

*The Graffiti written on the chalk face almost 100 years ago in the tunnels at La Boisselle.* (Picture Courtesy of La Boisselle Study Group)

BRITISH
FRONT LINE

G[
FR[

*An approximation of the front lines on 1 July 1916. The left line is British, and the right German. La Boisselle is in the top centre of the picture, where the two lines are so close. The large crater is Lochnagar and as can be seen was where trenches once lay. (Aerial Photograph courtesy of the La Boisselle support group)*

*Adjacent to the Glory Hole is the Lochnagar Crater, blown by the British at the start of the offensive of 1 July 1916. At three hundred feet across and seventy feet deep, it was the largest man made crater blown in the First World War. The people standing on the ridge in the background gives an idea of the magnitude of this crater.*

undisturbed for nearly a hundred years, was a very moving and sobering experience.

On my return to Cornwall, my enthusiasm gained momentum daily and, thanks to some great help from Simon, I returned to my research and discovered that not only had my grandfather indeed been a tunneller but that John Albert James Johns, to give him his full name, curiously had two army numbers recorded in the National Archives Medal Rolls Index; one for service as a private (21045) with the Duke of Cornwall's Light Infantry (DCLI) and another for service as a sapper (132290) in the Royal Engineers (RE).

Pop actually started his war by volunteering on 24 April 1915, along with many other Cornishmen, not for the Royal Engineers, but for the 10th (Service) Battalion DCLI (Cornwall Pioneers) which was formed in Truro by the Acting Mayor, Isaac Roskelley, on 12 April 1915, with Brevet Colonel Dudley Mills as the Commanding Officer and the famous Cornish novelist and poet Sir Arthur Quiller Couch (known as Q)

*'Pop' in 1915.*

as his second in command. It was reported in the *Western Times* on 30 March 1915 that Sir Arthur informed a meeting of the Cornwall recruiting committee at Liskeard that he had been asked by the War Office to raise two companies of Pioneers in Cornwall.

It was further reported in *The Cornishman* on 15 April 1915:

> *that the duties of a Pioneer Company are (1) to serve as infantry when required, and (2) to be especially efficient with:*
>
> *(a) Pick and shovel; for entrenching, road making and repairing, embanking, demolition of enemy works etc.*
> *(b) Cutting tools; wood clearing, felling and shaping of timber for bridges etc.*
> *(c) The moving of heavy material, blasting, the construction of obstacles, wire entanglements etc.*

*The cap badge of the DCLI and crossed pick and rifle collar badge of the Pioneer Battalion. The collar badges were removed if the Battalion was serving as infantry. (Picture Courtesy of Cornwall's Regimental Museum, Bodmin)*

By 24 June 1915, 'A' Company of 10th DCLI was complete after Pop, along with 220 others, had been recruited by Major FD Bain at the Drill Hall, Redruth, to become part of that Battalion. In the main, 'A' Company was formed from recruits from the west of Truro (mainly miners) and 'B' Company from recruits to the east of Truro (see Map 1). They were eventually billeted in their training camps, at Falmouth and Penzance, at times venturing out of the County into the South Hams district of Devon for field training.

What made my grandfather decide to join up will now never be known, but he was probably influenced by the wave of patriotism calling for every man to do 'his bit for his country', possibly coupled with a young man's desire for adventure. The outpouring of enthusiasm which swept the country on the declaration of war actually encouraged some young men to lie about their age just to join in. During research into the records of the men who eventually went to 251 Tunnelling Company, two recruits stood out for this very reason.

One young man, Sapper Richard John Rolling, signed his attestation papers at sixteen years of age, stating that he was nineteen years and

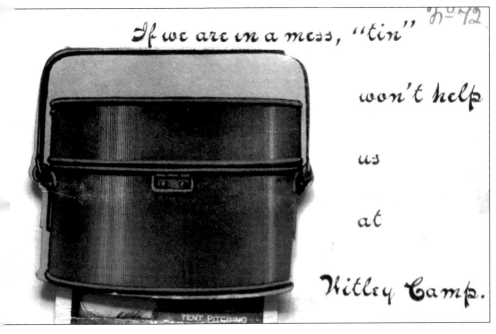

*If we are in a mess, "tin" won't help us at Kitley Camp.*

*As this postcard is numbered and has a play on words on 'tin', it was no doubt done especially for the 10th DCLI. The mess tin lifts to show the picture below.*

*Kitley Camp near Yealmpton in Devon, close to the famous Kitley Caves. The camp would have been in the 600 acres of grounds of the house, which is now a luxury hotel.*

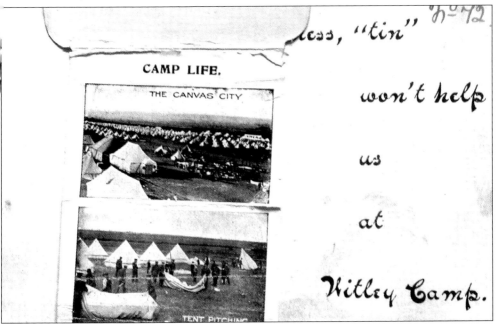

*...ess, "tin" won't help us at Kitley Camp.*

four months in April 1915. He was killed in March the following year in France, not even having reached his eighteenth birthday. In another instance, Sapper Edward Uren was only seventeen when he was sent to France. An appeal made by his mother for his return was rejected since his declared age at attestation was deemed to be of greater significance than that clearly stated on his birth certificate. Eventually the War Office did review this policy and changes were made, with instructions issued that any soldier under seventeen should be discharged and any aged between seventeen and nineteen should be placed in the reserve; unfortunately the changes were made too late to set Sapper Uren's mother's mind at rest - but he survived the war, serving with 251 Tunnelling Company for the duration.

Pop was born in Praze-an-Beeble, near Camborne, on 1 March 1895, the third of five surviving children of a family with a long tradition of mining in its heritage. The Fisher Act of 1918 raised the school leaving

*Three generations of miners from left to right: John Albert James Johns 1895–1962, James Johns (seated) 1838–1925 and James Henry Johns 1860–1925.*

*Looking across from Dolcoath Mine towards Redruth circa 1875. The hill on the right is Carn Brea where there is a monument to the Bassets, one of the major tin mine owners. The mine in the middle distance is South Crofty, which was the last mine to close in 1998, but which may be reopening in the next few years, owing to higher copper prices.*

age to fourteen, but this was too late for my grandfather who, at twelve, an age when a child of today would just be settling into secondary education, probably had no other option than to choose the route which meant that he would join his grandfather, father, brother and future father-in-law in the mines. Certainly, in the 1911 census, aged sixteen, he was recorded as a miner.

Parts of Cornwall, particularly in the mining areas, which are concentrated mainly to the west of the county, did not in those days have the idyllic landscapes associated with Cornwall that we all recognise and enjoy today. They were much harsher as a result of the countryside being torn and ripped apart by the constant drive to get yet more minerals out of the ground; environmental considerations played no part in the quest for copper, tin and arsenic in those days, as the photograph of the area around Dolcoath Mine clearly shows.

Families in Cornwall were relatively small compared to those in many other parts of the country; often only three or four children survived to adulthood. Houses were generally small two up and two down terraces of Cornish granite. They had no electricity or gas, even though only three miles away in Redruth, another strong mining area,

William Murdoch's house was the first in England to be lit with gas as early as 1792. Cooking facilities would have been provided by a small Cornish oven in a corner of the kitchen; washing was done in a lean-to in the rear yard.

There was the traditional outside lavatory, of course, but probably only an earth closet, as mains sewage systems did not exist at that time and indeed only reached some parts of the mining areas of Cornwall, such as Gwennap and St Just, as late as the mid 1960s. Life generally for the miner and his family was very hard. Overcrowding in damp houses with poor sanitation and poor diet, exacerbated by low wages, led to widespread disease; typhus, typhoid, measles, smallpox and diphtheria were all prevalent and all of them were often deadly to the young and the weak.

It was equally tough in terms of working conditions and wages; in earlier times the latter was often paid in the mining company's own currency (or 'chips'), which could only be used in the mine shops, often at inflated prices. This very unfair system was made technically illegal by the 1831 Truck Act and then enforced by the 1887 amendment to it, although the Cornish mines were slow to implement this particular law. The 'Cornish Penny', as shown on page 11, is an example of the chip that would have been issued at the mine where my grandfather worked.

*Praze-an-Beeble from the village green today.*

The working day was long, and conditions were wet, claustrophobic and dangerous; such an appalling working environment generated a degree of comradeship between the miners and a mutual support that was probably not so evident in other occupations. They looked out for their own when underground, and the miners' families would look after their own above, often taking in lodgers to give shelter to fellow miners whilst in addition, of course, generating a little extra income. If a miner was killed or maimed, his family would be looked after by his fellows, if necessary even taking the children in as part of their own family should there be no one else to look after them. Many unofficial 'adoptions' took place in this way.

*The 'Cornish Penny'. This replica is made of tin from the South Crofty Mine, near Camborne.*

Each eight hour shift was frequently preceded by a long walk to the mine, a climb down hundreds of yards of ladders and then as much as a two mile walk to the face. Then, with the shift finished, the journey was done in reverse to get home. The miners' diet was primarily potato, this being wrapped with a pastry crust to form the famous Cornish Pasty, which could be taken down the mine for crib as it was easily carried and would be reasonably sustaining; crib is a Cornish expression for meals taken during break times at work.

The Cornish tin miners' reputation was considerable and they were especially valued for their remarkable stamina and productivity. Mine owners, particularly overseas ones, were always looking for Cornish miners and in the goldfields of Australia a Cornish miner could be paid £3 per week against the £2 paid to other miners.

In an interview with a *Cornish Post* reporter on 24 August 1939, Major Guy Taylor, a well known and respected mining engineer who served with 172 Tunnelling Company, said that,

*In every mining camp he had visited in most parts of the World, Cornishmen were looked on as the miners who taught others how to mine properly... Cornishmen had the characteristic very markedly of hanging together when they got abroad and wherever they were to be found in any numbers, they had formed Cornish societies, under which they got together every week for 'sing songs', smoking concerts etc.*

*Miner working underground at level 234 fathom, which is 1,404 feet. The mine is at Cooks Kitchen, which was part of South Crofty Mine. The lighting was for the benefit of the camera; his usual illumination would have been a candle affixed either to his hat or the wall beside the face. (Photo courtesy of Royal Cornwall Museum, Truro)*

Smoking concerts were live musical performances for an audience of men only, usually held in hotels, where the men would smoke and talk politics while listening to music!

Despite the hardships of their job and the privations of their lives, the men retained their sense of comradeship, solidarity and community, keeping up a cheerful outlook, singing together not just on the way to and at work, but also at the Methodist Chapel on a Sunday and, of course, many also sang with the numerous male voice choirs for which Cornwall is famous.

The County's reputation for mining was confirmed with the opening of the Camborne School of Mines in 1888. Funded by the Bassett family, and based on an idea first proposed by Sir Charles Lemon fifty years earlier, the CSM, as it very quickly became known, rapidly built an international reputation for the quality of its teaching. It still exists today as a part of the University of Exeter. Many of the officers in the tunnelling companies who had been mining engineers before the war, studied at this school.

Such was the importance of the tin and copper mines of Cornwall that a whole raft of related industries grew around them. Hayle, a small town on the north coast to the west of Camborne, became synonymous with mining, having two major employers in the town. Harvey and Co, who at their Carnsew Foundry employed 1,200 people, became the world's largest supplier of beam engines and other mining equipment that was sold all over the world in the mining areas of countries such as Australia, South Africa and the Americas. In the early 1800s the adoption of gunpowder for rock breaking was a huge technical advance in tin mining and by 1836 thirty tons a year was being used in Cornish mines. In 1867 dynamite was patented by Alfred Nobel and both of these explosives were being imported at great cost. In 1888 the National Explosives Company built a factory in the sand dunes three miles north of Hayle, where both dynamite and nitro-glycerine were manufactured. The company employed over 1,800 people and during the war supplied the majority of the explosives to the armament manufacturers in Britain.

Drilling and blasting into granite was an everyday event for Cornish miners, so they were already experienced in the use of explosives. This was traditionally a perilous process, but one made much safer when William Bickford, inventor of the safety fuse, moved from his native Devon and set up his factory just outside Camborne. Bickford's made a range of fuses and their No. 8 fuse was the standard detonator used by the Royal Engineers in the course of military mining in the First World War. In Camborne, Holmans manufactured mining equipment and was the world's largest supplier of rock drills; for example, in 1900 over 2,000 of these drills were in use on the South African Rand alone. Holmans employed 3,000 people across three factories in the town and other mining equipment produced by them included compressors and pumps. These pumps were supplied to and used by the tunnelling companies during the war.

There is a strong sense of its Celtic heritage within Cornwall, but the Cornish are also a very patriotic people, and were ardent Royalists, going right back to the English Civil War, Pendennis Castle in Falmouth being the last Royalist stronghold in England to fall. When war was declared, although slow to enlist for the first six months, miners soon rushed to join up; one gold miner, Lance Corporal Treloar, travelled from Brazil to enlist and returned when he was discharged, on a travel warrant issued by the Royal Engineers.

> *As the war continues, and apparently is no nearer a close now than at the start, Cornishmen who had figured that the war would not last over three months are sitting up and taking notice, and each week a good many are packing up and buying their own tickets to England with the intention of helping the old country out...canvass a steamer on its way to England, and you will find that every Cornishman homeward bound has money and has left a good position. He is simply going because he figures he is needed.*
> (The Cornishman *11 November 1915)*

Dolcoath Mine alone lost 230 men to the recruitment drive in just twelve months, 193 of these being underground workers. Even though the loss of the men had a significant impact on production, the mine owners still welcomed the recruiting officers into the mines. Eventually the government ordered a suspension of the recruitment of miners from any mines in Cornwall that produced Wolfram; this material was urgently required by the munitions companies as it was used to strengthen the steel in artillery shells.

It is often assumed that Cornish miners were large, stocky men but frequently this was not the case; granddad was of a similar build to many of his fellow workers in being 5ft 6in tall, having no more than a 34-inch chest and weighing around 10 stones in weight. Short of stature they might have been, but it may be said that the Cornish miners were well prepared physically and mentally for some of the harsh conditions they were to encounter in France: dust and fumes from blasting, wet and cramped working conditions, disease, death and injury, were all common occurrences for them, to be endured and made the best of.

# Chapter 2

# Preparations for Mine Warfare: 1914

I shall return to the Cornish and my grandfather later, but in order to fully understand why the tunnelling companies were formed it is necessary to go back to the start of the war in 1914.

The war made the careers of a number of men; amongst them was the extraordinary John Norton-Griffiths, the 'father' of British tunnelling operations in the Great War. He was born in Somerset; despite his parents best efforts, he had no time for book-learning and, following a chequered pattern of schooling, went to work as a trainee draughtsman at Wetherby & Jones in London. He soon tired of this, and on impulse went to Knightsbridge Barracks where, after lying about his age, he became a trooper in the Royal Horse Guards. Within twelve months, although still only seventeen, he conceived a desire to go to South Africa with an old friend, Percy Kimber, and persuaded Percy's father, Sir Henry Kimber, MP for Wandsworth, to buy him out of the army. He initially worked on the land for the Natal Land & Colonisation Company, a business owned by Sir Henry. However, that did not last long either and he was soon working in the mines of Johannesburg, first as a miner but quickly becoming a mine manager. At the outbreak of the Boer War he became Captain and Adjutant to the bodyguard of the Commander in Chief of the British Forces in South Africa, Field Marshal Lord Roberts of Kandahar and Waterford; it was here he met Kitchener and the two became friends.

After the war he returned to mining and engineering, setting up his own company, Griffiths & Co, undertaking projects such as the building of 125 miles of the Benguela Railway in Angola and obtaining several tunnelling contracts. As Alexander Barrie says in his book *The*

*Sir John Norton-Griffiths. (Photograph courtesy of Pen & Sword)*

*Tunnellers of the Great War,* he was a man who *had unshakeable faith in his own ability as a man manager. He judged men quickly – often instantly - and seldom changed his opinions later on.* No doubt it was this skill, together with his charm and persuasion, that won him many contracts both at home and overseas.

He was not only a very successful businessman, but was also elected MP for Wednesbury, Staffordshire, in 1910; a self-made man with little formal education, who was a forthright and principled politician, but at times could be somewhat unpredictable having, for example, been arrested for striking a heckler at one of his political rallies. He was given the rank of major at the beginning of the war, was awarded the Distinguished Service Order in 1916 and promoted to lieutenant colonel in 1918, having temporarily held the rank in 1916. He also received the Russian Order of St. Vladimir in 1917, the Order Star of Rumania in 1918 and the Legion d'Honneur in 1919.

At the end of the war he founded the Comrades of the Great War Association, which later joined with other organisations to form the British Legion (Royal British Legion from 1971). He was made a baronet in 1922.

It is generally accepted that this country was not in a ready state to fight a land war, but most of those in power at the time did not recognise this. The regular army was only 247,500 strong, with about half being posted overseas throughout the Empire, and in addition some 733,000 in various types of reserves; this against Germany's 4,000,000. Lord Kitchener, the very popular soldier with a first-class military career, built upon a formal military education and coming from a family with a military background, was appointed as the new Secretary of State for War. He foresaw that it was going to be a long war which would need many more soldiers, even when taking into account the French Army of around 2,900,000.

On 28 July 1914, the First World War effectively commenced with Austro-Hungary declaring war on Serbia. Britain declared war on Germany some seven days later on 4 August 1914 when the Germans refused to accept Belgium's neutrality. The Liberal Government, led by Herbert Asquith, hoped it would be no more than a short 'bloody nose' for Germany and all be over by Christmas. Even after the declaration of war some of the Cabinet entertained the hope that Britain could avoid sending soldiers to fight. Lord Kitchener did not agree and when appointed Secretary of State for War immediately predicted that Britain was in for a three year struggle, noting: *I am put here to conduct a great war and I have no army.*

Lord Kitchener suggested that the Government introduce conscription, but Asquith rejected this on political grounds, leaving Kitchener with no alternative but to increase military numbers by means of volunteers; hence the use of the famous 'Your Country Needs You' advertisement featuring the face of Lord Kitchener, which first appeared on the front cover of the *London Opinion* of 5 September 1914, to recruit men for the New Army (Kitchener's Army).

His recruiting campaign saw 750,000 men enlisted by the end of September 1914, followed by a generally steady stream of 125,000 per month until the following June, when numbers started dropping. By mid 1916 the coalition government, which succeeded Asquith's Liberal government, had to concede that conscription was necessary, a policy which remained in place until mid-1919. Eventually 8,905,000 men would be enlisted from the British Empire, proving Kitchener right in his initial predictions of a long war that would make enormous demands on the Empire's resources, not least in the need for fighting men.

Norton-Griffiths was equally convinced of the need for recruitment to the extent of paying for his own advertisement in the *Pall Mall Gazette* on 31 July 1914, four days before Britain declared war on Germany, asking for volunteers from amongst those who had served in South Africa.

> *MP's INVITATION TO OLD FIGHTERS*
> *With a view to working in unity if duty calls, all*
> *Africans, Australians, Canadians or other Britishers who*
> *served in either the Matabeleland, Mashonaland or*
> *South African War and are not connected with any*
> *existing military or naval organisation and would be*
> *desirous of serving their Empire again are requested to*
> *forward their names and addresses with particulars of*
> *service to Mr John Norton Griffiths, MP, at 3, Central*
> *Buildings, Westminster.*

Lord Kitchener was against the idea of private armies, but such was Griffiths' success that he got agreement to form, at his own expense, the 2nd King Edward's Horse, which he did on 24 August 1914. This was an interesting choice as the 1st King Edward's was a unique regiment itself, formed originally as the King's Colonials during the Boer War, recruiting men who were from the Dominions resident in Britain. Norton-Griffiths served as a major and second in command, which was seen at the time as a largely honorary position.

*As the battlefields became quagmires, the trenches filled with water. (Picture by permission of the National Library of Scotland)*

Because of Kitchener's recruitment policy, the 100,000 soldiers sent to France in mid-August rapidly became a million by Christmas 1914. After fierce fighting on the Aisne and the Marne, and after the First Battle of Ypres, the German advance was halted. The arrival of winter and the associated appalling weather turned much of the front into a quagmire. The war on the Belgian and French fronts became a static one of trench warfare such as had last been seen in Europe at the Crimea; the British and German front line trenches were often only a hundred yards apart, and sometimes the distance was as little as thirty yards.

In such circumstances, the old military tactic of mining – that is, tunnelling under enemy fortifications and setting off explosives – became both a defensive and an offensive weapon; the Germans were generally ahead of the Allies in this aspect of war.

> *In places we were only 30-50m apart so that you are never quite sure when you might fly into the air. However, we lie 4-6m under the ground in great caves dressed up with wood and plank floor and railway sleepers for the ceiling, sometimes in two layers and everything is well protected.*
> *(Kriegsfreiwilliger* [volunteer] *Karl Losch, 199th Reserve Infantry Regiment, 3 April 1915)*

Lieutenant General Sir Henry Rawlinson, GOC IV Corps had, as early as 3 December 1914, made a request for a special battalion of sappers and miners to undertake mine work in response to German mining activity. Norton-Griffiths also saw the need for the army to counter further mining attacks by the Germans and wrote to the War Office suggesting the use of specialist tunnellers and engineers. He knew from his own experience that 'clay kickers', as they were known, many of whom worked for Griffiths & Co digging sewers in Manchester and Liverpool, would have no problem tunnelling in such conditions as prevailed on the northern flanks of the Western Front. His suggestion was initially disregarded by Sir John French, Commander-in-Chief of the British Expeditionary Force, who felt that the Royal Engineers could solve the problem. They, however, did not have the skilled, experienced and extensive labour force that such mining would require. Furthermore, much of their equipment, training methods and rule books dated back to the Crimean War.

Whilst this debate was taking place, Germany blew the first ten mines against the British on 20 December 1914 at Festubert, close to the Franco–Belgian border, where a number of Indian soldiers from 9th

(Sirhind) Brigade of the 3rd Lahore Division, were killed. According to the report from the German VII Corps, as a result of the attack which followed the detonations, the Germans captured nineteen officers and 815 men. They had blown just 750 pounds of explosive, a small amount compared to what was often used later in the war.

On 25 January 1915, more mines were fired under the British trenches two miles south of where the attack at Festubert occurred and, ironically, close to where 251 Tunnelling Company would be based. Fortunately, in this instance, a German deserter reported that the trenches had been mined and so no losses were incurred in the explosions, but the enemy still made inroads as far as the keep at Givenchy-lès-la-Bassée. Without some hard fighting by a Guards brigade, the sector and Béthune behind it could have been lost. Béthune was a key area as it was the location of the French northern coalfields, which provided more than 70% of the coal used by the French munitions factories; this would not be the last time that this sector came under sustained attack. On 3 February 1915 more mines were blown by the Germans, this time at St. Eloi, at the base of the Ypres salient, an area defended by the men of the 3rd East Yorkshires.

It is important to appreciate that mines were not just very powerful and destructive weapons, but that they also had a demoralising psychological effect. Infantrymen had a belief that they had an equal if not better than equal chance against an enemy that they could see; however, when the threat was an unseen one, possibly directly beneath where he was standing, the soldier was, not surprisingly, far more nervous. By now, strongly worded demands were coming from divisional commanders for mining support to put an end to the domination currently enjoyed by the Germans. Norton-Griffiths was summoned by Lord Kitchener who demanded that 10,000 clay kickers and miners, or 'moles' as they were known, be recruited. Although this was an impossible demand, it did give Norton-Griffiths the authority he required to recruit miners from anywhere in the country.

At the time, Griffiths Engineering Ltd had a tunnelling contract in Manchester, which Norton-Griffiths surrendered, so making his workers redundant. He immediately re-employed them to work on the Western Front, offering them six shillings a day – a very large amount, considering that an infantry soldier's basic pay was a shilling a day and even a Company Quarter Master Sergeant was on only four shillings and nine pence per day. While this monetary incentive was certainly an excellent way of motivating skilled miners to volunteer for work on the Western Front, it was to become an issue for the War Office that repeatedly raised its head for the duration of the war. Changes were made so that sappers initially went onto a 'tunnellers mate' rate of two shillings and two pence per day, the decision to bring them up to six shillings a day being made in the field by the Officer Commanding.

However there were still problems; in 1915 twelve miners from the 8th Wales Borderers were due to be transferred to the Royal Engineers as sappers on the tunnellers mate rate of pay. The men would not agree to sign the transfer, refusing to be constrained by Army Regulations. Prior to the war these men had fought long and hard for their rights for better pay in the pits at home and saw the six shillings a day rate as their right.

The need for miners was so great that Norton-Griffiths changed his mind in this instance and agreed to the higher rate. At this stage the Miners' Federation, which had been formed in 1888, became involved and an agreement was reached with the War Office whereby four sevenths (57%) of miners would be classified as skilled tunnellers and would be entitled to the higher rate and, once on that rate, would remain so unless the man himself opted out; few did. My grandfather, like many of those drafted into the tunnelling companies, was re-assessed in the field for this rate of pay, and within two months of arriving in France was on the six shillings a day rate. His certificate is still on his records and says:

*Qualification Certificate for the higher rate of Engineers pay*

*I certify that No 132290 Spr. Johns of 251st Coy R.E. has been tested by (tear in paper) and found to have attained a standard of proficiency in Tunnelling to entitle him to be remustered as a tunneller.*
*Date: 1-XII-1915*
*Consolidated Rate 6/- per diem*

*F Bullen*
*Captain RE*
*O/C 251st Coy RE*

Initially, Norton-Griffiths obtained agreement to form eight units, each having 227 men organised into four sections in the charge of six officers,

*Delegates from the Miners Federation after visiting the front line during the First World War. They were there as part of a consultation exercise with the General Staff. Although this could have been to do with the construction of trenches and dugouts, it is likely that the miners' pay was also discussed. (Picture by permission of the National Library of Scotland)*

although some companies had as many as 269 men. Attached to each company there was often an equivalent, or greater, number of infantrymen who were used to assist the 'moles', usually by carrying materials into, and removing spoil from, the tunnels. By the end of the war there would be twenty five such Tunnelling Companies as well as one New Zealand, three Canadian, three Australian, and one other, the Australian Electrical and Mechanical Mining and Boring Company. The latter, generally designated as the A.E. & M.M. & B. Co., was more affectionately known as the Alphabetical Company. It became a specialised company supporting all of the Armies in the provision and management of pumping systems and electrical generators.

As the number of tunnelling companies increased, so did the length of the sectors covered. Not one to do things by halves, on his frequent journeys to visit the tunnelling companies Norton-Griffiths travelled in the comfort of his personal Rolls Royce, which had been purchased from his wife by the War Office for the sum of £750 and delivered to France as part of the agreement.

The first unit formed, 170 Tunnelling Company, received no military training whatsoever, embarking for France in February 1915. They were immediately sent to Givenchy and were tunnelling within three days of their arrival. This lack of military training gave commanding officers a degree of concern as they were very worried that lack of military discipline might lead to mob rule taking over. Certainly there were some incidents, particularly over the six shillings a day that was promised but not paid to all; some who expected to be paid the full rate were categorised as 'tunnellers mates' and received the lower rate. Even so, in the main, the miners settled down very quickly, working their twenty four hourly two-shift system, with four days on and four days off.

They worked quickly and, on 17 April 1915, the first British mines were blown at Hill 60 (near Ypres), killing around 150 German soldiers with a further twenty taken prisoner; seven British casualties were reported. The turnaround had started but Norton-Griffiths needed more specialist tunnelling companies before the British could begin to change the course of the war underground and put an end to the enemy's dominance in this branch of warfare.

*Norton-Griffith's Rolls-Royce which, on his departure from the Front, he left in France for the use of Brigadier General Harvey. (Picture Courtesy of Pen & Sword)*

*Chapter 3*

# The Formation of
# 251 Tunnelling Company

As the use of underground warfare against the Germans grew, so did the need for experienced tunnellers, with the crisis point reached in June 1915. Norton-Griffiths toured the country looking for recruits, travelling to Cornwall in July of the same year.

Here he met the Mayor of Truro, who in March 1915 had been responsible for the formation of the 10<sup>th</sup> (Service) Battalion Duke of Cornwall's Light Infantry (Cornwall Pioneers), in response to the call by Lord Kitchener for the counties of the UK to provide soldiers ready to reinforce the BEF in France. Because many miners joined the 10<sup>th</sup> DCLI, it became known by the local newspapers as the Cornish Miners Battalion.

Many of those who joined, like my grandfather, had worked in the tin and copper mines of Cornwall, something which did not go unnoticed by Norton-Griffiths. When in 1915 Norton-Griffiths was looking for experienced, hard working and skilled miners, these were his type of men.

*The special skill of the Cornish miners is to be put to good use at the front. During the past fortnight a recruitment campaign has been carried on in the Duchy with the object of enlisting the miners in the tunnelling company of the Royal Engineers. The geological characteristics of Cornwall afford the miner there an experience in tunnelling work which make him peculiarly fitted for the operations in the trenches. Double rates of pay have been offered, bringing a miner's wages, if with wife and four children, to 36s and 8d per week. At Redruth and Camborne, the great centres of mining Cornwall, many highly skilled men are recruiting.* (*Manchester Evening News*, 4<sup>th</sup> August 1915)

# WANTED, CORNISHMEN !!

WHAT WE WANT FOR THE

## Duke of Cornwall's Lt. Infantry

## are CORNISHMEN.

At present a very small percentage of the Regiment are

**Cornishmen,**

still of that small percentage the following posts have been held by

**Cornishmen,**

during the last few years, in the

**Cornish Regiment.**

Quartermaster –
Pay 9/- per diem, with house and allowance and pension.

3 Serjeant-Majors –
Pay 5/- per diem, with house and allowances and pension.

Colour-Serjeants –
Three out of eight in the Battalion, 4/- per diem, with quarters and pensions.
The Officer's Mess-Serjeant and several of the best paid billets in the Regiment are held by
**CORNISHMEN to-day.**

### A Cornishman

Who enlists into the Regiment is made doubly welcome, and, from the fact that he is a
**CORNISHMAN,**
Has every inducement to be promoted.

It is the hope and ambition of all the Officers of the Regiment that the Regiment shall be for
**CORNISHMEN,**

as it once was many years ago, in the days of the Siege of Lucknow, where the **Cornish miner showed his worth.**

If parents who wanted a really good and comfortable career for their sons, would communicate privately with the Officer Commanding the Depot at Bodmin, he would be delighted to give them all information about life in the
**Cornish Regiment.**

T. R. STOKOE, Major,

Cdg. Depot, Bodmin, Cornwall.

## GOD SAVE THE KING.

*Posters being used in Cornwall by the DCLI for recruitment. (Picture courtesy of Regimental Museum, Bodmin, Cornwall)*

On 24 August 1915, the 10th DCLI moved from its training camp at Chyandour, near Penzance, to a camp adjacent to the National Explosives Factory at Hayle, when they were adopted by the War Office. The 10th went on to be one of the outstanding pioneer battalions on the Western Front, but the large majority of these early recruits, mainly from A and C Company, never fought with it, as they were transferred to the Royal Engineers.

*In the foreground are the remains of the National Explosives factory at Upton Towans in Hayle, or as they were locally known 'Dynamite Towans'. After leaving Penzance, the 10th were billeted in what is now, ironically, a holiday camp, which can be seen in the distance.*

Some two months after Norton-Griffiths' visit, 221 of those soldiers with a mining background, my grandfather among them, found themselves, on 29 September 1915, in the newly formed 251 Tunnelling Company Royal Engineers. This explains why my grandfather's army record shows two service numbers, one for the DCLI and one for the Royal Engineers. Interestingly, DCLI records at the Regimental Museum in Bodmin show no trace of these transfers or where the original recruits to this company went, but GOC Southern Command informed the Deputy Mayor of Truro of the decision by letter on 30 September 1915.

The First World War was not the first conflict in which Cornish miners had been involved. In 1857, at the siege of Lucknow, the 32nd Regiment specifically selected Cornish miners for mine warfare and for the construction of the Redan Battery, the strongest within the defences.

The 251st was formed on 28 September 1915 at Hayle, in Cornwall, by Captain Frank James Varcoe Bullen. He had also transferred from the 10th DCLI, having been previously transferred as a second lieutenant from the 7th DCLI to 10th on 17 May 1915. Captain Bullen was himself from a Cornish family and studying to be a mining engineer at the Camborne School of Mines. He was born in 1895 in the Pahang Straits, where his father worked for the Pahang Consolidated Company, and grew up to be fluent in Malay. He was promoted very quickly, being made lieutenant in May 1915, temporary captain on 11 August 1915 and was appointed as the first commanding officer of the 251st upon its formation; he returned to the 10th DCLI in January 1916. Subsequent commanding officers, and other officers identified to date as having served with the 251st are listed in Appendix 1.

Examination of the records has identified 169 of the original 221 soldiers who transferred from the 10th DCLI to make up 251 Tunnelling Company. A further twenty five have also been identified who, because of their service numbers, were almost certainly in the 10th DCLI and subsequently transferred to the 251st, making a total of 194. An additional eight Cornishmen were transferred into the 251st just after its formation, two of these having already joined the Royal Engineers directly, and the other six were transferred from 170 Tunnelling Company, which was already operating in France.

In the local press it was reported that a further ninety eight Cornishmen, forty six of whom have been identified, joined the Royal

*The officer in the picture is a young Second Lieutenant Frank Bullen. He was a brave man who went on to become a major, surviving the war, despite being shot on two occasions. He also served in the Far East during the Second World War. (Picture courtesy of Chris Bond, Cornubian Press)*

Engineers Tunnelling Companies directly in August 1915, no doubt as a result of an advertising campaign reported in the *Western Times* offering pay of thirty six shillings a week; more of them later. According to the *West Briton*, this group became known locally as the Cornish Tunnelling Company.

Details of the Cornishmen identified in the 251st will be found in Appendix 2; other Cornish Tunnellers found during my research working for other tunnelling companies are included in Appendix 4.

All units were required to keep a War Diary when abroad on active service, which was maintained either by the Officer Commanding or another officer to whom he delegated the task. For 251 Tunnelling Company, copies are now held at the National Archives and at the Royal Engineers' Museum at Chatham.

The diaries generally contain a handwritten account of day to day activities, although in the case of some units, they were typed. These diaries make it very clear that the 251st was formed in Hayle, contradicting other sources that state that it was formed in Rouen. From

*The War Diary of the 251st showing that the Company was formed in Hayle, Cornwall. The diaries show six commanding officers; however three of them, Captains Graham and Rowan, and Major Brown were only in command for very short periods, the three principal commanding officers being Majors Bullen, Humphrys, and Church. (Reproduced with kind permission of The Royal Engineers Museum, Library and Archive)*

individual soldiers' service records, it is evident that 221 men from the DCLI transferred to the Royal Engineers all on the same day, 29 September 1915.

A document came to light among the records held by the National Archives at Kew for Sergeant (132265) John Siddall. It is a memo from the RE Recruiting and Discharge Office at Chatham to Officer Commanding Records and clearly refers to the 221 men who were transferred from the DCLI.

*With reference to the 221 men who were transferred from 10th D.C.L.I. to the Tunnelling Co R.E. on 29th inst, will you please inform me if you have Army forms R241 concerning also regimental numbers allotted to these men.*

This transfer of men en masse by Norton-Griffiths was not unprecedented; in the summer of 1915, 178 Tunnelling Company was formed at Meaulte in France, with a total of over 200 men transferred from 53 Brigade.

The original tunnellers, with little or no basic military training, must have found it very difficult to accept army discipline; they were more used to working in civil engineering, where rank and standing was often less important than knowledge and ability. The word 'sir' was much more likely to be 'mate' or in the case of the 251st, 'Cap'n' or 'me 'ansome'; saluting would have been at best sketchy and at worst totally forgotten.

*These men were miners; they came overseas to mine, and knew and cared little about ranks and army etiquette and only just enough about a rifle to take the bare necessary number of parades when out of the line.....Every officer and NCO could and did frequently take up a pick and shovel and tackle a difficult piece of hard chalk face or set a "pair of legs" in treacherous ground. Each stood his ground when the job was sticky - e.g. when a gallery, undermined and charged by the Bosche, had to be charged and tamped in absolute silence. When the listeners reported danger it was for the officer or NCO to confirm their report personally and after a "blow" an officer and NCO were usually the first to don Rescue Apparatus and go below into the wrecked galleries, either to rescue or to explore.*

*Under such conditions it is not hard to understand the mutual good feeling which prevailed between all ranks or the friendly attitude of the sixty year old miner who in billets punctiliously saluted the dapper company commander, and in talking over the work when meeting in the mines addressed him with the familiar Tyneside expression "Ye B—-Ye". Such old miners were the salt of the earth. Fear they never showed, hardships they bore most cheerfully and under all circumstances their work came first.*
(from notes for lecture given in 1929 by Captain PT Hough MC, formerly 176 Tunnelling Company, Royal Engineers.)

As well as recruiting experienced miners, Norton-Griffiths also ensured officers sent to the tunnelling companies were equally well qualified; around 80% were civilian mining engineers brought in from all parts of the world. As these professionals were used to mining and its dangers and had experience of handling the type of men engaged in mining work, the tunnellers very quickly built up a high degree of respect for, and trust in, their officers.

Whilst this may have not been the military way of working, allowances were obviously made since, as will be seen, the unsoldierly tunnellers soon made great progress in their battle beneath the trenches.

*Chapter 4*

# The Life of a Tunneller
# on the Western Front

The miners were well used to working underground and life on the Western Front was in many ways very similar to that which they had left in the tin mines of their native Cornwall, but in some ways it was very different.

Deep mining, as my forefathers would have known it, commenced with a vertical shaft and stopped at a level (measured in fathoms) at which the first seams of ore could be extracted. Since tin mining was a commercial enterprise, only lode bearing ore would be removed, and this would be extracted by digging upwards along the galleries, leaving a large space behind called a stope. Tunnelling into hard rock such as granite was very slow and an extremely noisy process; large pumps were necessary to provide air for the miners and to extract water from the workings. In Cornwall, my grandfather would have been used to operating Holmans rock drills, which were driven by compressed air, but these could not be used in military mining.

As the mine expanded, levels got deeper and, by the time my grandfather left Dolcoath mine in 1915, there was a very complex system of some seventy miles of tunnel reaching a depth of 550 fathoms or 3,300 feet. At these depths it took some two to three hours a day just to get to the workface and back. Relatively few mine supports were needed for the tunnels and stopes, but the conditions they worked in were still very wet and dusty.

By contrast, on the Western Front, although there was also a complex network of shafts, tunnels, inclines, chambers, dugouts and listening posts, the deepest mine would be not much more than a hundred feet. The 251$^{st}$ were initially tunnelling in clay, a soft material that needs a lot of support, but later they would be tunnelling in chalk, which was more akin to the hard rock that they had been used to in terms of the need for supports but much softer in consistency than granite. In the construction of military mining systems, the first actions were usually to drive a number of inclined tunnels, the entrances to which would usually be some distance behind the front line. These inclines pushed out under the front line and No Man's Land, the area between the opposing lines of trenches which were typically thirty to a hundred yards apart. At the end of the inclines, a lateral gallery would be dug joining the access inclines together.

In this gallery a number of vertical shafts, fifty to a hundred yards apart, would be sunk with another lateral gallery joining them together. This would have been repeated at different depths, usually three to five levels according to the terrain and how deep the enemy were working; the goal being always to be deeper than, and therefore underneath, the enemy. Off these galleries further short tunnels were driven, sometimes

*This plan shows a typical defensive mining operation. Mine entrance adits are back from the front line and shafts are within the galleries to descend to lower levels.*

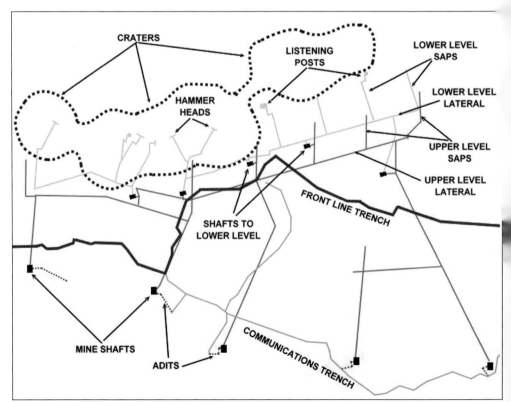

CRATERS

LISTENING POSTS

LOWER LEVEL SAPS

HAMMER HEADS

LOWER LEVEL LATERAL

UPPER LEVEL SAPS

UPPER LEVEL LATERAL

SHAFTS TO LOWER LEVEL

FRONT LINE TRENCH

MINE SHAFTS

ADITS

COMMUNICATIONS TRENCH

ending in hammerheads, which would become listening posts. The above describes a typical defensive mining system.

From these laterals, longer offensive tunnels could also be driven to finish under the German lines; the goal usually being to blow a mine and so destroy the enemy's trenches and dugouts.

The Royal Engineers' manual in use at the start of the war, laid down that straight tunnels as small as 3 feet by 2 feet, with a steep downward gradient, should be dug. It was soon accepted that these tunnels were not practical for mining warfare on the Western Front. The tunnelling companies initially adopted a size of 4 feet by 2 feet 6 inches with some even as large as 5 feet by 4 feet, these tunnels having a shallower gradient and sometimes changing direction at intervals, much like the trenches on the surface. Interestingly, the New Zealand Tunnelling Company constructed even larger tunnels of 6 feet 3 inches by 3 feet 6 inches, although this company only worked in chalk; the properties of clay would have been made it far more difficult, but not impossible, to construct such large tunnels.

The larger tunnels made it easier to pass bags of rubble back from the face and miners could move past each other in them. In the case of the enemy blowing a camouflet, a small controlled explosion designed to be powerful enough to wreck a hostile gallery and kill its occupants, larger tunnels were safer. This was primarily because the greater space reduced the blast pressure and having turns in the tunnels reduced blast impact.

Some of the galleries constructed were later enlarged and used in the building of sector defensive systems. In these, there would be first aid posts, rescue stations and command posts, as well as subways that allowed the infantry to walk below ground in safety, beneath the depth to which artillery shells could penetrate.

The experienced miners understood the dangers of, and the self-discipline required for, safe and effective working underground, even if counter-mining and trench fighting were new to them.

Initially the tunnelling companies worked independently of the troops fighting above ground and were almost a private army fighting a war within a war – a claustrophobic, uncomfortable and at times frightening underground conflict with an unseen enemy.

It is hard to imagine just how difficult and terrifying, when compared to tin mining, it must have been working in those long narrow tunnels under No Man's Land or under the enemy lines, knowing that, and

*Tunnel at La Boisselle still intact nearly a hundred years later. The tram rails can still just be seen. (Picture Courtesy of La Boisselle Study Group)*

sometimes hearing that, the enemy were only a matter of feet above, or more worryingly, below the workplace. Silence usually had to be observed, since the slightest noise might result in serious consequences, so there could be no singing as they were used to in the tin mines back in Cornwall. Every step, sometimes in stockinged feet or with sandbags tied around their boots, and every stroke of the pick had to be as quiet as possible; even bayonets were used at times instead of the pick just to gently pry the chalk or clay away. As Captain (later Lieutenant Colonel) David Dale-Logan RAMC wrote later, *working underground is stressful enough but the enormous concentration required to construct tunnels in such conditions and, usually under great time pressure, must have been exceptionally tiring.* Just to add to the pressures, there was a complete ban on smoking underground.

The further the miner tunnels away from the surface, the greater is the need for an air supply; the principle is the same for a military mine as for a deep tin mine. However, whereas in a tin mine the air could be supplied by heavy duty but noisy pumps, with back-up machines in case of failure, underground on the Western Front it had to be supplied silently. In the early days of the tunnelling operations, the noisy traction engines that were originally issued promptly drew enemy attention and

*Shaft from first gallery at La Boisselle, still intact after all these years. This all had to be dug in silence, knowing that the enemy may be only feet away.*

*The Holman Air Pump which could pump air on both the forward and backward strokes. Holmans, a Cornish company founded in 1801, was one of the world leaders in mining equipment, but is now sadly closed, the works being converted into a supermarket and flats. (Picture Courtesy of Trevithick Society)*

consequent fire so these were replaced by blacksmiths' bellows situated and operated at the tunnel entrance. Tunnellers working underground lived with the knowledge that just one direct shell from the enemy falling on a mine entrance could interrupt or terminate this supply. Whilst this method was labour intensive, it did provide for a silent operation. Later in the war, use was made of the Holman Silenced Air Pump, a piece of equipment my grandfather would have been very happy to see, as it was manufactured in Camborne, Cornwall. In due course, depending on the technical situation, electrically operated pumps became more common.

Frequently the British accidently broke into the German tunnels and vice versa and sometimes this would lead to vicious hand-to-hand fighting underground. At other times they could break through and discover an enemy mine primed ready for detonation. When this happened, the mine was often removed but there was always a fear that the enemy might blow it at any moment.

If the miners disturbed an enemy mine or perhaps heard working overhead, they could disrupt the enemy's progress by deliberately firing a camouflet, a defensive mine carried and laid specifically for this purpose. It was important that the damage from the explosion so caused be contained within the tunnels themselves. Blowing large ground breaking mines could, for obvious reasons, only be done after consultation with the infantry in order that the men in the trenches close to the mine workings were not caught up in the blast.

Apart from these dangers, there was also the personal misery of working knee, and sometimes waist, deep in water for the whole shift with no change of clothing, and at the end of the twelve hour shift only having access to a drying area where they would try to regain a degree of dryness and warmth.

*Billets improved during the the war and at times were of solid construction; that said, the 251st frequently found themselves under canvas throughout the war.*

As Lieutenant J French MC, MM (254 Tunnelling Company) noted in his diary:

> *In wet sap again working past the knees in water and water coming down your back like a shower bath. After about three hours air so bad that we had to come out - candles would not burn.*

Not all dangers were confined to working underground, for occasionally the tunnellers were stood to arms, that is they had to be ready to fight alongside the infantry, or form part of a raiding party crossing No Man's Land under the cover of darkness. These parties would seek out enemy tunnels and, if the opportunity presented itself, lay explosives to damage enemy galleries, usually by way of a device with a delayed action fuse. The 251st always had an NCO and five men ready to accompany raids in their sector, their job being to establish where shaft entrances were located and what equipment was being used.

*A photograph taken following a successful raid on a German trench. These raids were designed to collect intelligence from behind the enemy lines, and the occasional souvenir, judging by the pickelhaube being worn by the soldier in the second row. (Picture courtesy of the National Library of Scotland)*

At first the infantry regarded the miners with suspicion and indeed, at times, there was some resentment shown towards them and there were understandable reasons for this. The excavations tended to draw the attention of the enemy to wherever the miners were at work, which led to increased shelling of the area by enemy artillery. By infantry standards the miners must have seemed unsoldierly in attitude and dress and, no doubt, the extra pay received by the miners must have rankled and created its own problems. However, over time a great deal of respect was shown to the miners by the infantry, who felt considerably safer with the miners working beside and beneath them, against a common enemy.

On their arrival at the front, the miners discovered that the existing mining equipment was in a poor state of repair with some of it dating back to the Crimean War and had been in store for many years. Very quickly, Norton-Griffiths arranged for civil mining equipment to be delivered and adopted a role as the liaison officer between HQ and the Front, having been appointed to this post by the Adjutant General, Sir Henry Sclater. This liaison was essential as each tunnelling company was assigned to a particular Army; in the case of the 251st, the First Army. Tunnelling companies remained on the same front irrespective of whether or not corps, divisions or brigades within that Army moved. This frequently caused confusion within the chain of command, especially with reference to who the tunnelling companies actually reported to and where their orders originated from.

Ultimately the miners became a very flexible force. As well as fighting alongside the infantry in the front line, they were employed later in the war, as mining operations declined, in the construction of trenches, tunnels and deep dugouts, some of which were large enough to house several battalions. From the spring of 1917, when the Germans withdrew on the Somme to the Hindenburg Line, and particularly in the final stages of the war, the tunnelling companies became bomb disposal units, clearing German mines and booby traps as the enemy retreated in the face of the Allied advance. After the Armistice, in parallel with this clearance of explosives, they were employed in French and Belgian towns on major infrastructure projects, such as reconstructing bridges, repairing canals and railways that had been destroyed by four years of warfare.

There were advantages in being a tunneller when it came to food, as one of the benefits the miners received was a generous supply of rations. Reports say that the quantity of food was good but the quality was poor,

*This was a typical menu for the day, four meals with breakfast served from 3.15am. This was a huge improvement on the meals back in Cornwall; in addition cigarettes, tea and rum were supplied. It must have been adequate as absentee rates for sickness, an important barometer of the men's morale, was little worse than the industrial average in Britain. (Reproduced with kind permission of The Royal Engineers Museum, Library and Archive)*

however, it was balanced and included meat every day, the ultimate aim being to provide 4000 calories per man per day.

One further advantage tunnellers had over all other troops was an effectively limitless supply of rum. Often a miner's water bottle would be full of rum because the one thing he had plenty of was water, particularly when the water seeped continuously through the chalk if he was working in the Arras or Somme Fronts. Although this water had come through the battlefields, doubtless passing over corpses on the way, it was filtered by the chalk into clean drinkable water by the time it reached where the miner was working.

As for the rum, some of the Cornish miners would even wash their feet with it, particularly the Methodists, who abstained from alcohol, as alcohol helped prevent trench foot, a condition caused by permanently working in water.

As Peter Barton says in his book, *Beneath Flanders Fields*:

> *Few on the surface knew the horrific details of the tunnellers' work, yet this silent, claustrophobic conflict was a barbaric struggle that raged day and night for almost two and a half years, and one which generated mental and physical stresses often far beyond those suffered by the infantry in the trenches.*

If the Germans were superior in military mining techniques at the start of the war, this state of affairs was slowly but surely reversed by the British tunnellers. The mining operations carried out on the Western Front were extensive in scale and, by the close of the war the British tunnelling companies had built many miles of tunnels and had certainly assumed almost total dominance in the war underground.

*Chapter 5*

# Béthune – 'Home' on the Western Front

On 28 September 1915 my grandfather found himself, on the day before he was officially transferred from the DCLI, travelling to RE headquarters at Chatham in Kent, where he remained until 9 October 1915. Apart from the few who had transferred to the Royal Engineers but were still recovering from illness, the men of 251 Tunnelling Company sailed to Rouen, embarking at Southampton on the 9th and arriving in France some eighteen hours later on the 10th, before eventually moving up to the front on 16 October 1915. He did at least have time to send his sister a silk postcard bearing the name of the Royal Engineers on 14 October 1915 and to have his photograph taken with three of his comrades.

This transfer of men from the 10th DCLI to the Royal Engineers had been planned early in September as some men who attested in that month were recruited directly into the Royal Engineers, but held in Cornwall and posted to the 251st when it was formed. Many of these

*According to his note on the reverse, Granddad's new address was 2 Coy, RE Detail, No. 4 General Base Depot, Rouen, France.*

*What a smart lot – Granddad is first left, in France in 1916.*

men had in all probability never before left Cornwall, and some had probably never been outside of their local area. We can only imagine what they would have been thinking as they left Southampton for Rouen, crossing the Channel to Le Havre and sailing along the Seine valley past the high chalk cliffs; chalk, a material they would soon have to get used to working with. They would have had little idea of what lay in store for

*Narrow and tidal as it is, British troop ships will have passed this point delivering men and equipment to Rouen.*

them, but in the tradition of generations of Cornishmen before them who had gone abroad to work, they would have taken it in their stride.

The River Seine is wide at Le Havre and Honfleur but then narrows quickly as it enters the French countryside and meanders its way through small villages. A journey along the Seine may not have been without its excitement in 1915; significant tidal changes and strong currents affect the river and the change between ebb and flood tides is dramatic, meaning that the passage along it might not have been as smooth as one would expect on a river.

Rouen, the medieval city where Joan of Arc was burnt at the stake, was the Base Supply Depot for the Royal Engineers and other sections of the BEF. It was also home to a number of camps and hospitals, including eight general, five stationary, one British Red Cross and one labour hospital, in addition to a Convalescence Depot. All of these facilities remained at Rouen for practically the whole of the war, with the wounded being transferred to them by ambulance train from the front. A number of those who died at these hospitals were buried in local cemeteries, the great majority being taken to the city cemetery of St. Sever, where 8,348 soldiers of the First World War lie buried.

Aside from these hospitals and numerous base camps, Rouen was a world apart from the hostilities and horrors of the underground and trench warfare the new soldiers were about to encounter.

Prior to their move to the front, the 251st were inspected by Major Norton-Griffiths on 13 October 1915. His diary entry noted:

> *This unit appears to be well organized and have a good looking lot of men. All miners. Some china clay workers. Propose suggesting to CE 1st Army that it would be wise to draft a few experienced men and officers from other Coys in the 1st Army into this Coy and then I think it should do well.*

The 251st were headed for Béthune (see Map 2), which was only 120 miles from the Base Depots, their HQ being at an old chicory factory just outside the town, alongside the Canal d'Aire à la Bassée (La Bassée Canal). As can be seen from the following photographs, Béthune was within artillery range, as it was not far behind the lines on the Givenchy, Cuinchy, Cambrin and Auchy fronts, which were to become the fields of operation for the 251st until the summer of 1918. They worked initially with the 170th, the first Tunnelling Company formed, taking over the

*Rouen, home of the general base depot for the Royal Engineers and one of the railheads to the Front.*

Bethune was the HQ for the 251st as well as where the 33rd Casualty Clearing Station was located.

It was within German artillery range, and heavily shelled, but was courageously defended and never taken.
(Pictures courtesy of the National Library of Scotland)

France undertook a major rebuilding programme after the war, ensuring that buildings were largely reinstated to their former glory; this is Bethune today.

sector when the 170th were moved to Noeux-les-Mines, a little to the south.

Givenchy and Cuinchy, the latter the home of the infamous 'brickstacks', (see Map 3) were at the time amongst the 'hottest' areas on the front and they remained so until the Advance to Victory. This is not surprising, as the land in that area is flat and wet, apart from Givenchy which, standing on an extension of Aubers Ridge, is about forty feet higher than the surrounding terrain and overlooked the land behind the British lines; it would have been invaluable to the German artillery, as it gave comprehensive observation for the artillery over the crucial Béthune coalfields. Strategically, therefore, this was a critical area for the British to hold.

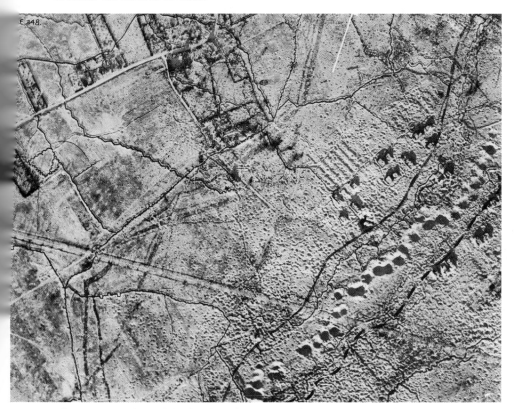

*This picture taken of the brickstacks in 1917 shows the extent of mining and counter-mining. The craters are clearly visible and the dotted lines are the two fronts. The dark shapes either side of the line are in fact piles of bricks. (Picture Courtesy of the Imperial war Museum)*

Colonel Guy Charles Williams, Controller of Mines First Army, who later became General Sir Guy Williams KCB, CMG, DSO, GOC Eastern Command during the Second World War, wrote the following letter to Lieutenant Colonel HJ Humphrys on 15 July 1931:

*You are right about Givenchy, it had great strategic and economic value and was one of the places that had to be held both on the top and underground. There will always be such places in every war that must be kept and consequently they will become objects for enemy attack in every form including mine warfare. Givenchy was the outstanding example on the British front. The Ypres salient was held for political and sentimental reasons rather than for purely military ones. The Givenchy Loos front certainly never yielded and we had it all the war; actually also after we took over further south, the front as far as Vimy was also always intact. I think it would be a good thing if the point was made in the official history that such important places like Givenchy were defended on their underground as well as their surface protection and that it stood the test notwithstanding many attempts to penetrate it.*

The Cornish miners were going to meet several different types of substrata from the one they were used to back at home, which would require new techniques. The geological structure of the area around Cuinchy and Givenchy changes from the chalk uplands of Artois to the south, to the waterlogged and clay ground of Flanders in the north, where through the ages clay deposits have built up to a depth of around twenty feet. This change occurs in the vicinity of the La Bassée Canal, which means that mining there was challenging. In clay, tunnelling is reasonably straightforward, but the wet quicksand they met would have required more specialist skills and equipment. It would be necessary for shafts to be sealed with metal collars bolted together, a process known as tubbing, and the tunnels themselves to be entirely lined with wood, a process unnecessary in the chalk tunnels further south. Once blue clay levels were reached, tunnelling became easier, but it was often still undertaken in very wet conditions. Beneath the blue clay lay chalk, which required different tunnelling techniques again, more akin to the hard rock faces that they were used to working.

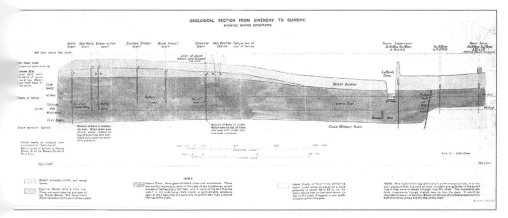

*This geographical section through Givenchy to Cuinchy showing mining conditions was produced in 1917 by Major Edgeworth David for the tunnelling companies. It clearly shows the chalk base and the clays. The original diagram indicated by colour the degree of difficulty a tunneller would have in working in this district; the brighter the colours the better the conditions. (Picture courtesy of National Library of Australia (MAP Edgeworth David Coll/21))*

Because of the geology of this area, the first tunnellers to be recruited were 'clay kickers'. To work, the clay kicker laid on a board and manipulated a grafting tool with his legs, an ideal technique in situations where picks could not be swung and in any case would not have been very effective; additional benefits of this method of working were that it was much less exhausting, far swifter and more efficient. A clay kicker could dig at twenty six feet per day against the German tunnellers' seven feet, as the process of clay kicking was a concept unknown to the Germans.

Once through the clay, the hard-rock miners of the 251st would have found the chalk easier to work than the clay, but there were long periods when sections of the 251st were working knee-deep in water tunnelling through clay. They must have soon got used to these new methods of tunnelling; by 1917 they held the 'all army' record for a 6 feet by 3 feet gallery, having tunnelled forty six feet in a 24-hour period. Shortly after they took the ten day record of 331 feet, breaking the two day, five day and seven day records along the way.

The clay-kickers and the Cornish hard rock miners were not the only ones with specialist skills. One of the Australian tunnelling companies was sent to an area near the Belgian coast with orders to tunnel through

*A model showing how a clay kicker would work in a confined area. (Picture courtesy of Allan Wright and Edward Swaim – www.wwi-models.org)*

quicksand. This required them to board the tunnels as they dug; a technique the Australians had learned in their native country, in the Victoria goldfields.

When cutting through chalk, the 251st could cut at a rate of around twenty feet per day, but chalk had its own inherent problems. Although it needed very few support props and was far less prone to collapse as it was cut, there was the danger of the chalk particles 'holding' carbon monoxide gas, which would be released when a mine was blown. Carbon monoxide is not visible and has no smell but was highly dangerous to the men in the tunnels; concentrations of carbon monoxide in the air of as little as 0.16% can kill and, if the concentration rises to just 1.25%, within seconds a man becomes unconscious and can die in less than three minutes.

To deal with the potential problems of carbon monoxide, mice and canaries became an essential part of the miner's toolkit, as they are more sensitive to lower concentrations of the gas. Mice were considered less dangerous than canaries; if mice escape they run to ground and are invisible, whilst birds, on the other hand, fly and eventually make their way to the surface. Losing a bird when at the front indicated to the enemy that there was tunnelling taking place in the vicinity, something which invariably led to targeted heavy shelling.

Canaries were thought of very highly by the miners, with each being carefully tagged and logged. When a canary did detect gas it would collapse but would frequently recover when returned to the surface. It is said that one unit ran a canaries 'home' to which, once a canary had 'collapsed' three times, it would be retired to live the rest of its life in peace. Grandfather always kept birds, and perhaps it was these canaries that gave him that interest in the first place. It would certainly have been different from what he was used to in the mines of Cornwall where gases were not such a problem. Danger in the mine where he had worked was indicated to the miners by the introduction of Eucalyptus into the fresh air pumping system.

A further problem encountered with chalk was caused by the constant collapsing and rebuilding of tunnels as mines and camouflets were fired. These explosions created finer and finer particles which, apart from

*A mine rescue team ready to go including the canary in a cage, albeit this photograph is of a civilian team. Canaries were used, as well as mice and rabbits, to detect carbon monoxide in the tunnels. (Reproduced with kind permission of The La Boisselle Study Group)*

damaging the lungs, when mixed with the water seeping through the roof from above created a glutinous liquid, not unlike freshly mixed Plaster of Paris, making mining more difficult.

*This picture shows a specially built museum example of a trolley used underground; the actual trolleys were of similar construction and designed to run on wooden rails to help cut down noise. (Picture courtesy of Memorial Museum Passchendaele)*

*The entrance to one of the tunnels at La Boisselle showing how low the entrances had to be. After all these years the tunnels remain largely in remarkably good condition.*

Spoil too was always a problem, as no tunnelling company wanted the enemy to know where the tunnel entrances were, this being a sure way of attracting enemy fire. But the waste had to be disposed of and in particular any chalk residue, being brilliant white, had to be carefully hidden or camouflaged when deposited on the surface to conceal it not just from the enemy in the trenches, but more especially from aerial surveillance.

*An officer listening with his 'geophone'. This picture must have been taken after 1916 as this instrument, developed by the Sorbonne, was not available until then. Earlier listening devices varied but some were as simple as a listening stick as still used today by water companies to find leaks. (Picture courtesy of Memorial Museum Passchendaele)*

Another problem with chalk is that it is a good conductor of sound. The activities of the German miners were easily heard and likewise they could hear the British mining. Great skill was required to detect where the enemy actually were and to try to second-guess just what they were planning. Listening posts were small saps constructed off the main galleries where the 'listener' would sit, making notes of the direction from which the sounds were heard. By linking the strength and direction of the 'noise' from the different listening posts, it was possible to calculate an approximate position for where the Germans were at work. In time this became a very sophisticated system using electronic devices connected to a central station, which then allowed an accurate plot of the enemy's underground activity in the location. Likewise, the Germans could detect British activity and so the miners would work in total silence. There was the added difficulty in that all of this activity was lit principally by candles placed in niches cut into the wall of the tunnel, although later on electric lighting was installed.

When the decision had been taken to blow a mine, explosives were placed in the mine at the selected point, and then tamped (a procedure whereby a quantity of explosive would be positioned, followed by a block of sandbags, followed by an air gap, a stretch of tunnel of several feet, followed by another block of sandbags, another gap and so on.) By adopting this approach, maximum damage could be inflicted on an enemy mine whilst minimising the damage to the tunnellers' own workings, as the blast would follow the line of least resistance, and with the air gaps and sandbags acting as shock absorbers, would deflect the blast in the desired direction towards the enemy tunnel.

Calculating how much explosive should be used was a skill in its own right as it depended on many factors such as the depth of the mine, the local geology, the proximity of friendly trenches and the type of explosive used. Whilst the Cornish miners were well practised in using explosives in a mine, they used it to remove ore in a lateral direction, not to create an upward blast to the surface.

Obviously, care had to be taken over the use of explosives. At first, guncotton was used but very shortly an explosive called ammonal, a mixture of ammonium nitrate, trinitrotoluene (TNT), aluminium

*This photograph, taken inside the tunnels at La Boisselle, clearly shows the tell-tale marks where candles were used for lighting.*

shavings and charcoal, was developed. It was three times more powerful than guncotton, and could not be set off with a naked flame or bullet, so it was a stable and relatively safe explosive to work with. The major drawback with ammonal is that it is very absorbent and any more than a 4% concentration of water in the atmosphere could seriously impede or, at worst, prevent detonation; not ideal for use in mines that were frequently a foot or more deep in water. This problem was largely overcome by using ammonal supplied in waterproofed bags or soldered waterproof tins.

Considering the trying conditions, working without being heard, the problems of getting explosives into place, and making sure that they detonated, to say nothing of the need to conceal their location and dispose of highly visible spoil, it is perhaps surprising that mining operations were as successful as they were. Much can be said for the skills and determination of both officers and men of tunnelling companies.

Field Marshal Sir John French, in his report to the War Office at the end of 1915 wrote:

> *I desire to call your Lordship's attention to the splendid work carried out by the Tunnelling Companies. These Companies, officered largely by mining engineers, and manned by professional miners, have devoted themselves whole-heartedly to the dangerous work of offensive and defensive mining, a task ever accompanied by great and unseen dangers.*
> *(*The Times *November 1915)*

# Chapter 6

# Operational Changes

Whilst the miners were beginning to make their mark, changes made at the end of 1915, at the very highest level, were going to have a major impact on the future work of the tunnelling companies. At the start of the war, the C-in-C of the BEF was Field Marshal Sir John French. Following significant British losses at the Battle of Loos in September and October 1915, and his alleged mishandling of the reserves, he was replaced in December 1915 by General Sir Douglas Haig (later Field Marshal). Haig, a member of the well-known whisky family, was a calm, resolute and dedicated soldier and a great believer in structure and discipline. From his experience in his previous command of the First Army, he understood the military possibilities of mine warfare, but felt that the tunnelling companies lacked coherent organisation.

*Field Marshal Sir Douglas Haig who passed out first in the order of merit at Sandhurst, earning him the Anson Sword. (Picture Courtesy of Australian War Memorial)*

On 1 January 1916 he appointed Colonel RN Harvey (later Brigadier General) as Inspector of Mines, his mission being to control and co-ordinate the tunnellers' efforts. Harvey, in turn, appointed three Controllers of Mines: Lieutenant Colonels GC Williams; AG Stevenson; and WBY Danford, one for each of the Armies in the field at that time, and set six rules for future operations. Barrie, writing in *War Underground, The Tunnellers of the Great War,* lists the rules:

> *1. There was to be no offensive mining unless it formed part of a thought out military operation involving the use of surface troops also.*

*2. Mining defences were to be designed to a definitive and approved plan.*
*3. The General Staff were to be kept fully informed about all important mining works.*
*4. The results of mine-firing were to be reported to the General Staff.*
*5. The Inspector was to advise the General Staff about the transfer of companies from one army to another.*
*6. The Inspector was to attend to all such matters as appointments, reinforcements, supplies of stores and equipment.*

These rules meant that the days of individual tunnelling company commanders and Major John Norton-Griffiths making autonomous decisions were over. There would be no more disagreements with brigade or local commanders as to who should give orders for tunnelling to be undertaken or for mines to be fired, as the timing of firing would now be fully regulated and co-ordinated. In effect, the tunnellers became integrated into the whole fighting force, no longer operating at the whim of a local commanding officer.

Major Norton-Griffiths requested a leave of absence for two months with effect from 1 April 1916 for 'personal reasons'. He never returned to the Western Front. It is not suggested that this was a direct result of the appointment of Colonel Harvey and his controllers of mines, but in many ways Norton-Griffiths had run the tunnelling companies as private enterprises and must have found the changes difficult to accept. To be fair, he had discussed the benefits of having a controller of mines with Major HJ Humphrys, later to become OC 251, as early as September 1915, which indicates that he recognised the decision as being the right one. Colonel Harvey might have missed Norton-Griffiths' expertise and drive, but he was to benefit from the use of the Rolls-Royce that Norton-Griffiths left behind in France for the use of the Inspector of Mines.

Following Colonel Harvey's appointment, new and modern equipment was introduced. This included such items as a new listening device called the geophone, which had been developed at the Sorbonne University in Paris, and new mine-rescue safety apparatus, in particular the Proto, a breathing device manufactured by Siebe Gorman that was similar, in principle, to equipment worn by divers today. Consideration was also given to the men's welfare and safety, in that Lieutenant Colonel Dale-Logan of the Royal Army Medical Corps, a specialist in miners' diseases and mine rescue work, was appointed to Harvey's staff.

Mining schools were set up, where basic training in military mining was given; that of the First Army was at Houchin. Instruction was also given in other specialist fields, such as mine rescue and listening, experimental work in pipe pushing and other activities which will be discussed later.

Mining tactics also changed to what was known as offensive–defensive mining. This involved constructing a number of tunnels side by side and if German tunnelling was heard a charge would be fired in one of the tunnels immediately. The remaining tunnels would then be diverted inwards towards the German tunnels and the same tactics used again. It was nerve-racking but exhilarating work for the British tunnellers and by operating in this fashion they started to show their worth, fighting their way forward with superior organisation, skill, energy and courage; as a result, the Germans were driven back. The war underground had developed in earnest.

The area around Cuinchy was one of the liveliest mining areas on the Western Front. This was brought home to the 251st shortly after their arrival, when on 10 December 1915 the Germans successfully blew an offensive mine that killed six Argyll & Sutherland

*This kit enabled the wearer to survive in an irrespirable atmosphere by combining oxygen in steel bottles with recycled exhaled breath 'scrubbed' of carbon dioxide using sodium carbonate; this absorbed any carbon monoxide in the air. (Picture courtesy of La Boisselle Project Group)*

Highlander infantrymen as well as four miners from the 251st: Sappers J Glasson; J Rule; and C Salmon, who are all buried at Cambrin Military Cemetery; and Sapper J Waters, who is buried at Béthune Town Cemetery.

This incident was one factor which brought about a change of commanding officer; on 20 January 1916 FJV Bullen, by now a temporary major, was succeeded by Lieutenant HJ Humphrys, and Major Bullen returned to the 10th DCLI.

Lieutenant Humphrys had already won a Military Cross, and had been recommended for the Victoria Cross by General Sir Charles Monro, GOC Third Army, for rescuing gassed men whilst he was with his

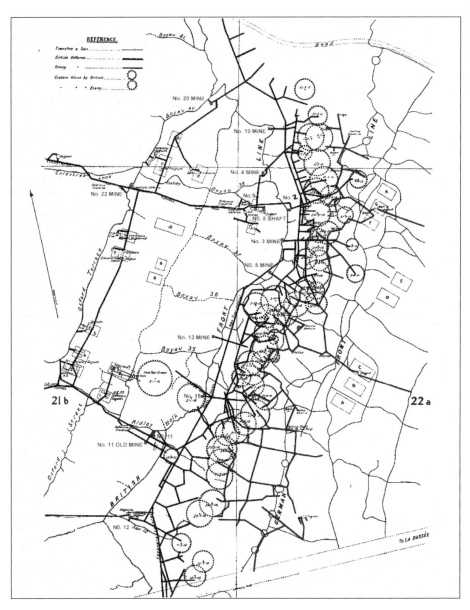

This illustration shows the tunnelling complex in the vicinity of the brickstacks at Cuinchy. The map represents a distance of only 500 yards so clearly shows the intensity of the mining activity. The dotted circles represent mine craters and the rectangular blocks show the brickstacks. Many craters were given names e.g. Midnight Crater because of the time when it was blown, whilst others were known by the date they were fired e.g. New Year Crater. (Map after Tunnellers, Grieve courtesy of Naval & Military Press)

previous company, the 179th; he was made temporary captain on 16 February 1916 and temporary major on 10 April 1916.

Major Humphrys was a trustworthy and capable mining engineer, who had been a junior Inspector of Mines in the coalfields prior to the war. A tall man, almost six feet in height, he joined 7th Black Watch in May 1914 and was transferred to the Royal Engineers in August 1915 as one of the seventy men and two officers from the Black Watch sent to 179 Tunnelling Company. As far as the 251st were concerned, Major Humphrys was an excellent choice to take command, as he had already been identified by Norton-Griffiths as probably the best mining engineer on the Western Front, and as an officer who he was keen to have command of one of the new tunnelling companies. On 9 April 1918

*Major HJ Humphrys DSO, MC. (Picture courtesy of Charles Kenyon and Simon Jones)*

Humphrys was transferred to 8th Royal Scots as a temporary lieutenant colonel and Captain Church, who was already serving with the 251st, assumed command.

On leaving the army in 1922, Major Humphrys returned to his previous career in the Mines Inspectorate, later becoming HM Inspector of Mines.

# Chapter 7

# 'Cat and Mouse' Underground, 1916

The War Diary held in the archives for the 251st is almost complete, in that it covers the period 27 September 1915 to 31 January 1919 but has some dates missing, notably 1 – 31 October 1918. What is immediately noticeable is that the *War Diary* does not actually commence in detail until 21 January 1916, the day after Major Humphrys' appointment as CO and twenty one days after Brigadier General Harvey became Inspector of Mines.

The first month of diary entries under the new regime records a great deal of activity; on 21 January 1916, the 251st blew their first recorded mine, using 1,000 lbs of ammonal and 1,000 lbs of guncotton. As was to be become the norm for this period of the war, the Germans retaliated quickly, blowing two mines on the following days, 28 and 29 January respectively, fortunately not causing any casualties.

As mining activity increased, additional support was sought from the nearby infantry brigades for help in shifting spoil from the tunnels as they were excavated. The first of the assigned infantrymen, comprising ten men and one NCO, from 100 Brigade, arrived; eventually there would be about 300 infantrymen assigned to the 251st, some of whom were to stay with them for a long time, remaining even when their own battalions moved back from the front line to their respective rest camps. These extra men could not be accommodated at the chicory factory and so were billeted at Annequin and Lieutenant Watson RE was detailed to take charge of them. Their introduction to the world of military mining would be swift; as a result of sounds heard only two days after their arrival, authorisation was given to blow two mines of 1,000 lbs ammonal each, an operation carried out on 3 February 1916 at 3.00 am.

Offensive mining was still allowed on occasion. Thus, when German mine waste that had not been hidden from sight was observed around the German front, the Controller of Mines immediately sanctioned the start of an offensive mine at Mine Point, which was blown later in the month.

February, however, was not going to end well for the 251$^{st}$, for on the 20$^{th}$ the enemy blew a mine in the Cuinchy sector and four miners were killed. Sappers W Cooper, EW Edwards, and Lance Corporal Nankivell are buried in Cambrin Military Cemetery, whilst Sapper Henry Ramage is commemorated on the Loos Memorial.

In spite of this enemy activity, great progress was made in other areas. Although it was only some six weeks since Brigadier General Harvey had been appointed Inspector of Mines by General Haig, it was becoming clear that the strategy of the tunnelling companies working in a co-ordinated manner with a distinct chain of command was already beginning to pay dividends. Away from the front line, experimental work was taking place at the newly created Mining School with the 251$^{st}$ working on pushing pipes into craters in order to observe the enemy. Pipe pushing was a technique whereby a 3 inch pipe would be pushed at a fixed depth through the clay or soil by a hydraulic machine or, on occasion, by a hand operated system. Apart from being used to observe enemy activity, these pipes could also be charged with ammonal explosive, which when blown would create a trench.

The tunnellers' welfare in billets was also addressed; Lieutenant Colonel Dale-Logan RAMC visited the billets, something which was to become a regular occurrence, to check on hygiene and sanitation in an attempt to avoid diseases such as diphtheria breaking out. As a result of this particular visit, arrangements were put in place with 33$^{rd}$ Division laundry to provide clean underclothes every ten days.

The 251st worked hard not only to control enemy mining activity but also to build defensive positions by stabilising the craters, particularly around Jerusalem Hill (see Map 3). Here they constructed a defensive line along the lip of the crater on the 'home' side to protect them from the enemy. Defensive firing positions were also constructed in case of enemy attack.

As a result of this type of work, camaraderie between the tunnellers and infantry started to flourish as the latter saw the benefits of having the tunnelling companies working alongside them. When urgent work was needed on the craters, an officer from the 251$^{st}$ reported daily to the infantry battalion commander, who then detailed extra working parties to assist in the operation.

With these intensive mining operations in progress, and with new galleries completed some three, or occasionally, even four or five levels down, there was little time left for formal military training. By the end of February the OC of the 251st was concerned that only half of his tunnellers had attended a musketry course and therefore knew how to handle and fire a rifle, something that might be required of them at any time.

As the 251st worked hard to overcome German superiority in mine warfare the intensity of the mining activity continued throughout March 1916, with the Germans blowing five mines against two blown by the 251st; the infantry in their trenches suffered no fatalities from these enemy mines. The tunnellers fared less well; Sapper Page was killed in an explosion at Jerusalem Hill on 2 March 1916 when it is thought that the Germans heard the British tunnellers working and blew a defensive mine.

On 7 April 1916, the tunnellers were working on a new lateral when they broke into an old German gallery. Listeners were posted, but no sounds were heard coming from the enemy. To ensure that the breach was sealed, a mine loaded with 1000 lbs ammonal was blown the following day. This time the enemy retaliated almost immediately by blowing a mine at 8.00 am on 9 April 1916 close to one of the lowest British levels, level 5, Cambrin Mine Point. In doing so, they caused what was to prove to be one of the worst days for the 251st in terms of casualties. Five men were killed as a result of the explosion; two Cornishmen, Sapper William Waller from Chacewater and Sapper Henry Wilkinson from Redruth, both of the 251st and Private Andrew Donaldson, 2nd Argyll & Sutherland Highlanders, who was attached to the 251st. It cannot be established with certainty, but it is likely that the other two killed were Private Walter Peebles, 2nd Argyll & Sutherland Highlanders and Private Thomas McGowan, Scottish Rifles, both of whom were attached to the 251st. My grandfather was taken to hospital on the same day, and it is my belief that the injury to his lungs and the following complications may well have been as a result of this explosion. Family legend has always maintained that he had been gassed, which he probably had, but not in the conventionally understood way. It is quite possible that following a blast in a low level gallery the resulting gases may well have affected him, especially if the air pumps had failed as a result of the explosion.

Like other soldiers injured on the front, he would have gone to the Regimental Aid Post, where he would have been assessed, then moved to a Field Ambulance and subsequently, in this case, taken to the 33$^{rd}$ Casualty Clearing Station (CCS) located at St. Vaast College in Béthune. Following further assessment at the CCS, the decision would have been taken to dispatch him via Ambulance Train to a Stationary, Base or General Hospital which were well away from the front line, often near the Channel ports; and from there he would have been returned to England by Hospital Ship.

Trains were not the only method used to transport the wounded, particularly if their injuries were such that they could not tolerate the shaking of the train; sometimes barges were used, as the following extract from a letter sent home by a wounded soldier shows:

> *I copped a slight flesh wound on Nov 4, told by shell, but now I have come to a conclusion that it was a bomb. I was in the Hohenzollern Redoubt repairing the parapet which had been blown in. I walked two miles to Vermelles, then I went by car to Cambrin, stopped there an hour or two, then they took me to the clearing station for the night. The next day they put me on a Red + barge, then I had 48 hours ride down the La Bassée canal and reached Calais on Sunday afternoon, stopped there till yesterday morning (10$^{th}$), got here last night. It is not a bad wound, it is just serious enough to get me to England, it is my left leg just above my knee.*
>
> Private George Goodchild, 7th Suffolks, to his mother<br>dated 11 November 1915.<br>(Courtesy of Harry Finch, www.goodchilds.org/theletters)

In Pop's case he was sent to No 18 General Hospital at Camiers, a tented hospital near Boulogne, part of a major camp generally known as Étaples Camp. He was admitted on 10 April 1916 and subsequently transferred by hospital ship to England and on to Abbots Barton Hospital in Canterbury, where he remained until 9 August 1916, being treated for pneumonia. He never rejoined the 251$^{st}$ but did eventually recover enough to be returned to the front and on 16 July 1917 he joined 185 Tunnelling Company, then working in the Lens sector. The lung damage caused by the pneumonia was something he lived with for the rest of his life.

An ambulance parked outside a dressing station. The dressing station appears to have been set up in the ground floor of a partly demolished building, possibly a chateau or a municipal building as it has quite ornate stairs going up in an arc on either side of the door. The ambulance is a Siddely-Deasy; unlike some of those used earlier in the war, the front of the cab is closed and more protected. (Picture courtesy of National Library of Scotland)

The college at St. Vaast (Béthune) used by the British as the 33rd Casualty Clearing Station. It was badly damaged from aerial bombardment, but was rebuilt and is still a school to this day.

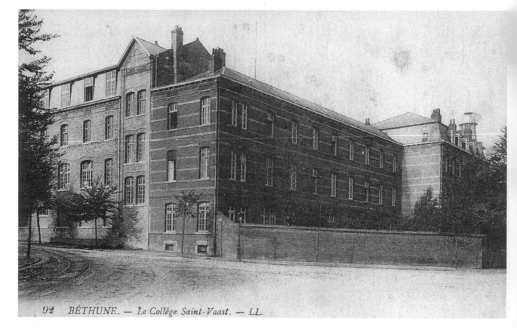

92    BÉTHUNE. — Le Collège Saint-Vaast. — LL.

*The ambulance trains ran from the Western Front to hospitals in such places as Rouen or Boulogne where soldiers could be placed on hospital ships to be brought back to England. This picture was to tell the people 'back home' how good the service was. The reality at the start of the war was cattle trucks with straw bedding, but this did improve later. (Picture courtesy of National Library of Scotland)*

*Pop (first row, second left) convalescing at Canterbury.*

Back at Cambrin, new defences were constructed by the 251st but mine warfare was still the primary occupation. Not all of the tunnellers' work was conducted underground, for on occasion they participated in raids into the German trenches in order to try to locate and destroy shafts with the mobile charges they carried; the capture of German equipment, listening devices and the like was always an added bonus. On 17 April 1916, with covering fire from 1st Queens, Second Lieutenant Fred Bullen, brother of the first commanding officer Major Frank Bullen, Second Lieutenants Deacon and Hunter and three tunnellers inspected and then destroyed a suspected shaft in a crater. These raids, whilst useful in terms of the information gathered, were not popular, as they usually resulted in men being killed or injured. This night was no exception, with Second Lieutenant Hunter being killed and Second Lieutenant Deacon injured. Lieutenant Bullen recovered the body of Second Lieutenant Hunter from the crater despite being under fire, and was awarded the Military Cross for his gallantry.

Only two days later the tunnellers would come face to face with the enemy whilst working underground. Following reports of hearing the enemy, Second Lieutenant Hansen was charging a mine when the enemy suddenly appeared; no shots were exchanged on this occasion, there were no casualties and the mine was successfully blown at 10.45 pm. Incidents such as this always required a detailed report to be prepared and sent to all relevant parties.

Captain Humphry's report, sent to Controller of Mines First Army on 20 April 1916, does not refer to the enemy appearing, even though it is clearly mentioned in the War Diary:

*I have to report that we exploded a mine at A.27.b.6.7 Mine Point, Cambrin, at 10.45pm yesterday 19th April. A sketch showing the general position and a larger scale sketch of our galleries are annexed. From the former it will be seen that we were driving a gallery '3 g' in the lower level under the enemy edge of the 'F' of the 'R.W.F.' craters. About 11 o'clock yesterday morning a small hole was discovered at the top left hand side of our gallery at the point marked 'A' on the large scale sketch. 2/Lieutenant HISLOP, who was on duty at the time, visited the place later and distinctly heard sounds of talking and distant working. He placed an armed listener in the post and put an empty sandbag in the hole, and decided to await developments.*

*It should be said that when the bag was removed there was a strong current of air blowing <u>into</u> our gallery sufficiently strong to blow out a candle. It was evident that either we had established connection with an enemy gallery or with the surface through the broken ground of the crater. 2/Lieutenant HISLOP stated that he could put his arm through the hole and the cavity above seemed a formed one like a gallery, also that the sound of the voices was similar to that travelling along a gallery and also no light came through the hole, so the data obtainable all pointed to our having established connection with an enemy gallery.*

*I listened carefully between 4 and 5 o'clock with an instrument and thought I heard sounds of voices and so did 2/Lieutenant O.J. HANSEN who listened later. We also heard sounds of distant working distinctly. After consulting these officers I decided to load up the end of the gallery with 500 lbs PERMITE and put in tamping to a sufficient height to allow a person to crawl over, and then when things had reached this stage one of the officers would enlarge the hole and more damage would be done to the enemy gallery since it would be wholly untamped.*

*It would appear that the gallery we broke into was one that was damaged at a point further back by our mine of 15.4.16. The distant sounds of working would be his work of clearing the gallery, which were probably just completed as we finished loading our mine. Our gallery '3g' was 30' away from his on 15.4.16 and assuming the above surmised correct this would account for the fact of our being able to work right under his gallery unobserved.*

Reproduced with kind permission of The Royal Engineers Museum, Library and Archive

The following day, 21 April 1915, the Germans blew another mine on the Cuinchy front at 4.40 am and about forty feet of British tunnel was destroyed. In the explosion, Lance Corporal WF Bloomfield, married to a French woman who lived in La Gorgue in France, and Private J. MacIntyre from Glasgow, both of them Cameronians, together with Privates T. Mulkerrin from Dumbarton and Private T. Potter from Leslie (Fife), both with the Argyll & Sutherland Highlanders, lost their

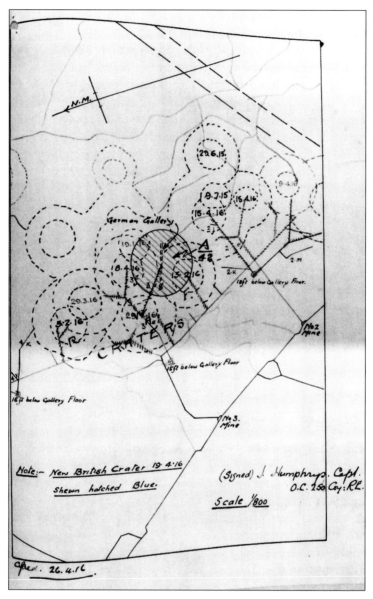

*This sketch produced with the report clearly shows where the mine was blown on 19 April 1916. As well as illustrating the level of activity that was taking place in this sector, it also shows the structured tunnelling approach introduced by Brigadier General Harvey. (Reproduced with kind permission of the Royal Engineers Museum, Library and Archive)*

lives. The underground war was often one of tit for tat, as both sides fought for dominance.

Further pipe pushing experiments were continuing at Le Quesnoy, where a pipe was pushed 133 feet in 2 hrs 5 minutes at a depth of five feet. This task was undertaken with the aid of a Sentinel Jack, a hydraulic ram invented by Stephen Alley of the Sentinel Steam Wagon Company. The pipe was then extended to 196 feet, loaded with 600 lbs of ammonal and fired. The resulting trench was quite level, about seven feet deep and fifteen feet wide; whilst the experiment was deemed to be successful it was thought that this technique would only work in clay as the pipes could not be pushed through chalk, although this technique was tried later in the war in the chalk areas surrounding Vimy.

More mining support arrived on 12 May in the form of the three tunnelling companies of the Australian Imperial Force. No. 4 Section of the Australian 3rd Tunnelling Company were attached to the 251st and billeted at Béthune. Although experienced miners they, like the Cornish tin miners before them, must have felt they had been thrown into an especially fierce and uncomfortable mining battle. Having gained a couple of weeks' experience on this front, they were transferred to Le Drumez to relieve 255 Tunnelling Company.

Meanwhile, whilst the greater part of the 251st continued with their work in the Cuinchy sector, No. 3 Section were moved to billets in Cambrin to take over that sector from 254 Tunnelling Company, thus making the 251st responsible for the work on two sectors.

As well as their mining and experimental work, the 251st also looked at other defensive measures and commenced the laying of land mines in craters that were judged to be too difficult to defend, as well as investigating various means of installing warning alarms for the men working underground in case of gas attack or enemy raiding parties.

These land mines would prove very useful a few days later, after the enemy exploded a mine by New Year Crater on 26 May 1916 and the 251st tunnellers broke into a German gallery near Queen's Crater. They found a mine tamped and ready for firing and heard the enemy talking and working just a few feet away. In total silence, a mine charged with 2500 lbs of ammonal was placed adjacent to the German gallery, which was close to where the land mines had been laid three days earlier. At 1.00 am the British artillery lightly shelled the area around the crater, and the land mines blew up, simulating a mine explosion. As they were expected to do, the Germans swiftly occupied the crater, with more men in support in the German trenches behind the crater. At 2.30 am, the mine that had been laid on the 26th was fired, taking with it the adjacent German mine. The British guns immediately opened fire with a heavy bombardment of the whole area, including the occupied trenches. It is not known what scale of losses were inflicted on the Germans that night but it is likely to have been high.

May was a month of intense mining activity but the tide was finally turning; the 251st were starting to gain the upper hand. In May, the enemy fired seven mines against eight fired by the 251st, an average of one mine every two days or so.

As a member of the HQ Staff of the Australian Tunnellers, May saw the arrival of one of the world's leading geologists, Major TWE David (later Lieutenant Colonel Sir Edgeworth David). Major David was a Professor of Geology (known as the 'Old Prof') and at fifty eight years of age he had talked his way into being sent to France. A Welshman by birth, he had been part of Sir Ernest Shackleton's expedition to the magnetic South Pole in 1909. When the Australian staff was broken up, Major David was attached to the staff of the Engineer in Chief RE for special duties.

Major Humphrys first met Major David on 17 May 1916 and over time a strong relationship developed between him and the 251st. As well as giving lectures on various topics to all of the tunnelling companies, he was also responsible for the drilling of 8,500 test boreholes to investigate the water levels in the areas in which the companies were mining. The water table in Flanders can vary according to the season and the results of Major David's investigations provided accurate geological information as to the type of material likely to be encountered at varying depths and how deep a mine could go before hitting the water table. All of this helped to establish which mining techniques should be used and assisted in calculations to determine how much explosive would be required to blow a particular mine, or type of mine. His knowledge of the geology of the area was to prove invaluable in the construction of both mine chambers and defensive positions. The maps he created of the boreholes were also used in the development of water supplies to the front line; these needed to supply, it was calculated, ten gallons of water per man (and per service animal) per day.

The Germans had the services of over a hundred geologists whereas the British relied on the duo of Major David and Captain WBR King, who had graduated from Cambridge with a first class degree in geology

*Major TWE David touring the front just after the Armistice. From left: the driver; Professor Charles Barrois of the University of Lille; Davids' military colleague Capt. WBR King and Major David. (Picture Courtesy of University of Sydney Archives)*

in 1912, and had joined the Geological Survey Organisation. He was commissioned as a second lieutenant in the Territorial Force in 1914 and in 1915 was sent to France to assist the Chief Engineer BEF, reaching the rank of lieutenant colonel. After the war, he became Woodwardian Professor of Geology in the Department of Earth Studies at Cambridge University.

Geologists and their understanding of the geology of an area played an important part, as without this knowledge water ingress from artesian aquifers would always be an issue. For example, in June 1916 the enemy blew the Red Dragon Crater at Givenchy and it was clear from the blast that the Germans must have been mining deeper than 254 Tunnelling Company, who were working in the same area. This surprised the 254th, as they did not believe it was possible to have mined any deeper. At the same time, the water table at the Bunny Hutch Shaft (see Map 4) had been penetrated but there was no knowledge of the depth at which this had occurred. It was clear that more detailed information was required as to where the water table actually lay, as this would constrain the depth to which they could mine. Geological surveys were conducted in the

Coventry and North shafts, which were located near the Bunny Hutch Shaft. Using a Horden boring set, holes were drilled until the aquifer was penetrated and water poured out. The hole was then filled with small bags of oats, haricot beans, rice, and wheat and held down with rods. After a couple of hours and the contents of the bag had swelled, Portland cement was poured in and left to set to seal the hole. Whilst this system worked well, it was a very slow and tedious method of working. Captain Fidoe, a tunnelling company officer, proposed a solution to speed this process up, following an exercise he had successfully undertaken when another officer mistook his instructions and dug a sump shaft 4 feet deeper than he should have done, and in the process bored into an aquifer. Instead of using bags of water absorbing ingredients, a pipe with a tap attached was pushed down the hole. The tap was left open to relieve the water pressure and Portland cement was poured down the sides of the pipe and left for a week until it set. The tap was then closed but could be used in the future to supply fresh drinking water to the tunnellers underground.

The data gathered in this manner was analysed and interpreted as evidence of the changes and dips in the strata at Givenchy; all future works were undertaken using these bores as reference points. As a result, a new mining system was laid out for Givenchy which was to prove crucial in later events.

June was looking promising in that a pioneer battalion was now working on the Cambrin front under the supervision of the 251st; whilst the experimental work with pipes culminated in a pipe being successfully pushed 120 feet in two hours and then loaded with 350 lbs of ammonal. When blown, a level trench was formed 15 feet wide by 5–10 feet deep. Instant trenches created in this way would be of great benefit to trench raiding parties as it would not only clear a path through the German wire but would also provide protection for the raiding party as they approached the enemy lines. The 251st themselves would benefit from such a trench later the same month.

The game of cat and mouse continued on 8 and 9 June, with both German and British mines being blown very close to one another. The tunnellers' skills were developing to a high level, particularly in their ability to work in silence; this was clearly demonstrated on 11 June when the Germans were heard working only six feet away from the tunnellers of the 251st. Despite being so close, the 251st, wearing sandbags around their feet to ensure silence, packed 600 lbs of ammonal into their gallery.

To avoid the blast being transmitted into their own tunnel and to ensure that the maximum blast went towards the enemy, the charge gallery was tamped with sandbags. Behind the ammonal, they placed 8 feet of tamping (sandbags) followed by an air gap of 5 feet, then a further 5 feet of tamping followed by an air gap of 8 feet and then a further 7 feet of tamping; the mine was successfully blown at 5.00 pm that day.

Successful mining operations such as this attracted interest at the highest level and prompted visits from dignitaries such as Major General Heath, CRE First Army, who visited with the Controller of Mines First Army on 11 June, to inspect the billets, to see for himself the work of the Company and to express his satisfaction at what he had seen.

An explosion was heard from the German lines on 20 June and, as no authorisation had been given and no action had been planned by the 251st, it was deemed likely to have been an accident in the German trenches. It was subsequently found to have been the result of a pushed pipe mine, this being the first time such a tactic had been seen to have been used by the enemy; it was perhaps slightly overcharged as it was observed to have blown a trench some 60 feet wide.

It was not only underground that the miners had to be careful; just getting to the mine entrances had its dangers. The enemy got to know the routes that the various shifts took and the times of shift changes and so frequently shelled these routes at the appropriate time. On 25 June, Second Lieutenant MA Phillimore RE was killed when a rifle grenade landed near him and exploded as he approached the shaft to the galleries of no. 3 mine in Cambrin.

Not all was doom and gloom, however, as the tunnellers must have thought 26 June one of their luckier days, for although the Germans blew a mine at 6.45 pm there were no casualties, possibly because the tunnellers were all enjoying the opening of the YMCA canteen and recreation room in their billet!

Sport played an important part in keeping spirits high in the billets and support of friends and relatives back in Cornwall helped in this aspect as shown by this extract from *The West Briton*:

*Sapper Richard Brown, of the 251 coy R.E., 1st Corp British Expeditionary Force, France, writing to Mr George Williams, secretary of the St. Day Rugby Club, says, :- 'Will you ask the boys of St. Day if they will give 2d. or 3d. each to get a rugby football and send out to us St Day and Carharrack boys at the*

*By 1916 the YMCA had over 1,500 workers in France and was allowed to open up rest areas and recreation rooms at sites near the front lines. This was before the days of the NAAFI which was not founded until 1921. (Picture courtesy of Arborfield Local History Society)*

*front, as they are longing for a good old game of rugby, and want to show some of the chaps out here how they used to play a rough-and-tumble game with the Redruth Reserves, Redruth Highway, and Lanner Clubs when they were at home.' In the course of his letter he adds: 'Tell all the boys at home we should like to see them out here soon, and tell —-we should make a man of him. Wishing you the best of luck, from old St. Day boys, Norman Triniman, Harold Knowles, Sam Bawden, Richard Brown and Corpl. Hocking.' Mr. Williams collected £1 2s. 11d. and purchased a football, which he sent with a supply of cigarettes to Sapper Brown, with the best wishes of the St. Day friends.*

June 1916 was the most active period of the war for the 251st with a total of twenty two mines blown, fourteen by the Germans and eight by themselves. The following details of a raid undertaken by the 9th Highland Light Infantry (HLI), supported by the 251st, clearly demonstrates how the infantry and tunnellers were now working together in close co-operation and how this was having a definite impact upon the enemy. Great detail and planning between the 251st and the 9th HLI, supported by the staffs of the 33rd Division and 100 Brigade, went into the preparation for this raid.

It was suspected that the Germans had some mine shafts located in two craters in front of Mad Point, a bulge in the German front line near Auchy-lès-la-Bassée (now Auchy-les-Mines), and the 251st wished to explore these craters in order to destroy the shafts.

The raid was to be led by Captain AC Frame of the 9th HLI, with an NCO and four sappers of the 251st led by Second Lieutenant Watkins RE, and was planned for the night of 27 June 1916. Four officers and 148 men of 9th HLI, together with the detail from the 251st, were given a detailed briefing, which included the examination of aerial photographs and lantern slide presentations, followed by a rehearsal in a field off the La Bassée–Béthune Road the day before the raid. The goal of the HLI was to advance to the German second line behind Mad Point and hold this for sixty minutes, so enabling the detail from the 251st to examine old and new craters and to destroy any mine entrances discovered. They were also to take as many prisoners as possible, capture any equipment they could find, and cause serious damage to the German defences and dugouts.

On the night of 26 June, heavy artillery targeted the German lines at Mad Point and the wire defences were breached, Lewis machine guns were set up and used throughout the following day and evening to prevent the enemy repairing the wire. On 27 June, the 251st pushed pipes at seven feet below the surface towards the craters and loaded them with 450 lbs of ammonal and the pipes were blown at 11.30 pm, creating a level trench. As the yellow flame and tearing wind from the blast died down, and with debris still falling down upon them, the raiding party rapidly moved forward along the trench with bayonets fixed. They quickly cleared the forward trench and continued the attack by swiftly taking the support trench. The raiding party now held 150 yards of German line and had penetrated some ninety yards behind the front line. At the same time, the artillery changed its range and, using four batteries of field guns, a howitzer battery and trench mortars, rapidly fired on what was effectively the perimeter of a rectangular box around the position being held; this prevented the Germans counter-attacking from either side, for to do so they would have to have gone through a barrage of heavy shelling and mortar bombs.

The raiding party further secured the left and right flanks of the captured trenches by placing men at either end, whilst a section went directly to the deep dugouts that had been identified from aerial reconnaissance and called for the Germans to surrender. A number of German soldiers came out from the dugouts, were immediately taken prisoner and escorted back to the British trenches; the dugouts were then destroyed, trapping inside any men who had not surrendered.

These tactics gave the men from the 251st who had accompanied the raid the protection they needed to inspect old and new shafts with three new shafts being identified. The tunnellers detail descended the shafts, entered the galleries, took eight German tunnellers prisoner and gathered up a collection of mining tools and equipment.

At 12.30 am, some sixty minutes after the first blast, 251 Tunnelling Company blew another mine, charged with 1500 lbs of ammonal, at a position midway between the Midnight and RWF Craters. This second mine served as both a diversionary tactic and a signal to recall the raiding party to their own trenches. During the return, the gunners maintained heavy fire on the 'box', providing cover for the returning party. To ensure the men did not get lost on what was a dark and overcast night, tape had been laid from the British to the German trenches for the men to follow on their way back. As the party reached their own trenches, delayed charges left in the new shafts by the 251st detonated, destroying the mine entrances as well as entombing any Germans left working deeper in the galleries.

On the return of the raiding party, it was established that papers from a German officer had been taken along with two machine guns, a number of rifles, steel helmets and a collection of mining tools and equipment. Thirty eight unwounded and seven wounded prisoners were taken, and a German officer and ten German soldiers were known to have been killed, with another two killed by shrapnel in the British trenches. An unknown number of enemy soldiers were killed when the dugouts and mine shafts were destroyed. British casualties amounted to eleven wounded, one seriously. There were many commendations the following day for what was to become known as 'the perfect raid'.

The next day, 9th HLI were relieved by the 2nd Worcesters and went back to its reserve line, whilst the 251st returned to the front line. This was not unusual, the trenches were wet, cold and exposed to the enemy and too much time in the trenches quickly sapped morale.

That is not to say the infantry had life any easier in the reserve lines, where they may well have still been under canvas, drill and training would continue, as well as the possibility of being called upon for carrying duties. Of course, the front line for the infantry was always a hard life, as is well described in the following extract from the anonymous diary of a nursing sister on the Western Front;

> *Three men of the S. W. Borders and five of the Welsh Regt. on advancing to occupy a trench found themselves cut off, with a 2$^{nd}$ Lieut. He advanced alone to reconnoitre and was probably shot, they said – they never saw him again. So the Sergt. of the W.R. (aged 22!) took command and led them for safety, still under fire, to a ditch with one foot of water in it. This was on the Monday night before Xmas. They stayed in it all Tuesday and Tuesday night, when it was snowing. Before daylight he "skirmished" them to a trench he knew of two hundred yards in advance, where he had seen one of his regiment the day before. This was in water above their knees. He showed me the mud-line on his trousers.*
>
> *This turned out to be one of the German communication trenches. They stayed in that all Wednesday, Wednesday night, and Thursday, living on some biscuit one man had, some bits of chocolate, and drinking the dirty ditch water, in which was a dead German dressed as a Gurkha. "We was prayin' all the time."*

Unfortunately, there were insufficient reserves within the tunnelling companies to allow for time out of the range of German shelling, so 251 Tunnelling Company were stationed either in the Front Line, or at their billets just a couple of miles away until April 1918.

> *Tunnelling Companies knew no Divisional or Corps rests. Their work was continuous. In the Company I was with, the work carried on in this routine from the formation of the unit in April '15 to the Company's first Sports Day in June '17*
> Captain PT Hough MC, 176 Tunnelling Company, from lecture notes, 1929.

The Battle of the Somme 1916 stretched along on a line from Gommecourt to Foucaucourt, south of the River Somme and in the French sector. It officially consisted of a series of thirteen battles that commenced on 1 July 1916 with the Battle of Albert, which was to last thirteen days. Meanwhile, the 251st at Cuinchy were on the southern edge of Aubers Ridge, thirty five miles north east of Gommecourt; it was hoped that increased mining activity in this area would lead the Germans into believing that the attack on the Somme was just a diversionary tactic and, to reinforce this idea, July started with a blaze of mine explosions, with eleven being blown in this area in the first nine days of the offensive.

On 2 July at 12.15 am the British fired mines at Railway Crater and Mine Point, followed by another at Mine Point at 12.45 am, all of this coinciding with a raid led by 2nd Worcesters. Two officers, two NCOs and five men of the 251st joined the raid specifically to enter, survey, and destroy German mine galleries, something they did with great success.

The number of these raids increased and during the Battle of Albert occurred every three days or so. Such was the success of the raid on 27 June 1916, more use was made of the 251st's ever increasing skills in pipe pushing. A raid on 5 July 1916 led by 2nd Welsh Fusiliers commenced with the blowing of a mine containing just 108 lbs of ammonal at 11.00 pm and, was followed at 11.05 pm by two mines just under the lip of A of the ASH craters, one containing 15 lbs of blastine and the other 1,500 lbs of ammonal. A three inch pipe had been pushed by a hydraulic pipe pusher earlier and loaded with 220 lbs of ammonal and this was also fired at 11.05 pm. This opened up a trench and, with the guns providing a covering barrage, the raiding parties had safe access across No Man's Land into the enemy lines. Pipe pushing in this particular area, where drilling was difficult, was no mean feat and, an operation to drill accurately for a distance of sixty yards could take eleven days; time and accuracy was of the utmost importance if a crater outpost was to be effectively removed as part of a planned raid.

Not all of the heavy work was done by the tunnellers themselves for, as mentioned previously, very often infantry or pioneer battalions would be tasked to work with the tunnelling companies. When urgent work was required on the defensive systems on the Auchy Front on 8 July 1916, the 13th Glosters (a pioneer battalion) and 112 other infantrymen were provided to undertake the work, whilst the 251st contributed two officers, four NCOs and twenty four men to supervise the operations.

There was, however, one thing that slightly soured this otherwise happy relationship between the tunnelling company and the infantry. Although the Germans were by now losing their superiority in mine warfare, they were still far quicker to occupy the crater formed after a mine was blown. On 16 July when the enemy were heard working underground at Vermelles Railway Triangle, No. 2 listening post in the British gallery was charged with 3,000 lbs of ammonal with a further 1,000 lbs being placed in No. 1 post, these listening posts being about fifteen yards apart. Almost immediately after the mine was blown and the crater formed, the enemy were seen to be occupying the lip on the British side of the crater. This was always very frustrating for the tunnelling companies and certainly a great deal of training was given to the British infantry so that they too might take this advantage; however, this was one situation in which the Germans always seemed to gain the upper hand.

Raids were also conducted by the Germans. On 31 July they raided the line at Auchy at 6.00 am, penetrating the British mining system by several yards, and then blowing a mobile charge. This raid happened during a change of shift and, although there was no material damage, four soldiers of 22ⁿᵈ Durham Light Infantry were killed, and one reported missing. Investigations showed that there had been insufficient guards at the entrance to the mining system. As early as 10 July, Major Humphrys had requested that 116 Brigade provide guards at entrances to all mine shafts, particularly as the Cambrin front was often left poorly protected. Major Humphrys had continuing concerns over the lack of protection for the mining systems and persistently informed those above him of them. On 1 August he visited Controller of Mines, First Army, about the protection of mine entrances and underground magazines and he followed this up the following day with a visit to HQ 8ᵗʰ Division, this time proposing the temporary closure of mine entrances no longer in use, so reducing the impact of enemy raids on the mining system. His suggestion was accepted.

By the end of July 1916, the 251ˢᵗ had blown fourteen mines whilst the Germans had retaliated with only four. The 251ˢᵗ suffered two further casualties, with Sapper R J Brown, from Gwennap, Cornwall and Sapper J Crozier, from Derby, killed after the Germans blew a mine at Jerusalem Hill.

In the nine months that the 251ˢᵗ had been operational in the Cuinchy/Auchy sector, their growing superiority over the Germans was almost certainly due to Major Humphrys' organisational skills and attention to detail as much as to his men's skill as miners. This was recognised at senior level, as a letter sent in July 1916 to HQ First Army, from Lieutenant General R. Haking, GOC IX Corps, confirms:

> *I am anxious to place on record the excellent work performed during the last few months by 251ˢᵗ Company RE under Major Humphrys on the Auchy and Cuinchy fronts.*
>
> *The Officers, NCO's and men of RE mining companies work in the dark not only as regards their actual labour, but frequently, I am afraid, recognition.*
>
> *This Company has been most successful with its defensive work never failing to give such worries of dangers underground and to take effective steps to avert it. They have been equally successful in working with the Infantry in offensive operations actually having been sent forward with reconnoitring Infantry to search and destroy hostile mine shafts and discover the enemy's system of working.*
>
> *I cannot speak too highly of the sound initiative and care devoted to all these exploits and no danger has daunted any one of all of the Company in their successful efforts to support their comrades in the Infantry.*
>
> *I have known all the details of the mining operations on this front since January 1916 and I vouch for the great difficulties to be overcome as it is one of the most active mining centres along the front of the Army.*
>
> *The constant strain has been supported by all ranks in the most cheerful spirit and I think Major Humphrys is to be congratulated on the results of this work and also the fine body of Officers NCO's and men he commands.*

(Quoted in 251 Tunnelling Company's War Diary)

On 6 August a commemoration service for the second anniversary of the commencement of the war was held in the Grand Place in Béthune; five officers and 180 other ranks of the 251ˢᵗ paraded in a march past General Monro, GOC First Army. This would have been one of General Monro's last duties in France as he was replaced the following day when acting command was given to Lieutenant General Haking. General Monro became Commander in Chief, India.

The ability of the German infantry to occupy a crater so quickly after a mine explosion, something at which their British counterparts still did not excel, continued to cause concern. Major Humphrys visited the CRE (Commander Royal Engineers) of the 32nd Division at his headquarters to discuss a proposal to improve infantry training in respect of this. Humphrys' idea involved constructing training craters that would allow the infantry to practise the consolidation of craters following the blowing of mines. The idea was accepted and on 10 August test bores were drilled near Beuvry to establish the suitability of the ground for such craters.

'Blow for blow' mining continued through August but perhaps with less enthusiasm. The numbers of mines blown fell, with the 251st exploding five mines, whilst the Germans blew only three. Yet the tables had turned, for not only had the 251st curtailed German mining activity, they now had the upper hand. In what seemed like a last ditch effort, the enemy exploded a mine between Midnight and RWF Craters at 7.20 pm on 1 September; one miner, Sapper WH Harris of Helston, who was underground at the time, was injured, dying of his injuries the following day and is buried in Cambrin Military Cemetery. After this very little was heard from the Germans and no further mines were blown by either side for the rest of that month.

As the intensity of the mining campaign diminished, Major Humphrys turned his mind to domestic matters. Ever aware of his men's' well-being, he recognised that many of the men, being Cornish Methodists, did not drink alcohol and preferred not to use a facility where alcohol was served. At the beginning of September he solved this minor problem by dividing the canteen into two, one half being 'wet' and the other 'dry'. A Company concert was held in the canteen later in the month, though the diaries do not record in which canteen it was held!

Lieutenant Colonel Dale-Logan continued to visit the billets, giving lectures on various health topics, such as the effects of mine gases, and showing an active interest in the maintenance of healthy living standards. On one of his visits he raised concerns about overcrowding and put in a request for additional huts.

As the year progressed, Major Humphrys' use of pipe pushing as an operational part of a raid was becoming widely accepted as standard practice. On 4 September he, together with Second Lieutenant Bullen, visited the HQ of 1st Dorsets in the Cambrin sector to provide assistance with the planning and preparation of a forthcoming raid. The plan devised required a pipe loaded with 270 lbs of ammonal to be pushed, using a Hughes & Lancaster machine, this time across the surface of No Man's Land near the Béthune–La Bassée Road for a distance of ninety seven feet. The charge was blown at 1.40 am on 8 September, destroying the enemy wire and allowing another raid to take place successfully.

On 14 September the proposed training crater was opened at Annezin. Two charges, each of 1,500 lbs of ammonal, were placed at a depth of seventeen feet, forty feet apart. A pipe was also pushed 112 feet using a Sentinel Jack and a trench was blown to the edge of the crater. After the explosion, practise in consolidation, demolitions, and attacks across craters with ladders, grapnels and alpenstocks were undertaken by the infantry.

With September a quiet month with regard to mine warfare, extensive work was carried out by the 251st in constructing dugouts to the rear of the communication galleries for the infantry. Major Humphrys had always recognised the Cornishmen as good miners who worked with a cheerful outlook and good team spirit and the speed with which the extra work on the dugouts was undertaken did not go unnoticed by others. The following commendation from the Corps Commander was received by Major Humphrys on 25 September 1916:

> *The Corps Commander wished me to place on record his appreciation for the excellent work all men working under your supervision have done in completing the scheme of underground work on the 32nd Division's front. After his visit this morning he realises that the task set was one of considerable magnitude and to have it completed in so short a time must have entailed the full energies of all concerned. He congratulates you on the results.*
>
> *The Army Commander has already been notified through the Chief Engineer of the Army of your group.*
> (Quoted in the 251st War Diary)

Despite the company's workload, the weekly concerts held in the canteen continued to be enjoyed by all. A company pierrot troupe was formed and the first performance given on 4 October. Enough leisure time was also found to play football against the 17th Highland Light Infantry. The results of this match are not recorded, but we must assume that the match was a great success, and hopefully the 251st won, as it was agreed that some of the profits of 1,300 francs (approx. £1500 today) from the first month's operation of the canteens would be used

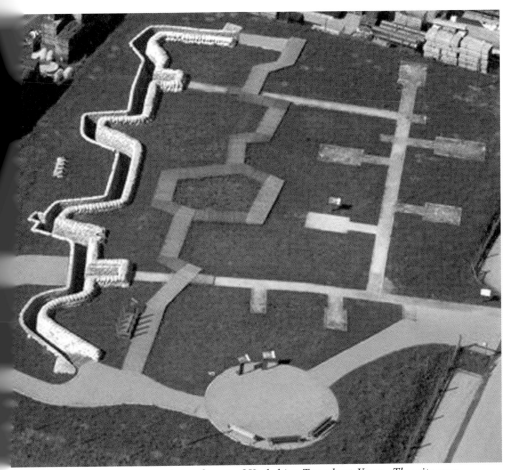

*The above photograph is of part of Yorkshire Trench at Ypres. The site was restored to the original layout; the trench line and exits from the dugouts into the trenches can be clearly seen. The square gravelled areas are where dugouts were located. (Picture Courtesy of City of Ypres-Tijl Capoen)*

to purchase football jerseys. Expenditure was also approved for supplementing rations, mainly by the purchase of vegetables grown locally and, to add even further to this new bounty, porridge was introduced for breakfast. 251 Tunnelling Company was settling into well-earned domesticity.

No doubt to the 251st it would have seemed much longer, given all they been set to do and what they had achieved, but 9 October was the anniversary of the Company sailing for France so a commemoration service was held that evening to remember those officers, NCOs and men killed in action during the year. Before this service, Major

*The divisional concert parties mirrored the Pierrot troupes that performed in the music halls and pier theatres at seaside resorts. The standard dress of ruffles and skull cap was a common feature of military concert parties. The troupe shown is from 8<sup>th</sup> Battalion Australian Imperial Force. (Picture courtesy of Australian War Memorial)*

Humphrys visited I Corps HQ to interview a German deserter who had come over to the British lines at Railway Embankment. The prisoner revealed the position of shafts, which had only hand pumps installed and which were being worked on by a small squad of men. Obtaining information in this way from deserters, who were usually willing to talk freely, was not unusual; one source suggests that the German Army had around 150,000 desertions throughout the war.

Defence schemes continued to be at the forefront of the agenda and on 13 October the Controller of Mines First Army visited Major Humphrys to discuss a scheme to build covered walkways, which were preferable to open trenches because of enemy trench mortar activity, from the reserve lines to ten proposed new strong points in the front lines, with a similar number on the support line. Work on this project commenced shortly afterwards for, as far as the blowing of mines was concerned, October was the quietest month to date. No mines at all were blown, a further indication of the superiority of the 251st over the enemy; this state of affairs continued into November.

Lieutenant Colonel Dale-Logan carried out a favourable inspection of the tunnellers' billets on 9 November but his deputy visited the camp on 15 November to discuss the siting of the new latrines. His work to keep men healthy must have been very much more difficult in some of the other billets he visited. It is said that 97% of the men in the trenches were infested at some time or another with lice, a problem exacerbated by the men only receiving baths two or three times a month, this being the only times that clean clothing was available to them, if they were so lucky. It was not known then that lice were the major carriers of trench fever, a debilitating flu-like illness, which was only discovered towards the end of the war. Even if it had been known before it is doubtful whether much could have been done to prevent lice being so prevalent.

The Company continued with the construction of defences; the new communication tunnels on the Cambrin and Auchy Fronts were inspected on 14 November by the GOC, 64 Brigade, with a further visit made by the Controller of Mines on 23 November. The latter also visited the work the following day to discuss the lighting of the communication trenches. He stayed for the weekly concert, which was also attended by the OC 257 Tunnelling Company, who had called to discuss the Company canteen. Obviously the canteen venture was attracting interest, which is not really surprising as the canteen accounts show expenditure in eight months of: 699 francs (£803 -2013) on Christmas cards; 2,085 francs (£2397 - 2013) on cakes; 9,500 francs (£10,735 - 2013) on vegetables and 25,281 francs (£29,073 - 2013) at various breweries! The approximations to today's values are obviously very rough, but it does illustrate the good profits the canteen was making.

The only mine to be blown in November was as a result of hearing the enemy working at Mine Point on 24 November. 500 lbs of ammonal was quietly tamped into place, and clearance was given to fire the mine. However, on the 25th the enemy was heard working for only four and a half hours, so firing was delayed. No sounds were heard the following day but, on 28 November, enemy activity was heard again and the mine was blown at 3.15 pm.

The 251st had by now constructed so many tunnels that, with some modification, many could be used as communication tunnels for the infantry. These tunnels made moving from one position to another much

*At the end of eight months the accounts show that they were carrying stock worth 4,913 francs (£5,650), 375 francs (£431) in returnable deposits on barrels and 2,475 francs (£2,846) cash in hand. (Reproduced with kind permission of The Royal Engineers Museum, Library and Archive)*

safer and messages could be carried more efficiently. Prior to this, moving men up to the front line, and messages, had to come along open communication trenches with all the associated danger from shelling or sniper fire. At the end of November the first of these subways, Robertson's and Wilson's tunnels, complete with electric lighting circuits installed, were handed over to the infantry to be used for this purpose.

On 11 December Major Humphrys visited the First Army Mining School to discuss a borehole that was required on the Auchy sector to support a planned trench raid. However, this appears to have been a

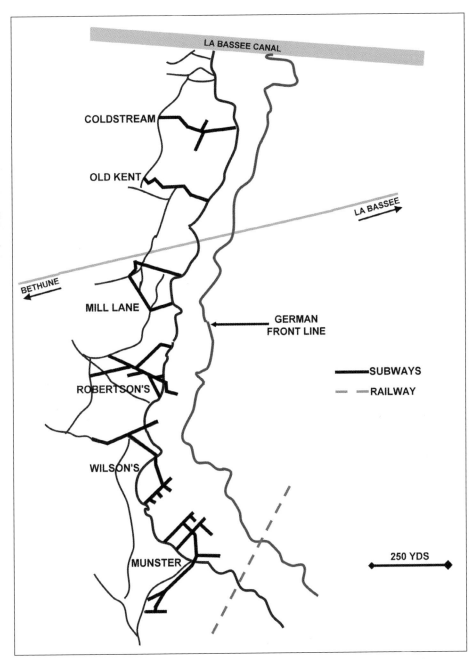

*By handing over these tunnels to the infantry, men could move up to the front line in comparative safety.* (Map after 'Tunnellers' Grieve)

difficult task, as on 16 December the raid was postponed because the borehole could not be prepared in time. It is not known if the enemy heard work progressing on the borehole, but at 4.30 am on 17 December the Germans blew a mine, destroying the borehole that was under construction. Fortunately, no casualties or further damage were reported and this was the only mine blown in December. Eventually the planned raid did take place with an officer and five men from the 251st taking part. Morale must have been high within the Company as, when it was decided that the raid into enemy trenches would take place, ten NCOs and men, twice the number required, volunteered to take part.

All was quiet up to Christmas Day, which was celebrated after Church Parade with a dinner at twelve noon, consisting of roast beef and veal, boiled carrots, turnips and cabbage, followed by hot Christmas pudding, bread and cheese, apples, oranges, walnuts and raisins. Christmas Tea consisted of boiled ham and bread and butter with jam. The meat, vegetables, nuts, fruit and ham were bought with canteen profits, another indication of how successful the enterprise was. The day was rounded off with a concert party in the billets performed by the Company Pierrot Troupe and Lena Ashwell, a well-known entertainer.

As 1916 came to a close, the 251st could look back on their part in what had been a hectic year of mining activity for the Tunnelling Companies, with 750 mines being blown by the British and 696 by the Germans. Once again, as had been the case in 1915, the most active areas were the Cuinchy, Givenchy, Hulluch and Loos sectors, along with Vimy Ridge.

In 1916, when at the height of its mining activities, the 251st blew sixty five mines in just six months while the Germans blew sixty two, a rate of almost one and a half mines per day. During this same period of conflict, a total of four mines per day were being blown by both sides along the whole length of the front covered

*Lena Ashwell OBE was an enthusiastic supporter of the British war effort. In 1915, she began to organise companies of actors, singers and entertainers to travel to France and perform free concerts to troops and by the end of the war there were twenty five of them. They travelled by London bus in small groups around France, carrying with them their equipment, including a piano.*

by the thirty two British tunnelling companies; when the comparison is made it is clear just how intensive the mining was on 251 Tunnelling Company's patch. Acknowledgement of the intense work being conducted, not just by the 251st but by all the tunnelling companies, was recognised by the C-in-C:

*The Tunnelling Companies of the Royal Engineers still maintain their superiority of the enemy underground...Many additional dugouts had to be provided as shelter for the troops, for use as dressing stations for the wounded, and as magazines for storing ammunition, food, water, and engineering material. Scores of miles of deep communication trenches had to be dug, as well as trenches for telephone wires, assembly and assault trenches, and numerous gun emplacements and observation posts. Important mining operations were undertaken, and charges were laid at various points beneath the enemy's lines.*

(General Sir Douglas Haig, quoted in *The Liverpool Echo,* 30 December 1916)

## Chapter 8

# Move to the Givenchy Sector, 1917

By early 1917, Germany needed miners back at home in the Ruhr to support the war effort and to mine for coal to supply power to the munitions factories; in addition, significant numbers were needed to assist in the construction of the Hindenburg Line, a German defensive position that was built during the winter of 1916–1917 on the Western Front, from Arras to Laffaux. To facilitate this, many thousands of German tunnellers and their engineering officers were withdrawn from the front line and were replaced by infantry, who lacked the skills and experience of the miners they replaced. Because of this, and coupled with the domination of the British tunnellers in the battle underground, German mining activity reduced significantly throughout 1917 and, as a result of the knock on effect, so did British defensive mining.

For the 251st, other plans were in progress and by the start of 1917 the Cuinchy-Cambrin-Auchy Front was well served by about a dozen tunnels, sometimes known as subways, more or less regularly spaced along the front, which were designed to get the infantry to the front line quickly and with effective protection; all of these tunnels were dug by the 251st. The work to construct tunnels through the railway embankment near Vermelles proved to be more difficult than expected, so the system was redesigned. In parallel to this, work also commenced on tunnel extensions for the 6th Division on the Cambrin and Auchy fronts, together with further defence works on the same fronts.

During January and February 1917 air temperatures plummeted, on one day dropping to 16°C below zero; the only cheer of the New Year coming from a concert given by the Royal Engineers band from Chatham, which visited the billets on 3 January 1917.

New equipment was developed as the war progressed and in particular improvements were made to the listening devices in use. On 20 January Major Humphrys attended the First Army School at Houchin for a course on the installation of electrical central listening stations. This equipment could convert disturbances in the ground caused by mining activity into electrical impulses and then reproduce these impulses into a telephone receiver. A number of these devices were linked together and transferred the information to a central listening station, so that an officer or NCO could monitor several listening posts at the same time. This was a great improvement on the geophones used up until then, particularly where galleries were very wet, as the equipment would be in a gallery but the listener could be based at a remote listening station, probably in the dry.

On 22 January there was a major change to the 251$^{st}$ when Major Humphrys left the Company to join the staff of I Corps as a 'learner'. Although he was a strict disciplinarian, he was sadly missed by the men, who held him in the highest regard. Every day he would be out amongst them, visiting sites and checking on the work being done. Their life was a hard one with little respite, but they knew that whenever and however he could, he would always act in their best interests. Their welfare was important to him and he always tried to ease their burden by ensuring that they were well billeted, well fed and had some sporting activity or entertainment organised for the limited time they had for rest. Captain EC Graham took command temporarily but was replaced on 6 February by Captain G Rowan MC.

January had been a quiet month, but on 4 February at 6.00 am the Germans blew mines on the Auchy sector, but with no casualties to the mining system or British personnel. The diary reports little activity during the remainder of February and early March, though the first of the new central listening stations became operational in February, in the Cuinchy sector, and was found to work very efficiently.

On 23 March Major Humphrys unexpectedly returned to take command, and Captain Rowan went on special leave on 24 March. The reason for his sudden departure is not known and he did not return to the 251$^{st}$ but joined 179 Tunnelling Company on 7 April 1917. On Major Humphrys' return he spent the first week visiting all of his sections and brigades, infantry divisions and corps within the sector, to bring himself back up to speed with the work that had been done in his absence.

Officers from one of the Special Companies RE, which were

responsible, amongst other things, for gas weapons, visited the 251st billets at the chicory factory in Béthune during April to discuss the requirements for the special facilities which would have to be constructed for the gas shells which were to be stored there. Four Special Companies of Royal Engineers had been established; 186 and 187 were assigned to the First Army to deal with the release of gas as a weapon. Although both Britain and Germany had signed the 1899 Hague Declaration concerning Asphyxiating Gases, which outlawed chemical warfare and the use of poisonous gases, both countries contravened it during the conflict – the British, of course, arguing that the Germans had started it!

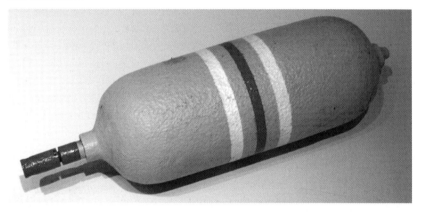

*All ordnance containing gas was clearly marked with coloured bands. The red (central) ring indicates it is an irritant gas and the two white bands confirm it is phosphorous. Out of the estimated 1.45 billion shells fired during the First World War, 66 million contained toxic chemicals. (Picture courtesy of Memorial Museum Passchendaele)*

April saw the widespread introduction of gas blankets, which were hung at the entrances and exits of the tunnels. These blankets were designed to filter out poisonous gas and to prevent it entering or spreading in the tunnels. Once fitted, they were inspected by the divisional gas officer from one of the special companies to ensure that the installation was satisfactory. Gassing and the effects of gas were a constant danger in the tunnellers' lives as Captain Graham of 185 Tunnelling Company, states in his book *The Life of a Tunnelling Company*:

*In the course of our work, we consequently absorbed more gas than was good for us, so much so that we were beginning to feel the effects. To add to it, the enemy bombarded the town next night with H.E. and gas. ....We got in a little later and just as we had finished the enemy opened up again, so it remained for us to warn our scattered crew and run the gauntlet. We swallowed more gas, however.*

Work on behalf of the infantry also continued, constructing trenches, saps and dugouts. Some of these shelters were not small underground rooms solely for use by officers or as brigade HQs, nor were they simply rest areas for soldiers, but were large spaces deep underground where a considerable number of infantry could be housed. Lighting and fresh drinking water was laid on, facilities were provided for sleeping and cooking and, just as importantly, so were latrines; larger dugouts often had medical facilities as well.

These shelters had a number of exits which would lead either into a gallery or directly into the trenches. It was important that the design

*The congested interior of a dugout, claustrophobic but safe from artillery shells. (Picture courtesy of Memorial Museum Passchendaele)*

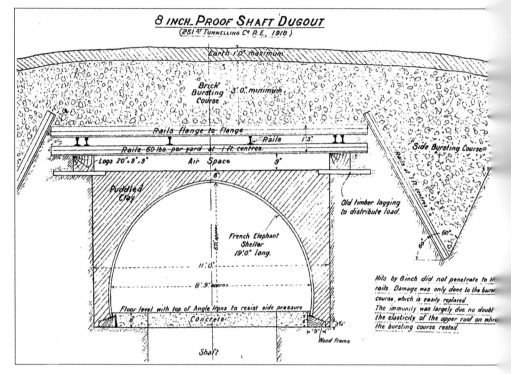

### 8 INCH PROOF SHAFT DUGOUT
#### (251⁵ᵗ TUNNELLING Cº R.E., 1918)

*Dugouts were very well designed to keep the men safe. This is a design by the 251st that was proof against from 8-inch shells. (Reproduced with kind permission of The Royal Engineers Museum, Library and Archive)*

would allow several hundred men or more to swiftly take up firing positions in the forward trenches. Shelters constructed by 251 Tunnelling Company at Givenchy would billet even greater numbers of men, but the design principles remained the same and effective movement out to the trenches remained paramount.

The advantage of deep dugouts and shelters, initially constructed to assist offensive operations, was that they protected troops from heavy enemy shelling which would sometimes continue for several days before an attack. Buried deep beneath the ground the infantry might be safe, but their existence was claustrophobic and it could be very frightening in such an environment listening to the sounds and feeling the upheavals of the maelstrom above their heads. Electric lighting was installed although at times it failed, leaving the troops in total darkness for a while; not a worrying scenario for a miner, but one that may have been a concern for others. There was always a back up system, such as candles or tilly lamps, but until these were lit darkness would prevail. Boredom would have been an issue too, as Captain Graham wrote:

*I suppose it will remain a mystery to our dying day how each one of us spent the hours in a dugout. Hour after hour would slip by in an aimless manner, and, of the twenty-four hours, perhaps eight would be passed in sleep, four in strolling around the work, and two in eating, leaving ten unaccounted for. Although some of us were keen readers, we could not concentrate our thoughts for long on anything except the lightest of literature. And yet we'd be stuck for the major portion of twenty-four hours in the dugout. How we eked out the time with perhaps a single companion I cannot now imagine. I fear our brains were often blank, and much more of that kind of life would have left our brains a perfect wilderness. No doubt the constant strain of the last three years was beginning to tell for all of us - constant touch with danger, with death jogging at one's elbows, was apt to put our nerves on edge.*

Some dugouts were exceptionally large, such as the modified existing cave system at Arras developed initially by the British and then handed over to the New Zealand Tunnelling Company, where over twenty four thousand infantrymen lived for days prior to the attack at Arras on 9 April 1917. Even an underground hospital was constructed with over 700 beds and an operating theatre. Part of this system in Arras, the Wellington Cave, is open to the public and is well worth visiting.

The dugouts and shelters certainly prolonged the life of many a soldier but life in some of them could be hellish, as described by Captain JD Hills MC, Croix-de-Guerre, in *The Fifth Leicestershire 1919*:

*At various points along* [the line] *these tunnels exits were built up to fortified shell holes, occupied by Lewis gun teams; these were our only supports. Down below lived Company Headquarters, the garrison, one or two tunnelling experts and the specialists, stokes mortars, machine gunners and others. It was a dreadful existence. The passages were damp and slippery, the walls covered in evil looking red and yellow spongy fungus, the roof too low to allow one to walk upright, the ventilation practically non-existent, the atmosphere, always bad, became in the early mornings intolerable, all combined to ruin the health of those who had to live there. But not only was one's health ruined, one's 'nerves' were seriously impaired, and the tunnels had a bad effect on one's morale. Knowing we could always slip down a staircase to safety, we lost the art of walking on top, we fancied the dangers of the open air much greater than they really were, in every way we got into bad condition ....Battalion Headquarters had a private tunnel, part of the mining system, which could be used in emergency, but as this was unlit, it was quicker to use the trench. The main tunnel system was lit, or rather supposed to be lit, with electric light. This often failed, and produced of course indescribable chaos. Although the tunnels had all these disadvantages, it is only fair to say that they reduced our casualties enormously, for during the three months we lost only three officers slightly wounded and eighteen men; of these at least four were hit out on patrol. We also managed to live far more comfortably as regards food than we should otherwise have been able.*

For the 251$^{st}$, construction of defensive works continued to be the norm throughout April and no casualties were reported underground. However Second Lieutenant Bullen and eight other men, all from No. 4 Section, were wounded by shrapnel from shell fire whilst on the La Bassée Road on their way to their place of work. Major Humphrys showed his virtue as a commanding officer by taking time out the following day to travel to 33$^{rd}$ Casualty Clearing Station in Béthune to visit the men.

On 10 May, the Controller of Mines, First Army, called to say that two Sections of the 251$^{st}$ were to relieve 254 Tunnelling Company on the Givenchy sector, whilst 170 Tunnelling Company were to take over parts of the Cambrin and Auchy sectors. Three days later, at 7.00 am, the southern portion of sector worked by the 251$^{st}$, about 1,900 yards long, was handed over to the 170$^{th}$. At the time of handover there was a continuous mining lateral on this sector, with the exception of two portions, one 150 yards and the other 300 yards in length, and three tunnels; there was no mining opposite this sector.

These three tunnels were, in effect, subways and had twenty feet of head cover all the way back to the reserve line. They were 550, 330 and

280 yards long respectively and were lit by electric light. Dugouts, machine gun emplacements, mortar pits, rifle grenade emplacements and underground loophole defences had already been established. There were thirty three listening posts with microphones installed, all wired to central listening dugouts.

No. 1 Section of the 251st had been on this part of the Cambrin sector since December 1915, driving 2.4 miles of galleries and in that time had blown nineteen mines while the enemy fired nineteen mines against them. No. 4 Section had been on the Auchy sector, driving 447 yards of galleries since June 1916 and had fired six mines, whilst the enemy fired eight mines against them.

During their time in these sectors, the officers and men of these two sections had between them been awarded: seven Military Crosses; one Mention in Despatches; one Distinguished Conduct Medal; one Meritorious Service Medal; eighteen Military Medals; and a Croix de Guerre. This was a remarkable collection of awards for just two sections of one company in such a short period of time. On the last day of May, the 251st was well over full strength, with twenty officers and 628 men, of whom 302 were infantrymen attached to the Company.

Back at the billets, sporting events continued to be promoted and on 27 May the War Diary entry is given over to a boxing contest, which comprised not only the championship bout for the 251st, but also contests against 182 and 170 Tunnelling Companies and the 66th Division. GOC, 197 Infantry Brigade attended with a large number of officers and men, whilst the band of the 66th Division provided entertainment in the canteen.

The next day, Major Humphrys visited the Givenchy sector and later, with Captain Hansen, went to see further experiments being conducted at Le Quesnoy in the use of ammonal-filled tubes to cut through barbed wire, a development of Bangalore torpedoes. The tubes were three inches in diameter and three feet long and weighed around ten lbs. On this occasion they very effectively destroyed a belt of wire twelve feet deep, certainly in a way which was superior to other methods being used at the time.

June started with No. 4 Section setting yet another all army tunnelling record when they drove forty five feet of timbered gallery, measuring six feet by three feet, in just twenty four hours. The following day they broke the record again by driving and timbering forty six feet of gallery in twenty four hours and then, for the following four twelve hour shifts,

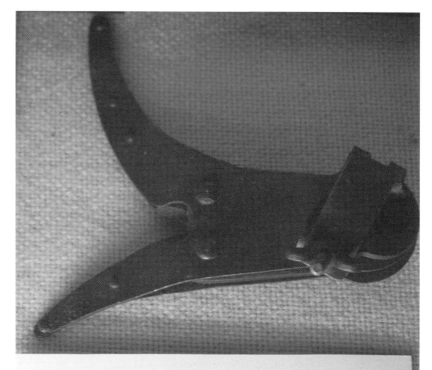

**WIRE CUTTER No 1 Mk II**
These were designed to fit over the nose-cap of the Lee-Enfield No 1 Rifle. Although of ingenious design they proved to be ineffective in cutting the German pattern barbed wire, and, in any case only worked if the wire was in tension.
Most were thrown away or reduced to scrap.

*This No.1 Mk II wire cutter was designed to fit over the nose cap of the Lee Enfield rifle. (Picture courtesy of Cornwall's Regimental Museum)*

achieved drives of twenty, twenty five, twenty, and twenty six feet, a total of ninety one feet in forty eight hours.

These tunnels could have been used for offensive mining, that is, tunnelling into or beyond No Man's Land and firing mines under enemy held positions. The purpose for doing so could either be as part of a major offensive, where the best example from the British viewpoint would be at the Messines Ridge, or for some local tactical benefit, the latter of which was the usual case. In January 1916, Brigadier General Harvey had issued orders that there was to be no offensive mining without his permission because he did not want to provoke unnecessary underground fighting.

There were exceptions to this rule; and one is certainly worthy of mention, although the 251st took no part in it. On 7 June 1917, at 3.10 am, the largest group of offensive mines ever blown was detonated at the Messines Ridge. The shockwaves and the explosion would certainly have been heard by the 251st, as it was clearly heard in London and was recorded as a minor earthquake at a seismic station in Switzerland. The attack, which had been proposed nearly twenty four months earlier by Norton-Griffiths, involved a total of twenty five mines charged with almost one million pounds of explosive, being laid under the German trenches on the Ridge. On the night, nineteen mines were blown, the rest having been abandoned or the decision taken not to fire them as it was deemed to be unnecessary. For a number of days prior to the 7th June 1917, it is reported that some 2,200 field guns fired in excess of three million shells at ten miles of German defences stretching from Hill 60 to Le Gheer. Twenty minutes after the artillery ceased, the mines were fired. After the detonation, combined with a massive rolling artillery barrage, the German front line defences were almost completely destroyed. Numbers in battles such as this are always difficult to ascertain, but it is generally accepted that following the subsequent attack by the British infantry who met very little resistance, over 7,000 stunned German prisoners were taken, with over 10,000 Germans being killed or missing as a result of the explosion and the week long offensive that ensued. The effect on the morale of the German army was considerable. Ludendorff, in his memoirs as quoted by Grieve, records:

*We should have succeeded in retaining the position but for the exceptionally powerful mines used by the British, which paved the way for their attack...The result of these successful mining operations was that the enemy broke through on June 7th...The moral effect of the explosions was simply staggering.*

One abandoned mine did explode later in 1955, possibly because of a lightning strike on a newly erected pylon. Many pounds of explosive still lie buried eighty feet below ground to this day, one mine still charged with 50,000 lbs of ammonal.

After the British triumph at Messines Ridge, Germany ordered all the serving geologists over the age of forty back to Germany; the others were transferred to fighting units. This decision to withdraw the geologists, coupled with the earlier one to send miners back to work on the home front, had a significant impact on the quality and capacity of the German mining capability; the threat underground was now greatly reduced, but not yet removed.

Whilst some Sections of the 251st were still busy constructing tunnels and counter-mining, the others were working on the defensive system at Givenchy. This system, with its subterranean elements, was designed by Lieutenant Colonel GC Williams and Major Humphrys and described by him:

> *...that the front line should consist of a number of detached posts, strongly fortified, access to which should be obtained by interconnected underground tunnels, well lighted and connected to dugouts and forward headquarters, all of which should be constructed by the tunnelling companies*

As part of this system, machine-gun and Stokes mortar emplacements were also constructed. The Stokes mortar was designed by Sir Wilfred Stokes, as a counter to the equivalent German light mortar.

Trench raiding parties continued to make frequent forays into enemy lines and provided a useful source of intelligence for both the infantry and the tunnellers. The 251st had successfully mastered the use of pipe pushing to create open trenches for this purpose and now proposed using existing tunnels to get a raiding party nearer to the German lines, constructing shafts from the tunnels through which the raiding party could emerge. After several trials, the first large scale raid was planned and carried out by the 2/4th East Lancashires with the 251st supporting the operation. The planning was notably detailed, with three tunnels to be used, which would allow 200 infantrymen to emerge less than fifty yards from their objective. All of the tunnels were linked by field telephone and in one tunnel an advanced dressing station was built so that any injured soldiers could receive immediate treatment.

Decoy mines to the left of the sector to be raided were charged with 2,000 lbs of ammonal. These were fired at 8.27 pm to distract the enemy, at which point the infantry emerged from the tunnels. Second Lieutenant Woods and five sappers from the 251st joined the raid to search for

*Battalion Stokes mortar emplacement. This particular one was at Ploegsteert for the use of 18th Battalion AIF. (Picture Courtesy of the Australian War Memorial, Canberra)*

German mineshafts, destroy shaft heads and remove any interesting equipment such as listening appliances and detectors. The 2/4th East Lancs took numerous prisoners, including an officer, sustaining only slight casualties themselves. It is estimated that the Germans suffered 250 casualties. One and a half hours had been spent in the German trenches and the raid was one of the most successful of the war, prompting a personal visit on 14 June from the Commander in Chief, Field Marshal Haig, to congratulate the raiding party.

Morale must have been boosted again when, on the same day, a letter was received from the Inspector of Mines, confirming that No. 4 Section had again broken all records whilst working on the Givenchy Front. They had, by driving 331¼ feet of six feet three inches by three feet gallery in ten days, broken the ten day and two day records for all

Armies, the five day and seven day clay gallery records for all Armies, and were just six inches under the seven day chalk gallery record. This was a remarkable feat, given that the digging during the last six days had been done with a push pick (broadly similar in size and design to an ice pick) and whilst working twelve hour shifts.

As tunnelling continued, a number of disused enemy tunnels and galleries were discovered. On 15 June, No. 2 Section broke into an old enemy gallery just 250 yards south of the Béthune to La Bassée Road. It was believed that the gallery was no longer in use, so the hole was closed off but with electronic listening equipment left in place to detect any German movement should they make an attempt to reopen it.

The next day the same Section broke into another gallery, which they penetrated for eighty feet until a collapse was encountered and the Germans were heard just a few feet away, working to clear the fall. For situations such as this, mobile charges were carried by the tunnellers and one was set and detonated. After the smoke had cleared, it was obvious that a 15 feet block of debris now existed between the galleries.

On 20 June, 197 Brigade in Givenchy was relieved by 6 Brigade. Before he left, Brigadier General Banon, GOC 197 Brigade, sent a letter to the 251st, expressing his appreciation of the Company's work, a copy of which was retained in the War Diary:

> *In giving up command of the Givenchy sector, Brig 197 Infantry Brigade wishes to express his appreciation of the excellent work performed by Major Humphrys MC and the officers and the ranks of the Tunnelling Company. The Brigade is greatly indebted to the wholehearted co-operation of Major Humphrys and his command who have always shown that they are not only ready to undertake work to further operations against the enemy but make good all they undertake and do, and get their work completed in a workmanlike manner in record time. Brigadier-General Banon wishes all ranks every success and trusts that he may work again with the Tunnelling Company.*
> *Brig HQ 19/6/17*
> *(Signed) Capt C.J. Gasson*

A few days later, on 25 June at 11.00 pm, the Germans launched a raid on the Givenchy sector, following a bombardment that caused some slight damage to the shaft heads. However, they did not gain access to the mining system but four hours later eight Bavarians were found in the British lines and were taken prisoner by an Australian rifleman and a lance corporal from the 251st. Two days later another German was captured by the 251st near the Coventry shaft on the Givenchy sector and was handed over to the infantry.

Greater pressure of work was placed on the 251st when just one section was ordered to relieve two sections of 253 Tunnelling Company who were working on the Neuve Chapelle–Armentières front. This meant that 251 Tunnelling Company was now responsible for maintaining a sector which ran from 250 yards south of the Béthune–La Bassée road to Houplines (two miles north of Armentières), a distance of eighteen miles.

Even more work was to come their way. On 19 July, Major Humphrys and Captain Church visited 253 Tunnelling Company's HQ at Le Drumez (see Map 5) to discuss a detachment from the 251st taking over the British Mission attached to the Portuguese 1st Division. Major Humphrys took the opportunity to ask for a further increase in manpower from the Controller of Mines, First Army.

In response to the discussions about manpower, two officers and ten men were left behind by the 253rd to act as guides to the mining system, and to provide information as required. Lieutenant De Mattos of the British Mission to the Portuguese was also attached to the detachment along with eight men from the Australian Electrical and Mechanical Mining & Boring Company. In addition, 135 other ranks from 23 and 35 Brigades and the 1st Portuguese Division were attached for duty, with Lieutenant De Mattos responsible for discipline in their camp. Two days later a further eight men from 251 Company HQ and six men from 253 Tunnelling Company were attached for duty.

Back on the Givenchy sector, Major Humphrys and Captain Hansen visited 6 Brigade and got approval for the construction of ferro-concrete shelters for the infantry's Lewis machine guns. The following day Major Humphrys visited 254 Tunnelling Company, who were also working in the Givenchy sector, to inspect the steel-lined shafts they were constructing in a soft sand area. Similar geological conditions would be encountered by the 251st, so this practical experience would prove to be very useful. Interestingly, it was Major Humphrys who had suggested using the steel shaft linings in soft sand areas, as he had witnessed a similar concept at Bentley colliery in Yorkshire when he was Assistant Inspector of Mines prior to the war.

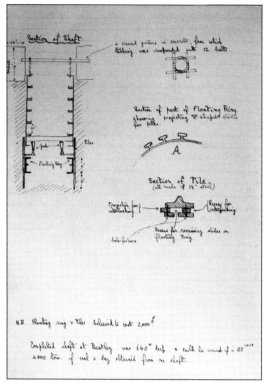

*Design of the shaft at Bentley colliery. The tubbing was 1.5 inches thick, 6 feet wide and in sections of 20 inches deep. The sections were sealed against each other using lead wool packing. They were made by Firth & Hadfield of Sheffield, a company formed in the early nineteenth century and still trading today as Firth Rixson. (Reproduced with kind permission of The Royal Engineers Museum, Library and Archive)*

*A steel tubbed shaft at Lancashire Farm, near Ypres. (Picture courtesy of the Tunnellers Memorial)*

The tunnellers were involved on 22 July 1917 in hand to hand fighting in the galleries in an incident on the Cambrin sector. The following description shows just how dangerous this type of fighting was, and how fortunate the 251$^{st}$ were to have a commanding officer of Major Humphry's calibre.

On 22 July the enemy broke into a British gallery in sector A21, which ran south from the bottom end of the Brickstacks almost to Mine Point. They penetrated to within sixty feet of the British line, but progressed no further, as Second Lieutenant Schneider and Lance Corporal Stewart, using their revolvers, exchanged shots with the enemy. The Germans fired a mobile charge at this point that blocked the gallery and the resulting fumes gassed several men, one of whom, Captain Hislop, lost his life. Second Lieutenant Schneider was awarded the Military Cross for his actions. His citation in the *London Gazette* dated 9 January 1918, states:

> *For conspicuous gallantry and devotion to duty. Assisted by an N.C.O. he attacked a party of the enemy who had entered our mine galleries and drove them back with revolvers. He then returned to the shaft and fetched explosives, intending to cut off that portion of the mine which had been temporarily lost. Whilst fixing the charge, however, he was rendered unconscious and gassed by the explosion of a charge left by the enemy, but it was due to his prompt action and gallantry that the enemy did not secure a large portion of our mine gallerie.*

Major Humphrys, immediately visited the site with Captain OJ Hansen, and acted swiftly to set out a plan to ensure that the gallery was fully secured to prevent the enemy from penetrating any further. Under cover of darkness that same night, a twelve feet long tunnel was driven from a listening post, accessed from a crater in No Man's Land. At the end of this tunnel a gallery was constructed, eight feet long and three feet square. Work commenced at 2.00 am and was completed by 5.15 am. A reconnaissance of the crater was undertaken by Lieutenant Walker, who listened on his geophone for ten minutes and then, at 5.45 am, the gallery was packed with 450 lbs of ammanol.

The mine was fired at 8.30 am, exploding 120 feet nearer the German line than the mobile charge that the Germans had exploded the day before. Major Humpry's quick thinking and swift action had closed the

German galleries without any further fighting underground and had prevented the situation from developing into something far more serious. Military Medals would subsequently be awarded to Sapper Swallow and Private Grubb for their actions on the day.

The following two letters, taken from the War Diary, expressing congratulations from both the Corps and the Divisional Commander, show that Major Humphrys' excellence as a commanding officer was duly recognised:

*24th July 1917*
*From Lieutenant General R. Haking, Commander XI Corps*
*I wish to congratulate you and all ranks concerned in the successful result of your operations when attacked by the Germans in our gallery at A.21.7.7 on the 22nd July. Your prompt and energetic action showed great resource and a soldierly appreciation of the best means of countering the enemy's attack without loss of time.*

*II OC 251st Tunnelling Company RE*
*Forwarded to you –*
*With the Divisional Commander's Congratulations*

Major General Sir Cecil Pereira, who was then GOC of the 2nd Division, wrote:

*25th July 1917*
*I have received the accompanying mine explosion report of the 18 J 17 of the 251st Coy RE dated 22/23rd inst. I consider that the action taken by the OC 251st Tunnelling Coy RE showed the greatest initiative, determination and ingenuity.*
*Owing to his good work a very unpleasant situation has been avoided.*
*I wish to add that the skill of the tunnellers has given the greatest confidence to the Infantry.*

On 28 July 1917, as a result of the experience of the German withdrawal from the Somme to the Hindenburg line and leaving behind a number of hidden explosive devices, courses on handling enemy booby traps started at the First Army Mining School. Major Humphrys and four other officers of the 251st attended a lecture on the subject given by the OC of 174 Tunnelling Company.

*Deep dugouts, often set out like these, were safe from 8 inch shells. (Picture courtesy of Memorial Museum Passchendaele)*

Because of the difficulties encountered in mining operations, civil or military, engineers were always keen to learn something new; on 1 August Major Humphrys and Captain Hansen, in the company of an officer from 250 Tunnelling Company, who were working in that sector, visited a site near Wytschaete on Messines Ridge where some reinforced shelters, constructed by the Germans, had been captured by the British during the attack of 7 June 1917. Major Humphrys was particularly interested in how different types of shellfire had affected the structure, since concrete shelters were a major part of the scheme for the defence of the Givenchy sector.

A couple of days later, on 30 July 1917, the enemy were heard to be working close to one of the listening posts in the Cambrin sector. Working extremely quietly, with the men wearing sacks tied over their feet, the 251st loaded a mine with 2,000 lbs of ammonal and permission was given to fire the mine at 7.15 am the following day. The new listening equipment again proved its worth; information gathered from a microphone that had been left connected to the central listening post established that the enemy were still working, just fifteen feet away from the charge at the time of firing.

On 5 August a commemoration service was held in the billets for the third anniversary of the outbreak of war, with the fallen of the Company named and remembered.

On the Givenchy sector, sounds of German mining activity had been detected since May 1917; now the enemy were heard working within twenty feet of the Willow South listening post. One of the galleries located underneath the Germans was loaded with 9,000 lbs of ammonal and fired at 7.00 am on 10 August 1917, so forming a large crater named the Warlingham Crater, after the founding district of the 17<sup>th</sup> Royal Fusiliers. Neither the 251<sup>st</sup> nor anyone else in the other tunnelling companies would have known it at the time, but the 251<sup>st</sup> had just fired the last major British mine of the war.

More change was on the way when the Controller of Mines First Army called to say that it was his intention to hand over part of their eighteen mile long sector to 170 Tunnelling Company, releasing men from the 251<sup>st</sup> for work further north. The 251<sup>st</sup> had been working this part of the Cuinchy sector since October 1915, but now the southern part, about 450 yards long, was handed over at 9.00 am on 7 August. At the same time an additional eighty one men from No. 3 Section and a further fifty Portuguese were assigned to the work at Le Drumez (see Map 5).

The 3<sup>rd</sup> Australian Mining Company, under Major Sanderson, took over a section of the Red Lamp, Fauquissart and Chapigny sectors in front of Le Drumez on 12 August. They received a warm welcome from the enemy who, at 4.30 am, fired two mines at Duck's Bill and Fauquissart, but no damage was caused to the mining system.

Major Humphrys visited the detachment at Le Drumez in the wake of an enemy raid that had taken place on 14 August in the Mauquissart and Duck's Bill sectors at about 4.45 am. Second Lieutenants Woods MC and Walker of the 251st were on duty in the trenches at the time of the raid and did well in defending the line by organising the Portuguese troops in the vicinity. One prisoner was taken and several Germans killed, with one British soldier reported missing. The actions of officers and men of the 251<sup>st</sup> were again praised in a letter from the Corp Commander, expressing high commendation for the excellent services provided by the 251<sup>st</sup>. Two further Military Medals for gallantry following the trench raid by the enemy were awarded on 14 August, making a total of thirty one Military Medals won by the 251<sup>st</sup>.

Conscription had started in March 1916, following the passing of the

Act in January 1916, but the infantry was still short of men. On 26 August, the Controller of Mines First Army called at 251's billets to inform Major Humphrys of the anticipated withdrawal of all attached infantry from the tunnelling companies. Consequently, Major Humphrys visited the detachment at Le Drumez to reorganise work allocations.

At the end of August, to help reduce the manpower needed to maintain mining systems in that area, the decision was taken to flood the Ducks Bill system on the very low lying Winchester Front, thus making it unavailable to the Germans. Major Humphrys visited the sector together with Captain Evans to decide on the best location to bring this about.

By the end of August the Company strength stood at twenty officers and 613 men; of these, 211 were attached infantrymen. About 250 more infantrymen were with the detachment at Le Drumez.

Following the decision taken on 26 August, the permanently attached infantry left for their respective infantry base depots on 13 September. A large proportion of these men came to France in 1914 and many of them had been with the Company for almost two years, having volunteered to remain with the 251st rather than with their infantry battalions. In September, Lieutenants Walker, Rees and Cock, together with 163 men, returned to HQ from Le Drumez, the remainder being left to supervise the Portuguese Mining Company, who were constructing ferro-concrete shelters. The returnees arrived just in time for the opening of the Company gymnasium, complete with Swedish bars and wall ladders.

The roads behind the front, which were part of the supply route, were frequently very congested. Major Humphrys visited Béthune and suggested that there was a case for mining timber and other stores, which were sent from the Company HQ to the RE forward dump at Pont Fixe, to be carried by barge along the canal instead of by road. The canal route was much more direct, only four miles long, and water transport would be much more economical in time as greater loads could be carried by the barges. The supplies required by the tunnelling company were now significant, with seventy to eighty tons of material being required for a single major ferro-concrete shelter.

Although the British had fired their last mine, the Germans had not; two explosions occurred on 17 and 18 September. One of these explosions may not have been a mine as it occurred just behind the enemy's line at Fauquissart and did so in such a way that it is believed that an ammunition dump in a dugout or crater had exploded. This theory was supported by aerial photographs taken soon after, which showed that a new crater, about eighty feet in diameter on the side of a road well behind the German lines, had been formed at the time of the explosion reported on 17 September. The following day the Germans blew a shallow mine on the Givenchy front at 7.30 pm but again, rather oddly, the explosion occurred on the enemy's side of No Man's Land. No damage was caused on the British side either above or below ground and there were no casualties. On 18 September, Major Humphrys visited HQ 1st Portuguese Division to discuss augmenting the Portuguese Mining Company with miners drawn from Portuguese infantry battalions, thus strengthening the overall position.

By the end of September the withdrawal of some of the attached infantry had reduced the strength of the Company significantly. It was now down to twenty two officers and 417 men, a hundred of these attached infantry. Six officers and about eighty other ranks of the Company remained at Le Drumez.

October started with the Germans firing a mine on the Givenchy sector but, apart from two small craters, there was no damage or casualties either above or below ground. On 6 October, a further commendation for the Company came from GOC 2nd Division, who expressed his appreciation of the work done by the Company during the time the 2nd Division had been in the same sector.

The following day a commemoration service was held in the billets, it being the nearest Sunday to the second anniversary of the arrival of the Company in France. On the actual anniversary, 9 October, a special dinner, which included roast veal, was given to celebrate the formation of the Company, followed by a concert performed in the billets by the 25th Division's Concert Party.

On 14 November, Major Humphrys returned to England to unveil a memorial to Lieutenant MA Phillimore at St. John the Baptist Church, Shedfield, near Botley in Hampshire. Second Lieutenant Phillimore was originally with 11 Essex, but was transferred to 251 Tunnelling Company. He was killed on 25 June 1917 and is buried at Cambrin Military Cemetery. He must have been a very popular officer as a collection was held amongst his fellow officers and sufficient funds were raised to purchase the memorial plaque erected in his local church.

On 22 November, XI Corps was replaced by XV Corps but, as was usual for the tunnelling companies, the 251st remained in the same

*The tablet erected in memory of Second Lieutenant Phillimore in St. John the Baptist Church, Shedfield, Botley, Hants. (Photograph courtesy of the Parish Administrator, St. John the Baptist Church)*

sector and billets, still part of First Army. Whilst divisions and corps could be moved from one Army to another, or withdrawn to rest areas away from the front, so leading a fairly itinerant life, the tunnelling companies tended to remain in the same location for long periods. As a result, there were some advantages that the tunnelling companies enjoyed over the infantry. Although the tunnelling companies were constantly at work with their four day on, four day off shift pattern, and no collective time away, this did enable them to operate in a slightly different way.

As an example, four pigs were purchased by the company canteen committee and then fattened up before being slaughtered to provide extra meat rations; arrangements were also made with a local landowner for the planting of cabbage plants, the 251st providing the labour and the landowner supplying the plants, with an agreement that if they still occupied their billets when the cabbages had grown, then they would only pay for the original cost of the plants when the cabbages were harvested.

Superiority in the mining campaign having been gained, and with the last British mine having been fired, the possibility of using the tunnels for other purposes was considered, particularly with regard to the extensive defensive systems of machine gun posts, brigade headquarters and deep dugouts that were now being built in this crucial sector.

In December, Captain Irvine of the US Army and Captain Ball from the First Army Mine School visited the Givenchy sector to examine the dugout accommodation that had been constructed by the 251st. Such was their interest that later in the month Captain Hansen visited 127 Brigade with reference to the dugout accommodation on the Givenchy sector and took the Brigade Major on an inspection around the sector and through the mining system.

With all mining systems in a waterlogged area, where the water table was never too far from the surface, as those systems became more complex, problems occurred. At Chapigny, for example, water broke through in December from the old German mines in considerable volume. Major Humphrys and Captain Church visited the system as the water continued to rise and found that it was a foot deep in the gallery at the bottom of the northern shaft and up to the top of the gallery in the southern shaft. The decision was made to flood the galleries completely. A connection was made between the top of the shaft and a surface drain so that surface water could run into the mining system, rendering it useless to the enemy.

Major Humphrys proposed new ways that the 251$^{st}$ could employ their skills when, on 11 December, he visited the senior signals officer at XV Corps to discuss pushing pipes under the railway near Armentières. This time the pipes were not to be packed with ammonal but to carry signal cables. Unfortunately, on this occasion pipe pushing was found to be impracticable and it was decided to recommend driving a tunnel through the embankment instead, which of course would still be a task for the sappers to undertake.

As the end of year approached, on 15 December, further assistance arrived when two companies from the 1/8th Manchesters were assigned to the 251st. The timing was fortunate as they arrived in time for Christmas Day and, no doubt, enjoyed partaking of the three fattened pigs slaughtered for Christmas dinner. The day started at 3.15 am with a breakfast of liver and bacon being served followed by Church parade at 11.00 am. Dinner (lunch as we would know it today) was at 12.30 pm for HQ and three of the reliefs, the other remaining on duty; irrespective of the festivities, all shifts were required to turn out in the usual way. The menu consisted of roast pork with apple sauce, sage and onion stuffing, carrots and potatoes. This was followed by plum pudding, apples, nuts and a pint of beer per man. The loyal toast was given and absent friends remembered. Tea consisted of tea, sweet biscuits and tinned apricots, followed by a concert in the evening.

The absent friends remembered at the festivities would have included Sapper Henry Wilson Thomas from St. Agnes, who died that day at 33rd Casualty Clearing Station, Béthune, from gunshot wounds received earlier. Sapper Thomas' mother received a telegram on 29 December 1917, four days later. It is still part of his service record, although now barely legible:

> *Dec 29th regret to inform you Officer Commanding 33rd Casualty Clearing Station reports 25th Dec died 25th Dec 132352 H.W. Thomas RE from Gunshot wounds perforated and lesion of spine.*

As was apparently usual, and as a mark of courtesy, all post addressed to his mother would have been held back by the Post Office until the telegram was delivered.

After the Christmas festivities, the 251st enjoyed the mutual support so often given by the tunnelling companies when, on Boxing Day, one officer and twenty five other ranks from 176 Tunnelling Company reported for duty to help drive a tunnel at Pont Fixe, which was to carry power cables, and also to assist with the installation of a suction pipe for a water-cooling pump at the power plant located there. On New Year's Eve three more officers and 150 other ranks from the 1st Battalion Portuguese Miners reported for duty, now attached to the 251st. The Commanding Officer of the Portuguese Mining Company took command of the attached Portuguese infantry and assumed responsibility for the billets occupied by Portuguese troops.

Looking back, 1917 could be considered as a year of consolidation. The Germans' supremacy in mine warfare on the Western Front enjoyed in the early years of the war was over, whilst their capacity for offensive mining had been significantly reduced. After Messines, the main thrust of the work for the 251st and the other tunnelling companies was the new defensive positions constructed for the infantry, work which was going to prove to be so very important in the spring of 1918.

*Chapter 9*

# 'Stood to Arms', 1918

By now, the war effort required even larger sums of money, and it was seriously damaging the British economy; the Government had to raise money to help to balance the books. War bonds were issued, which all patriotic citizens were encouraged to buy; the bonds were an attractive proposition, with their offering of a 5½ per cent yield, all free of tax.

The soldiers fighting at the front were not excluded from this campaign to encourage financial investment in the country's war effort. On 4 January, at morning parade, all of the men were lectured by Major Humphrys about the benefits of war savings and economy bonds. This lecture was repeated by Lieutenant Ritchie the following day for the benefit of the men who had been on duty the previous day; by the end of January 1918, of the 333 men serving in the Company, 155 of them, almost fifty percent, had subscribed to the scheme to a total amount of £2,068 10s. The average amount subscribed per head was £6 10s 6d. The men were able to purchase the bonds at the Field Post Office, which had much the same facilities as any local village Post Office at home.

The 'save and lend' campaign was continued through February and into March. On 31 March a prize was awarded to the highest contributor in the Company but sadly there is no record of who the lucky winner was. The prize giving ceremony was followed by a roast pork dinner, with meat supplied from the company's own pigs.

No mines were blown by either side during January, which meant a nice quiet start to the New Year. However, those serving at the front must have been worried by other news. The Russian government had succumbed to the Bolshevik Revolution on 7 November 1917. The new government almost immediately sought an armistice and withdrew from the war a few weeks later, on 15 December; it would only be a matter of time before German troops on the Eastern Front would be transferred to the Western Front. These troops were battle-hardened soldiers who had fought their way to within eighty five miles of Petrograd (now returned to its original name of St. Petersburg), then the capital of Russia. With this in mind, much effort on the part of the 251st went into the building and strengthening of defensive systems, dugouts and machine gun posts in readiness for any new offensive by the German Army. An offensive was expected in the near future and, in preparation for this, all Armies had been ordered to ensure that strong defences were in place.

The company was at full strength; two officers and seventeen other ranks were at Le Drumez, in the XV Corp area, where the 251st were supervising the work of the Portuguese Mining Company. At the home billet, Company strength was augmented by an infantry carrying party comprising one officer and 152 other ranks. On 13 February, another five officers and 148 other ranks from 165 Brigade reported to 251's HQ for temporary attachment to the Company.

It was suspected that Germany would make use of tanks as part of the expected offensive; in anticipation of, and in preparation for this, on 10 February Major Humphrys visited the HQ of the Tank Corps, along with Lieutenant General Holland, GOC I Corps and Major Tulloch, OC 185 Tunnelling Company. They were there to look at ways in which obstacles could be created that would render the tanks ineffective or, at the very least, hinder their progress; another task that would be aided by the expertise of the tunnelling companies. During the course of the day the Australian 3rd Tunnelling Company blew a number of craters and British tanks were made available to try to negotiate these obstacles. Two tanks were used in the exercise; amid clouds of exhaust smoke and a great deal of engine noise, they struggled to climb the steep walls of the craters. The information thus gained was of immense use to the 251st in its work of preparing anti-tank defences. At the time it was unclear what the German capability was in terms of heavy tanks; in fact they only had twenty of these machines, (plus twenty captured allied ones) compared to the allies 7,700, although many of these latter, almost half, were very lightweight.

The United States of America had declared war on Germany on 6 April 1917 following the sinking of seven US merchant ships by German submarines. Although by the summer of 1918 the Americans were sending 10,000 men per day to the Western Front, their initial impact was slow. On 16 March 1918 an officer from the US Army arrived at the billets and was attached to the 251st for a few days to gain experience

*An A7V German tank captured by the Australians. It weighed around thirty tons and carried a crew of seventeen, including one officer. (Picture courtesy of the Australian War Memorial, Canberra)*

in how the tunnelling companies operated in conjunction with the infantry.

Ludendorff was unsure at what stage the Americans would come into the war in significant strength. Germany still had to leave a sizeable force of around one million men in the east until the peace treaty of March 1918, but many other of its better, battle hardened, soldiers were redeployed to the west. He decided to launch a Spring Offensive with the intention of splitting the French and British armies and defeating each before the Americans became strategically and significantly involved.

The first part of the plan, Operation Michael, which commenced on 21 March 1918, concentrated on the British Fifth and Third Army in the area between St. Quentin and Arras, south of Givenchy-lès-la-Bassée. Although great swathes of ground were gained by the Germans and the

Fifth Army suffered massive casualties, the operation was called off on 5 April after the Germans failed to secure Amiens. However, Operation Michael had drawn British forces from other areas to defend Amiens, and this movement of troops left the rail route through Hazebrouck and the defences of the major supply points to the Channel ports of Calais and Boulogne vulnerable.

It was known with certainty that Ludendorff would attack again, this time further north. Naturally expert in the use of explosives, the 251st was employed in the work of preparing charges ready for the destruction of roads, bridges and railways in case of attack; to be fired, if necessary, in order to delay any German advance. Even when the expected offensive commenced to the south of their position, it would seem that the 251st felt confident about their readiness as they still found time to plant the Company allotment with potatoes!

*General Erich Ludendorff. After the failed 1923 Munich Beer Hal Putsch, he was tried for treason alongside a certain Adolf Hitler but was acquitted. (Picture courtesy of George Grantham Bain Collection)*

On 1 April Major Humphrys visited all of the ammunition dumps in his sector identified as requiring demolition in case of a rapid advance by the Germans to ensure that they were suitably prepared. He may have known, but his men would not, that two days later orders would be received for Major Humphrys, promoted to the rank of temporary lieutenant colonel, to take command of 8th Royal Scots. On 5 April he left 251 Tunnelling Company to take up his new post. On 18 March 1918, he had been awarded the Distinguished Service Order for the events of 22 July 1917, during which a considerable portion of front line had been saved by his actions. His citation reads:

*The enemy having broken into our protective tunnelling system, he at once grasped the situation and extended another branch of the tunnel into an old crater, thence driving a shaft down onto the captured tunnel. The mine was charged, tamped and fired, the resultant crater effectually blocking the tunnel at a good distance from our front line. Major Humphrys undertook and supervised this work throughout, carrying it out in the open within a few yards of the enemy front line, and by this action, the enemy were undoubtedly prevented from blowing up a considerable portion of our front line.*

For three years he had remained unscathed, despite serving in one of the hottest sectors of the front. He was wounded just a few days into his new command and was taken to hospital, having developed nephritis, a potentially fatal kidney infection. To help his recovery, he was transferred to an administrative role in Egypt, working with prisoners of war, returning after the war to his work in the Mine Inspectorate.

On 6 April 1918, Captain (shortly to become Major) James Church was appointed Officer Commanding 251 Tunnelling Company. Captain Church, born in England, was a highly experienced coal mining engineer who was working in Canada at the outbreak of war. He joined the 19 Alberta Dragoons as a trooper and was soon promoted to corporal; he was transferred to the Western Front as part of the Canadian Expeditionary Force in February 1915. He was resting in billets one evening when Norton-Griffiths turned up in his Rolls Royce. He had heard about Church's mining experience, and informed him that he was to join 251 Tunnelling Company as a second lieutenant, which he duly did on 26 October 1915. Such was the speed of the posting that when his orders arrived a few days later his commanding officer knew nothing of it. Norton-Griffiths had proved himself time and again to be an excellent judge of character and the fact that a corporal in the Dragoons would eventually become a major in command of a tunnelling company, and that during his time with them he would gain the DSO and MC, bears this out.

Just three days after Church's appointment as OC and, two years to the day since five miners were killed in a mine explosion, 9 April was again to prove to be an eventful day for the 251st. The next three weeks were probably the most challenging for the Company in the whole of the conflict, for as well as their usual tunnelling work, they were to stand to arms and fight in the trenches alongside their comrades in the infantry.

In preparation for the anticipated German offensive, Major General Hugh Sandham Jeudwine, GOC 55th (West Lancs) Division, in whose sector the 251st fell, initiated a very strict regime from February 1918. Respirators were to be worn by all officers and men between 10.00 and 10.15 am every day so that they became well-practised in donning the

*All ranks had to practise wearing their gas respirators for fifteen minutes every day, so that when gas was released they were well experienced in using such restrictive equipment. (Picture courtesy of Memorial Museum Passchendaele)*

apparatus very quickly. Every man had to fire ten rifle rounds daily, irrespective of where he was working, and to facilitate this musketry practice, thirty yard ranges were constructed near billets. All of the men in his division knew the positions they had to take up in case of attack, whilst supply routes were planned to ensure that adequate supplies of ammunition and rations could be sent up to the men.

The fortifications at Givenchy, principally designed and built by the 251st in preparation for this expected offensive, included concrete machine gun posts and deep mined dugouts that would prove to be very effective. The dugouts were some forty feet underground in order to provide protection against the severest of shelling and had entrances protected by reinforced concrete canopies weighing up to 200 tons; they were designed to ensure an easy exit for the troops when they had to move up to the front line to repulse an attack.

Around Givenchy, a complex defensive system was constructed; a network of ferrous-concrete pillboxes with long subways linking together the many dugouts, thus allowing for the safe movement of the infantry (see Map 6). The mined dugouts could house up to two battalions of men and came complete with boreholes, which provided fresh drinking water, pumps to keep the dugout dry and ventilated and tiers of bunks to provide sleeping accommodation. So great were the numbers of men crammed into the dugouts that one area became known as the 'Bunny Hutch System'. This subway maze linked Moat Farm, a heavily fortified area behind the lines, to the front line itself, allowing the infantry relatively safe access to the front line trenches even when subjected to the heaviest of shelling by the enemy artillery.

The existing mining system at Givenchy was in itself a defensive structure. A 350 yard tunnel was created between the two strong points of Givenchy Keep and Marie Redoubt, again giving the two battalions in these strongholds easy access to their positions.

Electric power and lighting to the dugouts and subways was supplied from a power station established by the Australian Alphabetical Company in a cellar at Pont Fixe on the La Bassée Canal. This was one of the largest power stations on the front and could generate 101 kW of electricity, supplying not only Givenchy but also the system at the Hohenzollern Redoubt, south of the Auchy sector.

From January 1918 the concept of deep dugouts was generally adopted along the length of the British front, and the British tunnellers, supported by attached infantrymen, built almost 200 of them, each capable of accommodating anything from fifty to 2,000 men. To put this into perspective, in March 1918 there were more soldiers living underground than there are inhabitants living above ground in the same area today. On 8 April 1918 the front, from the River Lys to La Bassée, was held by the Portuguese Corps to the north, I Corps to the right, with 55th (West Lancs) Division holding the flank at Givenchy. The 55th Division had no tanks and very little support from the air; the battle, when it came, was going to be fought by the infantry and support units that included 251 Tunnelling Company.

The next phase of Ludendorff's plan, Operation Georgette, was launched at 4.15 am on 9 April 1918, when the area around Givenchy came under heavy artillery fire. At 4.45 am the 251st were stood to arms, effectively turning them into infantry, and awaited orders from 55th Division HQ at Béthune. In the meantime, Lieutenant Barker and three men were posted on the canal bank to observe any movement from the north.

A captured divisional order dated 6 April 1918, showed that the objectives in this area were to take the ground and the British position in the triangle formed by Givenchy, Festubert, and Gorre:

> *In our attack our three regiments will be opposed by at most six companies in front and at most two reserve battalions in Festubert and Givenchy. One battalion in divisional reserve is south of the La Bassee Canal, in Le Preol. It will be prevented by our powerful artillery fire from taking part in the fight for Festubert and Givenchy. The troops are elements of the English 55th Division, which, after being engaged on the Somme, has suffered heavy losses in Flanders and at Cambrai, and was described by prisoners in March 1918, as a division fit to hold a quiet sector, that is below the average quality.*
> (Major J. Stirling, The Territorial Divisions, 1914-1918)

Believing they would take this sector with ease, at 9.00 am 4th (Ersatz) Division, supported by 43 Reserve, 18 Reserve, and 1st Bavarian Reserve Divisions, advanced. By 9.30 am, the Germans had reached the village, occupying the ruins of Givenchy Church and attacked battalion headquarters. Captain Church organised the removal of the RE stores that had been accumulated and despatched them to Béthune. He then gave orders for charges to be prepared and laid ready for any demolitions which might be needed.

Earlier in the day Captain Auret was sent to find the day relief shift, which had been caught by the enemy attack en route to the mining system and finally returned to billets with them at 9.00 pm. He immediately set out to return to Givenchy to take charge of the relief who were still working in the mining system.

At 3.00 pm Sergeant Newell of the 251st was sent with twenty men to a defensive position on the Sailly Labourse–Tuning Fork line, at its junction with the Béthune–La Bassée road. At 5.40 pm Captains Evans and Walker, together with Lieutenants Morgan, McGregor, Marsland and Baker, twenty NCOs and 149 other ranks, proceeded to man the Essars defences in compliance with orders from XI Corps. In doing so they were placed under the orders of 166 Brigade, located at nearby Gorre Chateau. (see Map 7)

*The Chateau at Gorre, originally a priory, was the headquarters of 166 Brigade as well as the officers' quarters of 251 Tunnelling Company; it was destroyed in 1918. The Gorre Indian and British Cemetery is in a corner of the woodland of the original chateau.*

*The 55th Divison's memorial at Givenchy. The inscription on the memorial reads: Around this site from the 9th to the 16th April 1918 the Division, continuously attacked from the canal to Festubert by three German Divisions and with its left flank turned, held its ground and inflicted severe loss upon the enemy.... This most gallant defence, the importance of which it would be hard to overestimate...', an extract from Sir Douglas Haig's despatch dated 20 July 1918.*

The 166th were repeatedly attacked by the Germans, but the enemy never penetrated their line; however, it did take practically every rifle in the division; infantrymen, pioneers, gunners, trench mortar units, entrenching companies and part of 251 Tunnelling Company, to hold that position. During the course of the action, Sergeant W Dunstan from Stithians and Sapper E Curtis from Lanner were taken prisoner by the Germans; they were finally released on 17 December 1918 and 29 November 1918 respectively. By the end of the day and after a gruelling battle, 55th Division held a line over six miles long; this was certainly the Division's finest hour and after the war Givenchy was chosen as the site for the Divisional Memorial.

The Germans kept up the onslaught, shelling Béthune with heavy calibre naval guns and continuing to shell roads and gun positions. The 251st dug new defence trenches from Essars to the La Lawe Canal and it was whilst manning these defences, on 10 April, that Lieutenant Barker and four other ranks were wounded, and two men, Sappers J. Martin MM of Hazleslade, Staffs and T. Osborne of Hertford, were killed. Sapper Martin is buried in Lillers Communal Cemetery and Sapper Osborne is commemorated on the Loos Memorial.

Captain Church, who had visited the detachment at Essars, returned to the billets and moved 251's HQ to Lannoy, at the same time ordering the 1st Portuguese Mining Company HQ to relocate to Gonnehem. On 11 April, he again visited the 251st detachment at Essars and found that, although still under heavy fire, they were maintaining their position and holding the trenches. Lieutenant Rees was tasked with demolishing the crossroads at Locon and, together with Lieutenant Morgan and nine other ranks, he proceeded to this position; on arrival he found that the ground had been destroyed by enemy shelling and the plan to destroy the roads in the vicinity was abandoned. Later that day an unusual incident occurred. A bi-plane with British markings and the number E23 flew low over Lannoy–Gonnehem, waggling its wings to attract attention and then indicating that the troops below should retire. Suspecting that this was an enemy ruse, Captain Church ordered that the plane should be shot down if it returned.

As the defence of Givenchy continued, 6-inch guns were moved up and placed next to the billets of the 251st, so that on 11 April the billets were prudently moved a further 300 yards to the north-west, removing them from the danger of any enemy shells targeting the guns. Six NCOs from the First Army School of Mining reported for duty to help supervise the 1<sup>st</sup> Portuguese Mining Company. The 251<sup>st</sup> began preparations for the demolition of part of Rue Du Bois in the vicinity of Le Hamel. In spite of all the forward planning, the tunnellers were running very short of explosives. Sergeant Pooley of the 251<sup>st</sup>, a Cornishman from Redruth, made three trips under heavy shellfire from Oblinghem to the Company Magazine, which was located one mile to the east of Béthune. In total he brought up 8,000 lbs of explosive and was awarded the DCM for his bravery. His citation dated 3 September 1919 reads:

> *He has been in charge of the company mining stores and explosives for the past 34 months, and has performed his duties in a most praiseworthy manner. On the 12<sup>th</sup> April 1918, when a division was without explosive, he made three trips under shell fire from Oblinghem to the company magazine one mile east of Bethune and salved 8000 lbs of explosive which was urgently required. His fearless devotion to duty and determination have made his services invaluable to the company.*

At 4.50 am on 13 April the culvert on the Rue du Bois was blown successfully by Lieutenant Rees and nine other ranks and preparations began for the demolition of the bridge over the La Bassée Canal on the Gorre to Loisne road. This was one of the main crossings into Béthune and in the event of the enemy breaking through the demolition of this bridge would have significantly slowed the German advance.

On 14 April at 11.30 pm Captain Evans and his detachment were finally relieved from the trenches at Essars and returned to billets. After five days of heavy fighting the casualty toll for the 251<sup>st</sup> was eleven wounded and two killed.

Three days later, on 17 April, Captain Auret, two further officers and thirty eight other ranks returned from the Givenchy sector, where they had spent nine days working underground during the enemy attack. Meanwhile, the work on new defences continued, with four officers and a hundred other ranks starting work in the vicinity of Fosse Annezin, constructing 417 yards of trench (see Map 8).

The next day, 18 April 1918, Sergeant Newell and six other ranks returned to the billets carrying Captain Walker, who had been wounded. They had been part of 'A' Relief, which consisted of three officers and thirty nine other ranks, who had proceeded to the Givenchy front on 17 April for a forty eight hour shift. They found themselves instead fighting alongside the infantry when the Germans attacked and broke into the Bunny Hutch subway system at 7.00 am. 'A' Relief fought alongside 1st Black Watch and held out until 2.00 pm when, with 200 men wounded and no further ammunition, the officer in charge surrendered.

Captain Walker was injured in the leg by machine gun fire during the initial attack and Sergeants Newell and Menedue were carrying him on a stretcher, having been taken prisoner. On their way out of the subway system through the Moat Farm exit, they overcame two German sentries who had been posted there and, together with three others, evaded their German captors. They all succeeded in getting back to the British lines, except for Corporal Knowles, a Cornishman from St. Day, who was killed during the attempt; he is commemorated on the Ploegsteert Memorial. In the confusion, three more men escaped after hiding behind sandbags in the dugout system and arrived back at the billets just after Sergeant Newell's party, but Sappers Whitford from Carn Brea, Sapper A Finch from St Agnes and Sappers A Knight and W George from Scorrier were taken prisoner; they were released on 12 December 1918, 16 January 1919, 18 April 1919, and 2 December 1918 respectively.

Captain Ritchie sent Lieutenant Woods to investigate the situation in that area and he returned early the following morning, confirming that the Germans were now holding the Bunny Hutch subway system and trenches.

Captain Church took this information to GOC 1st Division and at 11.00 am on 19 April a decision was taken to send Captain Auret and seven other ranks to the Bunny Hutch system with instructions to deny the Germans access to the magazine located in the Coventry Shaft. On 21 April, Captain Church again called on GOC 1st Division to establish the policy to be pursued at the Bunny Hutch subway now that the Germans were occupying part of the system. It was decided, with the sanction of I Corps, that the system should now be abandoned; a small charge of 250 lbs of ammonal was blown at the junction of the Bunny Hutch subway with the Piccadilly exit to seal it and to prevent the Germans from making use of the numerous galleries and mined dugouts within it.

Such was the maze of subways and galleries that the 251st had constructed in this sector that they now had yet another role to play in their support of the infantry. Lance Corporal Jose and four other ranks, acting as guides, accompanied two companies of the 1st Northants through the defence systems at Givenchy in readiness for an attack, which was planned with the objective of retaking that portion of the ridge lost on 18 April. The 1st Northants were joined by 1st Black Watch and after a hard fight successfully drove the enemy out of Bunny Hutch, Scottish Trench, Ware Road, New Cut and Piccadilly (see Map 4). Lance Corporal Jose returned to billets the following day with two men, the other two being reported missing, one of them believed to be Sapper Ninnes from Manaccan.

*Sapper John 'Posty' Ninnes, 251 Tunnelling Company RE. A quarryman, he was taken prisoner of war on 20 April 1918. He was sent to Altdamm prisoner of war camp in Germany and released on 26 December 1918.*

Keeping the subway systems from filling up with water was a constant battle and after the success of the counter-attack this became a priority; it was essential that the subways were usable again. Lieutenant Landrey and ten other ranks were sent to Pont Fixe to connect pumps for the Givenchy Keep system to prevent it from flooding. Following a gas attack, Lieutenant Landrey and all of the other ranks were taken to the Field Ambulance suffering from the effects of gas; Lieutenant CT Landrey of Bodmin died on 21 April following this attack; he is buried at Lapugnoy Military Cemetery.

*Hand pumps like this were operated for three days continuously to keep the subways usable, if not dry. (Picture courtesy of Memorial Museum Passchendaele)*

With the electric pumps still out of action, Lieutenant Woods, together with ten other ranks, was sent to the Givenchy sector manually to operate hand pumps in the Givenchy Keep dugout system, this keeping the water down until the installation of a reliable power plant could be arranged.

A Petter set was obtained from the Alphabetical Company and a pumping set which ran on petrol was borrowed from 350 Electrical & Mining (E&M) Company RE on 22 April. Lieutenant Gibbon and ten other ranks were sent to install the newly acquired mechanical pumping sets at the Givenchy Keep shaft, with Lieutenant Woods and his party continuing to maintain the hand pumping system in the meanwhile. On the same day, 22 April 1918, a message was received from the Engineer in Chief GHQ congratulating the 251st on the *gallant defence of their home.*

By 25 April 1918, the manual pumps had been working for three days, keeping the dugouts and galleries usable by providing air, even if the water levels were still very high. The new pumps were installed but one of the petrol pumps had to be returned as it was faulty. However, the other pump started working at 4.00 am that morning that reduced the water levels in the system considerably and a replacement for the faulty pump was delivered by 350 E&M Company. Now that the pumps were working effectively the decision was taken to dismantle the electrical power plant at Pont Fixe.

Although Ludendorff's offensive had gained further ground, by the end of April he accepted that it had lost its momentum and that there would be no further success on this sector and called off the attack. The 55th Division had fought courageously to hold off four elite German divisions but they would be the first to admit that, without question, the defences constructed and, in the main, designed by the 251st, together with the speed of the repairs made to those defences, contributed enormously to this success; so too did the men of the 251st standing to arms when events compelled them to do so.

As Captain EJ Ritchie, adjutant of 251 Tunnelling Company, wrote:

> *This battle justified the Controller of Mines policy of deep dugouts, as without the deep dugouts, there is no infantry in the world that could have held Givenchy Ridge that day, because the intense bombardment in the early morning would have wiped them out, whereas our casualties through shell fire were comparatively light up to the time of the general attack.*
> (Simon Jones, Underground Warfare)

For 251 Tunnelling Company, the period 9–25 April 1918 must surely rank as their finest hour. The months of planning, the tireless construction of defensive systems and, despite their early lack of musketry training, their ability to fight shoulder to shoulder with the infantry meant that when their time came they stood up to the mark. It is not surprising, therefore, that shortly after these events, on 6 May 1918, the 251st received the following telegram commending their efforts from Field Marshal Sir Douglas Haig:

> *Please convey to Captain Church and to all ranks of the 251st Tunnelling Company my congratulations on their very gallant behaviour.*
> (Copied entry from 251's War Diary)

Later, Lieutenant Colonel Dale-Logan DSO MD DPH in a paper read to the North of England Institute of Mining and Mechanical Engineers (see bibliography) said:

> *... At Givenchy the miners helped to save a critical situation; indeed, if it had not been for the work of the 251*[st] *Tunnelling Company, it is almost certain that Béthune, with its valuable coalfields, would have fallen ....*

Ludendorff discontinued the attack on 30 April 1918 when he reached the conclusion that his Fourth and Sixth Armies were no longer capable of continuing with it. Even though the Germans had failed to take Givenchy, Operation Georgette was a qualified success to the extent that the Germans gained significant ground in most other sectors in the area. However, it failed in its strategic intentions. German success at Givenchy would have made the local French coalfields available to them, would possibly have left the British cut off, and could have contributed to forcing the allies to accept defeat.

# Chapter 10

# Stemming the Tide, 1918: Building New Defences

By the end of the Spring Offensive on the Arras and Somme fronts, total British losses by 30 April 1918 were some 250,000 men killed, wounded or taken prisoner. General Gough was dismissed and the Fifth Army temporarily disbanded, having suffered heavy losses.

After the Battle of the Lys, the Germans had suffered enormous losses, with an estimated 348,000 casualties, numbers they would not be able to replace, unlike the allies, who had manpower and equipment arriving daily from America. Despite this, it was felt with certainty that the enemy would attack again, and so the order came for more defences to be dug behind the new British Front. It was still crucial to the war effort that the coalfields around Béthune and the railhead at Choques be protected and remain in allied hands. As can be seen from Map 8, the British Front Line to the north had been pushed back. Following the success of the defence of Givenchy the 251ˢᵗ were moved to an area north west of Béthune, to construct a system similar to that at Givenchy; a complex of mined dugouts, trenches, machine gun emplacements and subways.

The pressure of mine warfare had now been replaced by the need for speed; it was imperative that these new lines of defence were completed as quickly as possible in case of further attack. As it turned out, this was in many ways a wasted effort, but no one knew that Ludendorff had to all intents and purposes abandoned his attack on this objective and that, indeed, the war was coming towards its end. 251 Tunnelling Company continued to work feverishly to complete their set task of helping to build a defensive ring around Béthune.

On 1 May, Captain Evans accompanied CRE XIII Corps on an inspection of the trenches at Hinges–Bellerive (see Map 8), whilst the Controller of Mines called on Captain Church to discuss moving his headquarters and billets to a new site; following this visit, Captain Church set out the next day to find a suitable location. The selection was a difficult one as the Company was going to be spread across a wide area, on trench work from Annezin to the Hinges–Bellerive line, on the Givenchy front, and making trial borings at Lillers station to ascertain the water levels in an area where dugouts were to be constructed. As the camp needed to be some distance from the new defensive lines under construction, a site in the vicinity of Allouagne (see Map 7) was decided upon, very close to what is now Lapugnoy Military Cemetery.

On 4 May No. 1 Section, under the command of Lieutenant W Reed, began clearing the brushwood on the site of the new camp in preparation for the erection of Nissen huts. Such was the discipline of the Company that all of this camp construction work took place without any interference with the tasks they were undertaking on the defence systems.

On 6 May Lieutenant Schneider and five other ranks, who had been at Givenchy, rejoined the Company, now based at the new camp, this leaving just five men behind at Givenchy.

On 18 May, it was announced that a number of awards had been made to the 251st in connection with the recent battle at Givenchy. A bar to his MC and promotion to captain went to Lieutenant GW Walker MC; the DCM to Sergeants Newell and Menadue; the MM to Sappers W Jose, C Turner, NS Hoskin and W Weller, and on 24 May a further seven MMs were awarded: to Sergeants H Newell DCM, J Weatherstone and J Winterbottom, Corporal P Richards, Lance Corporal S Bagley, and Sappers D Campbell and G Strachey. The *London Gazette* citation, dated 3 September 1918, for Sergeants Newell and Menadue typifies the courage and attitude of the tunnellers of the 251st:

*For conspicuous gallantry and devotion to duty. This N.C.O., with another, was in charge of a position of underground defence that was overrun by the enemy; they, however, refused to surrender and remained below with an officer, who was unable to walk, having always in view the possibility of an escape in the confusion. Their anticipations were justified, and in spite of a heavy machine gun fire and shell barrage, they succeeded in carrying the wounded officer into safety and in rescuing six other men. The happy result of this enterprise was due to the courage and resource of these N.C.O's, who were equally responsible for its success.*

Lieutenant Fred Bullen, the brother of the first Commanding Officer of the 251st, was awarded a bar to his Military Cross for his gallantry in the defence of Givenchy. His citation reads:

> *For conspicuous gallantry and devotion to duty. When the enemy had broken through, he organised a post, collecting some machine gunners who were retiring. While doing this he was all the time under heavy shell fire, and was twice buried. He held the position for an hour, and must have inflicted considerable casualties on the enemy.*

By the middle of May, on the Hinges front the initial trench work was nearing completion and suitable sites had been identified for the construction of dugouts. No. 1 Section commenced work on dugouts for 9 Infantry Brigade in the grounds of Chateau L'Abbaye. The next day the newly promoted Major Church and Captain Auret went to Mont Bernenchon to see the boreholes that had been sunk, from which they

*Military Medal awarded to Lance Corporal William Jose of Scorrier for his actions on 18 April 2014 during the battle of the Lys. (Picture Courtesy of the family of Lance Corporal Jose)*

could assess the suitability of that site for further dugouts.

At the end of the month, Major Church visited the Givenchy sector and found that all of the galleries were now clear of water following the installation of the new Lister electric set that had replaced the Petter. He then accompanied machine gun officers from XIII Corps to Vendin les Béthunes to establish suitable sites for machine gun battery positions on the Béthune–Chocques road.

The fighting in Givenchy had taken its toll on the strength of the Company; at the end of May it was 255 strong, being short of a Section sergeant, three carpenters, a plumber, thirty tunnellers, thirty three tunnellers' mates and four Class A batmen.

The start of June saw the 251st on the move again when Major Church and the 251st found themselves 'evicted' from the Nissen huts at Allouagne and under canvas near the sandpits at Fouquereuil; their old camp at Allouagne was handed over to the 3rd Division as its new headquarters. The Company were now working with XIII Corps and were no longer with the First Army; they were now under the command of the Fifth Army, which had been reformed on 25 May 1918 under General Birdwood. At Givenchy, the sector was handed over to the 3rd Australian Tunnelling Company, whose first task there was to make four new deep dugouts. On 15 June, OC 3rd Australian Company called to collect all plans, listening and survey records for Givenchy held by the 251st and, in the spirit of the co-operation which existed between the tunnelling companies, Major Church visited Givenchy the following day to ensure a smooth handover of the work.

Following the transfer of the 251st to the Fifth Army, Major General HS Jeudwine sent the following letter to I Corps on 22 June:

> *As the 251st Tunnelling Company has now I understand handed over the Givenchy system to the 3rd Australian Tunnelling Company may I be allowed to express the appreciation of my Division for all the good and gallant work which Major Church and his Company have done for us since we have been associated in the defence of Givenchy. We have never called on them in vain, and often they anticipated our needs. We have valued them equally as comrades whether they were using the pick or the rifle. Major Church himself has been especially helpful.*
>
> (Copied into the Company's War Diary)

Plans for further defensive measures continued to be made and, on 4 June, Major Church went to reconnoitre the roads in the Vendin-lez-Béthune area to establish where demolition charges should be laid ready for detonation should a German advance occur. He also visited Mont Bernenchon to look again at the viability of plans to construct deep dugouts in that vicinity. He delivered his report to the staff of 4th Division and CRE XIII Corps and a few days later work commenced in both places.

Throughout early June, the need for larger mined dugout systems became apparent; a signals dugout at Le Cauroy, near Hinges, and a Brigade HQ dugout at Le Vertannoy were constructed by the 251st.

To further bolster the defensive system in their sector, the 251st were set to digging more trenches between Vendin and Annezin; all of this work was co-ordinated by the Controller of Mines Fifth Army, who visited the sites frequently to monitor progress and give new orders. The

*Remains of machine gun pillbox at Bienvillers-au-Bois. The reinforced concrete walls are in excess of three feet thick. (Picture courtesy of Pen and Sword)*

line was to be strengthened with a proposed new style of machine gun emplacement, and skeleton plans for this were drawn up and shown to CRE XIII Corps on 12 June. The new plans were accepted and so a request was made for additional labour and for lorries to transport the hundreds of tons of concrete that would be needed in the construction of these gun platforms.

These new designs may have arisen from discussions, at the highest level, about the difficulty the Fifth Army had in holding off German attacks during the Spring Offensive. It was thought that this may have been at least partly due to a failing in the design and positioning of the machine gun posts; at Givenchy (under the First Army), a strong defensive machine gun system had been constructed, as shown in map 6, and had proved to be very effective.

The construction of these machine gun posts needed careful designing. They had to give protection to the gun crew, whilst the available firing apertures should not restrict the sweep of the gun.

The sweep of such a gun emplacement is quite small, so each post would form part of a linked battery of guns. Positioning batteries in this way provided fire cover across the whole width of the front against which the enemy were attacking. Access to each post varied, with some being reached from a shelter or trench behind, whilst others had ladders going down vertically into deep dugouts below.

Since the Company was by now working in many different places on a variety of projects, work was allocated by section; Section No. 1 had responsibility for the machine gun battery at Vendin; Section No. 2 worked on the defensive trenches on the Vendin–Annezin line for XIII Corps; Section No. 4 were building the dugouts at Vertannoy, whilst Section No. 3 was working on both the dugout accommodation at Mont Bernenchon and setting road demolition charges. The distances from base camp meant that some of Section No. 3 were billeted with 9th Field Company at L'Eclème. There was always more work to do and they were tasked to build another machine gun battery position in the vicinity of Bas d'Annesin, on the La Bassée Canal, and another just south of Chateau le Abbaye.

Perhaps not helped by their workload and the pressures it placed upon them by the conditions in which they were working, or by the fact that they were under canvas again, the company suffered from a severe outbreak of PUO (Pyrexia of Unknown Origin), with three officers and fifty four other ranks falling sick. PUO is a term for specific fever symptoms and is now generally thought to have been a type of trench fever, a louse-borne disease which displayed flu-type symptoms. It was a nasty illness, made particularly unpleasant in that it could recur for the rest of the victim's life. On 24 June a Company Rest Camp was established where the sick could be isolated from the rest of the Company, rather than going to hospital; as a result of this measure the number falling sick moderated considerably.

The strength of the Company was still low at the end of June, with two officers and sixty four other ranks needed to bring it up to establishment; however, they were not unique in this situation as this deficiency of manpower was reported across much of the BEF at that time.

The shortage of men was alleviated when, by 5 July, twenty four other ranks from 179 Labour Company reported for duty. This proved useful, as the machine gun battery at Bas d'Annesin was obviously considered urgent, since work started there at 9.00 pm following a visit

*The above is a reconstruction of an officer's dugout that could be part of a complex system holding up to 2,000 men, or more. (Picture courtesy of Memorial Museum Passchendaele)*

to the site by Major Church and the CRE 3rd Division earlier the same day. They also visited Pont Avelette, where a dugout for a Lewis gun had been proposed. On the same day positions for other machine gun batteries and dugouts were reconnoitred at a site just north of Beuvry and to the south west of Le Quesnoy; the work on these being allocated to No. 2 Section, who had just completed the dugouts at Vendin.

Ten more infantrymen from the 4th Division were attached to the company to assist No. 1 Section with work in constructing a dugout magazine at company headquarters. This started just five days later, on 15 July 1917, although not before a sports meeting, with a number of field and aquatic events, had been arranged for the company.

Divisional work was progressing well on the laying of explosive charges ready for road demolitions should they be required, with five sites being handed over to CRE 4th and 5th Divisions. The need for more of this type of work was identified in the 45th Divisional area and the search for sites suitable for machine gun batteries and dugouts was underway at Pont l'Hinges.

On 21 July, the work on the machine gun batteries and dugouts at Beuvry was handed over to 176 Tunnelling Company and Captain Evans, who had been in command of that section, proceeded to Fifth Army HQ as temporary assistant to the Controller of Mines; by the end of the month he had been permanently appointed Assistant Controller of Mines for Fifth Army.

Planning and training in case of enemy attack commenced, with all ranks practicing moving to the positions they would take on the defence line, just as they had at Givenchy. Major Church operated in a very similar manner to that of Major Humphrys before him, insisting on visiting all sites daily, irrespective of the type of work going on, and on these visits he would frequently be accompanied by the Controller of Mines. On 5 August, Major Church went to Deauville on leave, but he still took the time to visit the signals dugout to inspect the Sentinel Jack pipe forcing equipment being used there.

With reports coming in of withdrawals by the enemy from some sectors, coupled with reports of desertions from within the enemy's ranks, there was a general feeling that the end of the war might be in sight; but the possibility that the Germans might still have one last push left in them could not be ignored. For the 251st work continued as normal, with preparations for the demolition of crucial railway junctions and crossings in the centre of Bruay still underway in case they were needed, and new dugouts were started at Oblinghem.

*Chapter 11*

# The Tide Turns:
# The Advance to Victory

At 4.20 am on 8 August the Battle of Amiens commenced and by the end of the day the allies had, on average, pushed seven miles into the German lines. Ludendorff referred to it as 'the black day of the German army' because morale had sunk so low that the fight had gone out of it and the retreat had started. This signalled the start of a new phase for the tunnelling companies, whose expertise was now not so much needed for setting explosive devices but for rendering harmless those booby traps, explosives, unused shells and ammunition left behind by the retreating Germans.

The 251st were one of the first companies to be engaged in this work; on 9 August three NCOs and eleven other ranks were sent to CRE 4th Division to help in searching for booby traps in areas vacated by the enemy. On 16 August two more NCOs, together with a further twelve other ranks, were also sent to the 4th Division for the same purpose. Although the Battle of Amiens had been a considerable success, not just in terms of land gained, but also in the demoralising effect on the German troops, Haig did not support Foch's proposal that the attack should continue when it ran into stiffening German resistance; instead Haig ordered a fresh attack by the Third Army between the rivers Ancre and Scarpe. The Amien offensive having been temporarily halted, some of the men from the 251st, Sergeant Cowan and six other ranks, who had been attached to the 4th Division, returned to the Company lines.

Despite the success of the Fourth Army at Amiens, the 251st continued with their defensive work, with Captain Auret visiting the Mayor of Bruay-la-Buissière (Bruay) on 12 August to discuss the dumping of waste from a shaft that was being dug near the level crossing in the town. Happily for Auret, he was able to combine duty with pleasure, enjoying an afternoon at XIII Corps horse show! On 31 August, Major Church met the Mayor of Bruay, together with Monsieur Johm, the Engineer in Chief of the mines of Bruay. They met to discuss the use of a site for an explosives magazine in preparation for any road demolitions that might be required in the case of another German advance.

The Portuguese Tunnelling Company, who had worked closely with 251st during the attack at Givenchy, rejoined the company on 16 August 1918; Major Church found suitable billets for them in the vicinity of Oblinghem and Lannoy and they were set to work at Avelette, near Hinges, on the La Bassée Canal. Later a further thirty two other ranks from 179 Labour Company, together with Lieutenant JK Forrester from the Australian Imperial Force, also joined the 251st; on 31 August, another Australian officer, Second Lieutenant HS Redmond, joined the company. By the end of August, the strength of the company had increased significantly, now standing at seventeen officers, 263 other ranks, with thirty two attached infantry awaiting transfer; eighty two men of 179th Labour Company were also listed as attached to the 251st, together with five officers and 109 other ranks from the Portuguese Tunnelling Company.

The beginning of September saw officers and men being sent on various courses to learn new skills. Lieutenant Barker and twelve other ranks were sent to a local concrete factory to attend a one week course in the construction of concrete block shelters; Lieutenant Roe and five other ranks attended a course on bombs; whilst Lieutenant Morgan accompanied nine other ranks to a Lewis gun course at XIII Corps' machine gun school.

As the Advance to Victory gained momentum, work on the defences slowed down and, moving up with the advancing infantry, priority was given to clearing booby traps, removing explosives, and undertaking construction work, such as rebuilding roads and bridges. The scope of this work was broad; for example, near the distillery in La Tourelle, just North of La Bassée, a number of anti-tank traps were uncovered, which required disabling.

The tunnelling companies worked in close co-operation with one another and any information about new devices that had been found, together with details of how to disarm them, were sent to the CRE of the relevant division as well as the Controller of Mines in order that the

*As some German dugouts were cleared, they were used as first aid posts to treat the wounded soldiers. (Picture courtesy of the National Media Museum)*

latest intelligence could be shared with the other tunnelling companies.

The afternoon of the 7 September must have been quite poignant for Major Church, as he attended the funeral, at Pernes British Cemetery, of Major Robert Manning, OC 170 Tunnelling Company. The two men would have known each other well, for at times the 170th worked very closely with the 251st; and Major Manning, like Major Church, had worked in Canada before the war as a civil engineer and had also been promoted from the ranks. It is not known how Major Manning died, but the last report he signed said that four booby trap mines had been found.

The following day Major Church and the OC Portuguese Mining Company assessed the work that needed to be done in clearing the Loisne River near Vieille-Chapelle (see Map 9), and a day later a hundred men from the 251st, together with three officers and seventy three other ranks from the Portuguese Company, commenced work.

Further manpower was required to complete their engineering works and this was forthcoming as, by the 11 September, the strength of the Company was boosted yet again with the arrival of 402 other ranks from 35th (Portuguese) Battalion; these men were to work under the orders of the 251st, repairing roads in XIII Corps' area. By the end of the month, the work on dugouts was completed and when XIII Corps was replaced by XII Corps, the new Corps staff visited the lines to discuss the work the Company was doing.

Meanwhile, the 251st was preparing to move camp again, this time to return to the original billets at the chicory factory in Béthune: billets which had been the base for the Company from the time of its arrival in France until 15 April 1918. Ironically, they moved from these billets, rifle in hand, during the defence of Givenchy; and now, on their return, they again fought with rifle in hand, working forward of the infantry, clearing mines for the advancing troops.

The War Diary for October is not available. This may be because it was partly destroyed in September 1940, when a German bombing raid damaged the War Office Repository in Arnside Street, London. However, it is more likely that it has been mislaid or was destroyed during enemy action, before a copy had been sent back down the line. What is known is that during October, as part of the Advance to Victory, the 251st moved billets again and were working at La Bassée, clearing booby traps as the infantry advance drove forward to liberate Lille on 17 October 1918.

To the people of occupied France the allied armies were certainly a welcome sight as they moved forward, liberating parts of France that had been under German control for over four years. Lieutenant HJ Redmond, who returned to his original company when the 251st was disbanded, sent a letter, dated 28 October 1918, home to his mother in Australia, in which he describes the welcome the liberating troops received from the local people:

*On our way chasing the Bosche, we passed through several villages with thousands of citizens who gave us a splendid welcome. My party and I were the first to go through and we had our work cut out to prevent the girls from strangling us by throwing their arms around our necks and hugging us. By the time we finished the day's march which was 25 miles we looked more dressed for a pantomime than for war. Red, white and blue [for France] and red, yellow and black [for Belgium] ribbons were all*

*over us and I had my arms full of huge bunches of fine flowers, which the civilians had insisted on me taking. It was some job keeping my chaps sober, as the people would offer them beer and spirits. These people are French who have been prisoners of Germany since 1914 and were mad with excitement at being released by our troops. One young lady who had studied English at one of the Universities would insist on coming as my interpreter for the day and marched along with us. All the guns, waggons, lorries, etc., were decorated with flowers, flags, etc., and the whole thing looked more like a gala day than real war, and made you forget that the struggle was still on. Everywhere I asked for billets the people could not do enough for us and I can honestly say I have never slept in a better bed than I did in those villages. Although the people were short of food, and when it was obtainable had to pay extortionate prices for it, they would rather starve and give it to you as they were so pleased at being released. I would not have missed the experience for a lot and consider that all the privations we have to go through have been simply paid for.*
Published in *The Northern Miner,* Queensland, 7 January 1919

These celebrations apart, there was still a lot of work being done, as the following report, an extract from the War Diary for November, shows. The tasks undertaken and completed by the 251st in just one week prior to 9 October 1918 were recorded as:

*Two road diversions round craters put in, craters filled in, three small bridges rebuilt, one bridge across culvert, 27 foot span commenced, roads and ditches repaired for 5000 yards. An area of 18 square miles has been searched for traps and unexploded demolitions, 42,393 lbs of explosives removed, and all roads examined, over 800 detached buildings and dugouts have been examined besides four villages and one half of the town of Fournes-en-Weppes.*

This was just the start; by the end of the war the tunnelling companies had cleared a total of over 2.5 million tons of German explosive.

Delayed action mines were found at Haubordin, just outside Lille, and these were cleared jointly with 170 Tunnelling Company. The Germans had placed charges on the bank of the Canal de La Deûle, which they had detonated, so damaging the wall of the waterway. One section was put to work, repairing the damage quickly and clearing the dam. These repairs prompted a note of appreciation from the CRE Fifth Army for the work done on the canal as well as that done in the clearing of booby traps.

Other sections were working on the Don–Lille and the Tournai–Lille railways, again removing booby traps and delayed action mines. Great caution was always needed in this work as booby traps are, by nature, difficult to identify. The tunnellers developed a sixth sense when undertaking this task; observation was the key quality required for success. Amongst the techniques used, was a compass attached to a stick and suspended over a suspicious area; if the compass needle deflected then this was an indication that shells had been hidden in the vicinity as it acted as a rather primitive metal detector, based on magnetism. However, this technique was not fool proof and the work was dangerous. Frequently these hidden shells would be left with a delayed action fuse – perhaps something as simple as a chemical placed under the shell head; over a period of time the safety wire would be eaten away and the striker plate would then fall on the detonator. Another tactic used by the retreating enemy was to loosen a step in a dugout and place a charge underneath, so that anyone stepping on the board would detonate the mine. Charges would also be placed under helmets, bottles and even corpses. Occasionally, as happened at Le Beuverie, what appeared to be booby traps turned out to be dummies. A great deal of time was lost in checking them out but this work had to be done thoroughly, even if it slowed down the allied progress.

By 8 November the 251st had cleared Haubourdin and Wavrin, so No. 2 Section was sent forward with the infantry into Tournai (see Map 10). On the strength of this, the 251st moved billets again, this time to Faubourg St. Martin, a suburb of Tournai.

Ludendorff had suggested beginning negotiations for an Armistice as early as September. In addition to the failure of his offensive and the disastrous events of August, he recognised that the successful allied blockade of German ports and the ineffectiveness of the German navy was resulting in the near starvation of the civilian population in Germany. With his troops surrendering in large numbers, he realised that the war needed to end; it was not, however, until 4.53 am on 11 November 1918 that the terms and conditions were agreed and the Armistice signed, to be effective from 11.00 am that day.

Surprisingly, no mention is made of the Armistice in the diary, or of any celebration of the war's end. There would be no mass partying; the war may have ended but too much had passed for celebrating. For the men who had fought it was just the knowledge and the sheer relief that there would be no more shelling and no more killing that struck home.

> *It is strange how calm the troops are now that hostilities have ceased. One is almost weighed down and oppressed with the knowledge that it is over. Is it because a mighty empire has crumbled and is grovelling in the dust? Or is it because on looking back one sees a long vista of crosses, desolation and desecration? The contemplation leaves no room for outward joy, but one has a kindling feeling round the heart with the happiness and certainty of seeing those we love and the knowledge that the suffering has not all been in vain.*
> Letter home from Captain HW Graham MC

The Armistice had been signed, but for the 251st, as for the other tunnelling companies, the war was still far from over.

Many booby traps and delayed action mines had already been cleared but the 251st continued searching and making safe the northern half of Tournai. Under Foch's instructions, to avoid any localised conflicts as the Germans withdrew, the allies were to progress no further than the line that they held at 11.00 am on 11 November, an order which remained in place for a further six days.

Clause A.VII of the Armistice stated that: *Roads and means of communications of every kind, railroads, waterways, roads, bridges, telegraphs, telephones, shall in no manner be impaired.*

As part of this and other conditions of the Armistice, the Germans had to provide detailed information on the location of all traps and delayed action mines. Although this meant that at least the locations and type of some of the devices were known, great care still had to be taken in disarming them, whilst not all locations had been recorded. To help in this work, Major Church worked with the Mayor of Tournai to enlist the help of the civilian population, who could identify where Germans had been billeted and which buildings had been held, so that these could be checked and cleared.

By 19 November the infantry were moving forward again in the wake of the wthdrawing Germans. Work for the 251st switched to finding and clearing the tank traps that had been left in the countryside on the western side of Tournai. The amount of explosives that had to be removed was so great that central dumps were established in each Corps area.

Apart from the clearance operation, work also began to help France and Belgium rebuild key transport infrastructure, such as railway lines and stations. For the 251st in particular, this meant working on the canal locks and bridges on the Escault Canal and River, the latter a major waterway flowing through France, Belgium and Holland to its mouth in the North Sea. More labour was required for this task and by 20 November assistance had arrived in the form of 1/7 Pioneer Battalion DLI, who were attached to the 251st for this work.

On 21 November, the 251st were transferred from XII Corps to VII Corps. As a result, their work was now based in the vicinity of Avelghem and Berchem and their billeting split, with No. 1 Section at Warcoing, No. 2 Section at Berchem, while HQ and Nos. 3 and 4 Sections were at Escanaffles. The Company operated in these areas until the end of November, its work rate hindered only by the lack of material and equipment.

Nearly six million men had left the UK to fight in the war and this had created worker shortages in some occupations at home, particularly in coal mining. With the Armistice now clearly holding and the Germans out of France and Belgium, priority was given to ensuring that men returned to the UK as soon as possible. On 1 December no work was done by the Company, as Major Church addressed the men on the subject of the selection process for repatriation to the UK; to assist in this process Lieutenant Morgan proceeded to Third Army HQ to act as liaison officer.

Whilst discussions were taking place at HQ, work continued on the lock at Espierre and drainage works were commenced at Warcoing, although two officers and fifty other ranks were given a day off on 7 December to go to Froyennes to see His Majesty King George V, who was on an official visit to the area.

On 10 December the coal miners serving with Sections 2 and 3 were recalled to HQ and the following day seventy five other ranks proceeded to the Fifth Army camp at La Madeleine for demobilisation. On the same day, Company HQ and No. 1 Section moved to Mons-en-Baroeul, near Lille.

Demobilisation continued in earnest and the following day, 11 December 1918, twenty eight other ranks proceeded to La Madeleine. As the disbanding of the Company was obviously now well under way, Major Church, together with the Controller of Mines Fifth Army, visited the old trench lines at Cuinchy and Cambrin for the purpose of obtaining articles of interest for the War Museum. Sadly, the diaries do not record what artefacts were recovered.

As the work eased off the tunnellers were increasingly impatient to be demobbed and repatriated to the UK. To keep them occupied, additional training was introduced after fatigues, as well as lectures arranged on such diverse subjects as 'Flying in the Royal Air Force' to 'The countryside in Alsace Lorraine' – an area that had been taken by the Germans from France in 1871 and was now returned under the terms of the Armistice.

Whilst many men hoped that they would be back home in time for Christmas, this was not to be; further work was assigned to the 251$^{st}$, rebuilding the bridge at the Rue Du Pont at Helchin. This required a further change of billets for a detachment of one officer and thirty other ranks.

At least this year what remained of the company could properly celebrate Christmas and a lorry was despatched to Aire to obtain supplies. All ranks returned to HQ to celebrate a special dinner prepared, with kindness, by the local inhabitants; this was followed by a dance, to which other ranks were allowed to invite their friends.

The start of 1919 saw the rest of the Company preparing to return to Britain; Major Church visiting the old HQ at the chicory factory in Béthune to check the stores that had been left behind when they moved forward in the advance. On Major Church's return, Captain Woods and nine other ranks were sent to the camp to ensure that all surplus stores were returned to the RE Base Depot at Rouen.

A few days later Major Church was writing personal confidential reports for all men in the Company and Captain Stevenson, the medical officer, was conducting medical examinations in the field, ready for demobilisation. On 18 January the demobilisation of the rest of the Company commenced with Lieutenant Mein, Second Lieutenant Campbell and fifty nine other ranks proceeding to the Fifth Army camp for transfer to England. One exception was Captain McGregor, who was appointed Deputy Director of Grave Registrations and Enquiries, Fifth Army, and became responsible for the next three months for arranging the transfer of isolated burials into cemeteries.

Three days later more men were sent for demobilisation and Major Church inspected all the billets and the horse transport stables. The horses that had served them so well throughout the war were also prepared for their repatriation; they were inspected by the Fifth Army

Veterinary Inspection Board, who gave them final clearance for their return to England, declaring them fit for travel.

Captain Woods had been given one special task to do before he could proceed to demobilisation; he was sent to the Base Cashier in Lille to pay the sum of eighty eight  francs to cover the cost of bayonets lost in December 1918 – no doubt taken home as souvenirs.

The War Diary ceased on 31 January 1919 and the records show many other ranks were returned to England and discharged in early February – after first undergoing a thorough delousing.

Major Church, as he returned to England to demobilise and board his ship for his return to Canada, must have reflected on the war 251 Tunnelling Company had endured. Tunnelling companies had no rest camps or reserve lines; instead they were effectively serving on the front line for the duration. The 251st had both started and finished their part in the static war in one of the most active sectors on the Western Front, initially tunnelling under enemy lines in record times to control and then eliminate German superiority underground. Subsequently they designed and constructed the effective defence system around Givenchy, a rare area on the Western Front never to have been broken by the enemy. They had courageously helped defend this, 'their home', in the Battle of the Lys, had with fantastic speed constructed part of a second defence line around Béthune and then, moving forward with the infantry during the Advance to Victory, had cleared booby traps and delayed action mines in both town and country. The dangers of the war had not finished for them on the 11 November 1918 but continued until all of these devices were made safe; even then they had carried on working, helping to rebuild key infrastructure for the inhabitants of France and Belgium and this work had gone on right up until the day of their return to England. On the way they would have witnessed the horrors of this war, seeing many friends and fellow soldiers wounded, maimed, killed and buried where they lay, their bodies still lying in France and Belgium today. Major Church had been a part of this fine body of men virtually from the start, serving under Major HJ Humphrys, who some would consider to be the best Officer Commanding of any of the tunnelling companies on the Western Front, and had the privilege of commanding them himself for the last ten months.

All the men of the tunnelling companies worked under very difficult conditions throughout the war, but the 251st surely had to be one of the best.

# Chapter 12

# 'One and All':
# A Basis For Success

The Armistice came into effect at 11.00 am on 11 November 1918. In December 1918, as the miners were being discharged from the army and returned home, the following special order was circulated to all tunnelling companies in France and Belgium:

SPECIAL ORDER OF THE DAY
by Field Marshal SIR DOUGLAS HAIG
KT GCB GCVO KCIE
Commander-in-Chief, British Armies in France

*A large number of men are now being withdrawn from Tunnelling Companies for urgent work at home.*

*Before they leave this country, I wish to convey to the Controller of Mines and to all ranks of Tunnelling Companies, both Imperial and Overseas, my very keen appreciation of the fine work that has been done by the Tunnelling Companies throughout the last four years.*

*At their own special work, Mine Warfare, they have demonstrated their complete superiority over the Germans, and whether in the patient defensive mining, in the magnificent success at Messines, or in the preparation for the offensives of the Somme, Arras and Ypres, they have shown the highest qualities both as Military Engineers and as fighting troops.*

*Their work in the very dangerous task of removing Enemy Traps and Delay action charges, on subways, dugouts, bridging, roads, and the variety of other services on which they have been engaged has been on a level with their work in the mines.*

> *They have earned the thanks of the whole Army, for their contribution to the defeat of the enemy. Their fighting spirit and technical efficiency has enhanced the reputation of the whole Corps of Royal Engineers, and of the Engineers of the Overseas Forces.*
>
> *I should like to include in the appreciation the work done by the Army Mine Schools and by the Australian Electrical and Mechanical Mining and Boring Company.*
>
> D. Haig FM<br>*Commander-in-Chief*<br>*British Armies in France*
>
> *General Headquarters*
> *4th December, 1918*

However, even before the end of the war, the outstanding efforts of 251 Tunnelling Company had been brought to notice; the following extract comes from a despatch dated 21 October 1918, addressed to Viscount Milner, the Secretary of State for War, from Field Marshal Sir Douglas Haig:

> *... The work of the Royal Engineers, both during and subsequent to the retreat on the Somme and on the northern battle front, has been particularly arduous. In addition to the heavy demands made upon them in the destruction of roads and bridges and such-like matters during retreat, and the labour entailed in the construction of new positions, they have frequently been called upon to take their place in the firing line. On such occasions their various units have behaved with the greatest steadfastness and courage, and, in circumstances such as those in which the 251st Tunnelling Company greatly distinguished itself at Givenchy, have added to the high reputation of their service.*

At over twenty six thousand words, it was a very detailed despatch and was published in full in *The Times*. The despatch went into great detail about Armies, corps and divisions, but the 251st were the only Company to be singled out within it; their record must have been quite remarkable to have been given such prominence.

Captain Grant Grieve and Bernard Newman, in their book *Tunnellers*, evaluated their efforts thus:

*Military historians rightly point to Givenchy as the key to the Lys battle. The Germans knew something about the art of fortifying villages, as their work on the Somme has shown. But at Givenchy they had to give us best, and more than one of their commanders has paid tribute to the work of the Tunnellers in the creation of this vital and impregnable position.*

As Major-General Harvey CB CMG DSO wrote in his forward to the book:

*...Even when the mining had ceased and our miners took to other work, they were constantly exposed to dangers in searching for booby traps, concealed charges, delay action mines etc. left behind by the Germans in their retreat. The amount of explosive thus collected amounted to no less than two and a half million pounds. In addition to this second main branch of work, the Tunnelling Companies proved their general usefulness by taking on every form of engineering work as it came to hand; construction of deep dugouts, repairs to roads, bridge building, water supply, drainage, and in times of stress they fought in the line with rifles, fully proving the claim of their originators that the Tunnelling Companies as organised for the Great War were the most valuable engineering units in France, and the most highly prized by the Commander of any formation who managed to get possession of even one Company of them.*

By the end of the war many miles of tunnels and subways had been constructed through the combined efforts of the twenty five tunnelling companies, Royal Engineers, the three Australian tunnelling companies, the three Canadian tunnelling companies and the New Zealand tunnelling company. The spoil from these tunnels and subways, which must have run into hundreds of thousands of tons, was all moved by the tunnelling companies, ably assisted by the infantry assigned to them.

As has been demonstrated, the 251st were a very flexible, efficient, determined and successful tunnelling company. They fought long, hard battles both above and beneath the ground, and helped to hold one of the few areas on the Western Front where the Allies never conceded ground. At times they came to within a whisker of doing so; at Givenchy

*Finally, the trip all the soldiers were looking forward to: going home. This is the* Golden Eagle, *which was requisitioned in WW1 as a troop carrier and again in WW2 when she served as an anti-aircraft ship. (Picture Courtesy of George Robinson from the original records by Stuart Cameron of www.clydesite.co.uk)*

*The picture shows a typical trench on the Western Front. Mine spoil would need to be carried (seventy sandbags on average for each foot driven) through trenches such as this to a dump as far behind the front line as practicable. (Picture courtesy of Cornwall's Regimental Museum, Bodmin)*

the front line was broken both to the north and south but the defences around the village of Givenchy held; with their ability to tunnel record distances in very short times, and by working closely with and fighting alongside the infantry they protected their position.

By the end of the war, out of the 221 Cornishmen who went to France as 251 Tunnelling Company, twenty three that we know of were never to return home, a small casualty rate, given that they were engaged permanently in one of the most active mining areas on the Western Front. Out of those twenty three, seven were killed after transfer from the 251st to other units; of the sixteen remaining, four lie in the Béthune Town Cemetery and eight in Cambrin Military Cemetery. The rest were lost underground and their remains have never been found. Three are commemorated on the Loos Memorial, and one on the Ploegsteert Memorial. Details of the Cornishmen who died whilst serving with the 251st, or who were part of the original Company but who were later transferred elsewhere, are listed in Appendix 3.

To date, only 194 of the 221 transferred from 10th DCLI to the Royal Engineers to form 251 Tunnelling Company have been positively identified. Of those identified, 178 (88.1%) returned home, a remarkable figure for any unit, and something that must be surely the result of more than luck. It is not suggested that the 251st was any more skilled than any other tunnelling company, but given its very high survival rate, a few points are worthy of discussion.

The average age of the miners in the 251st was 26 in 1914, young enough to deal with the stress of mining under such extreme conditions, but at the same time having had up to twelve years of mining experience in tin, copper or clay. This combination of experience and relative youth provided them with the resources they needed to do their work well and made them confident in their approach to that work.

*It is tedious work digging these mine tunnels, but the sappers are experts. It needs skilled men because it is easy to lose direction and dig in a circle, and also because the enemy may be digging in the same neighbourhood and these sappers can tell the sound of their own picks. If they detect counter-mining, there's a race for life, each side trying to finish a mine first and set off a mine. 'A dig for life.'*
*The Cornishman* 2 September 1915

All tunnelling companies used listening equipment to detect enemy activity, but these Cornish miners would be aware of the noises and sounds in a mine; as tin miners they would have been constantly, and perhaps superstitiously given a widespread belief in 'knockers' and 'piskies', listening for the creaking of earth and timbers which signalled a potential cave-in. This gave them an edge when mining below the enemy, they would be very aware of any change in the sounds in the tunnels, so allowing them to take defensive action early and in sufficient time.

The formation of the Company in September 1915, well after the formation of the first tunnelling companies, gave them the advantage of having, from January 1916, Lieutenant HJ Humphrys (a major by April 1916) as their Officer Commanding. Major Humphrys, who transferred from the 179th, might well be considered to be the best OC in the tunnelling companies on the Western Front, certainly something which was recognised by none other than Norton-Griffiths, who wanted him to take command of one of the new tunnelling companies being formed. As an experienced mining engineer and former junior inspector of mines and quarries, Major Humphrys had the relevant experience for the job in hand, as well as the ability to communicate with all ranks. His skills and the level of leadership he showed; both contributed to the extremely high success rate enjoyed by the 251st. The following extracts are from a tribute given by Captain DI Evans MC, one of Major Humphreys' Section officers, and later Assistant Controller of Mines Fifth Army.

> *No history of the 251st (T) Coy RE would be complete without an appreciation of Lieut. Colonel Humphrys, and it is at the request of numerous officers of that company that the following note has been compiled.*
>
> *Lieut. Colonel Humphrys was doubly fitted for the command of a Tunnelling Company in that prior to the war he was an Inspector of mines in Scotland with a wide knowledge of mining problems and was moreover an enthusiastic Territorial officer. It was not surprising therefore, that when mining warfare commenced in 1915, he was seconded from the Infantry to the 179 (T) Coy RE. It naturally followed that when command of a Tunnelling Company fell vacant he should have been immediately promoted and it was the good fortune of 251st (T) Coy RE to come under his command.*

*When Colonel Humphrys took over the 251st Coy it was in a very poor state – recruited hurriedly like all Tunnelling Companies from practical miners, supplemented by miners drafted out from other arms of service, and except for the Cornish miners, hardly any of the men knew one another. Esprit de corps and tradition were yet to be built up ....*

*[R]arely a day passed but he spent six hours in the mining front by his enthusiasm and unbounded energy he stirred the whole company into life. In a few months overhauled the whole mining system, .... Nothing short of the best possible would satisfy him and he invariably got it ...[T]o eliminate any temptation to drunkenness in the company (a crime which he frowned severely upon, not so much on moral grounds as on the grounds of impaired efficiency), he arranged for a wet and dry canteen in the company's own billets ... [and] his foresight in selecting the right NCOs and men for the right job was almost "uncanny"...*

*[T]he men of the Company – although subjected to rigid discipline – esteemed and respected him because they knew he had their interests deeply at heart and always gave them a straight deal, and it is difficult to conceive of a more fitting virtue in a commanding officer. His officers knew little of him except in matters pertaining to work. He mixed seldom with them in the mess, but rather to a combination of inherent shyness and lack of time. But no Company of officers ever served under a Commander who backed them up more whole heartedly. His theory was that if the Company did well, he was only the peg on which honours were hung and consequently – such was his sense of justice – should anything go wrong his was the broad back that accepted all responsibility.*

*Of his personal courage none of his men had any doubt. He was not the man to sit in his orderly room and direct from there the operations of his subordinates. If there was any 'sticky' job on, he was to be found in the thick of it ... .*

*A humourist of the Company once remarked that Colonel Humphrys was the only man he had ever met who really enjoyed the war. Such was not the case. His energy and enthusiasm were caused not by the love of war but by a strong sense of duty, an absolute assurance in the justice of the cause, and an*

*appreciation of the ability of the enemy, whom he was convinced*
*could only be defeated by everyone giving their utmost. It can be*
*truly said of him that he did his part.*
*(Personal papers of Captain DI Evans MC)*

Right from the start, when forming the tunnelling companies, Norton-Griffiths wanted to try to keep groups of men who worked and lived in close communities together in one company. Indeed, he said to Humphrys, who was a lieutenant with the 179th at the time, that he knew the Cornish were good miners, so he was going to recruit from that area. Although in past times they had made their living under harsh conditions, the Cornish were known for their constant cheerfulness, even in times of adversity, and would always work together as a team. All but three of the 251st identified were Cornish by birth, and the Cornish are well known for their clannish behaviour and for looking out for one another.

The coat of arms of the County of Cornwall features both a fisherman and a miner – both of whom believe implicitly in the motto, 'One and All'.

This esprit de corps and sense of tradition made a major contribution to the success of the Company. Whilst the 251st was, in time, going to be brought up to complement with miners from other areas of the country, and augmented by the 300 infantrymen that were permanently attached to it, the Cornish core was always present. At the end of the war, although some men had been transferred out and new tunnellers transferred in, the 251st was still predominantly Cornish, with over 72% of the men born and bred in the County serving with the 251st for the duration. Of those who lost their lives serving with the 251st, remarkably few were from Cornwall.

*Chapter 13*

# A Return to the Front

On leaving hospital in Canterbury on 9 August 1916 my grandfather was transferred to 99 Field Company RE in Seaford, East Sussex and, apart from a short spell in the 2nd Eastern General Hospital in Kemptown, Brighton, remained there until April 1917, when he was transferred to 3 Provisioning Company RE in Chatham. Here he remained until 21 May 1917, when he sailed for France; but this time, after disembarking at Rouen, he remained with 10th Company RE General Base Depot in Rouen, from which he was transferred to 185 Tunnelling Company on 16 July 1917.

It is not clear why he did not rejoin the 251st, but he had been away from his original unit for some fifteen months. By the time he joined the

*Seaford Camp was one of the many Kitchener Camps formed on greenfield sites on the South Coast. It was an accommodation and training base designed to hold 20,000 men. Eventually, the tents were replaced by Armstrong huts, the last of which was still standing in 2005, in the centre of a housing estate. (Picture reproduced by courtesy of Seaford Museum & Heritage Society)*

SEAFORD CAMP FROM THE GOLF LINKS

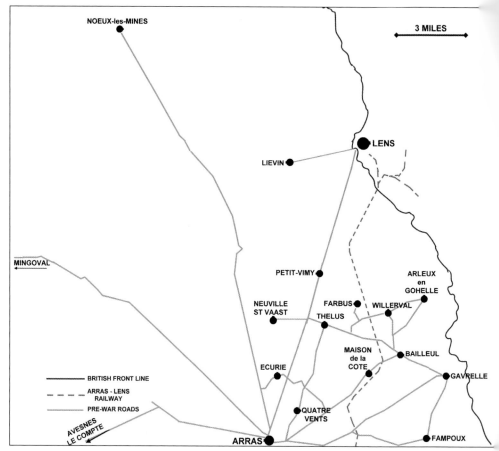

*Map 11. Map showing areas worked by 185 Tunnelling Company from July 1917 until the Advance to Victory starting in August 1918.*

185th, they were tunnelling on a front south of the La Bassée Canal and were therefore working in chalk; perhaps it was being a hard rock miner with previous experience of tunnelling in chalk, which meant his skills would have been well received by his new OC. This possibility is supported by the fact that Sapper Charles Butler, another tin miner from Cornwall, was transferred from 252 Tunnelling Company two months earlier and an old colleague of his from the 251st, Sapper Charles Kessell, joined the 185th just a couple of weeks later; he too was an experienced tin miner from the same district of Cornwall as my grandfather.

By the time Pop joined the 185th he would have seen some changes in attitude to the tunnellers. This is not to say that they themselves would have become any more military in terms of saluting or lining up for drill than they had been before, but he would have noticed a significantly improved relationship with the infantry who, as we have seen, by now saw the tunnellers' work as useful and, indeed, crucial to victory.

Pop would have joined the 185th at Écurie, near Arras, on the Vimy front, itself about sixteen miles south of the location where the 251st were working. For a short period of time Pop's section was attached to the Canadian Corps, working on the construction of dugouts, whilst another section was assigned to 170 Tunnelling Company for six weeks, working at Noeux-les-Mines, building subways. At the time this work was top secret, but details have since emerged revealing that it was associated with a scheme to discharge enormous quantities of gas through a system of 170 mines, across an extended front, for a duration of twenty four hours. The gas itself was to be stored in large cylinders buried deep underground, beneath the dugouts and subways. The idea stemmed from an incident earlier in the war, in which the German Army had flooded the French coal fields with mustard gas whilst civilians were still working in the mines. However, the possibility of gassing French civilians who were living behind the German lines as well as the targeted enemy troops led to the cancellation of the project.

The summer of 1917, following the Arras offensive of April and May, continued in relative peace for the 185th, apart from an occasional shelling. On 17 October a sports day was held at the sports ground adjacent to the Company billets, with the 185th competing against 172, 176 and 182 Tunnelling Companies. An event like this, which was attended by Brigadier General Harvey, Inspector of Mines, and Colonel Stokes, Controller of Mines, must have been widely welcomed and encouraged as it promoted goodwill between the companies as well as between the individual officers and men. A championship cup was donated by an American major attached to 185 Tunnelling Company, which was won by his own company.

On 18 October the unit was moved to Willerval, a destroyed village below Vimy Ridge, where dugouts were being constructed – no more tented camps or makeshift shelters, here they lived in the comfort of Armstrong huts; although the location was rather less comfortable, as this area was frequently the target of gas shells fired by the Germans.

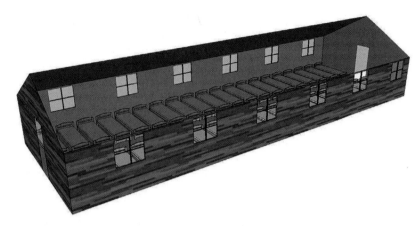

*An Armstrong hut of the type used on the Western Front. They were twenty yards long and seven yards wide and held up to forty men, with beds five inches off the floor and had straw mattresses. They were named after Major B Armstrong who was Director of Fortifications and Works. (Sketch courtesy of Brian Dury and Henry Finch from 'The Goodchilds of Grundisburgh')*

These were probably amongst the best quarters to be found on the Western Front, with a change house, baths, drying room and their own water supply from boreholes. Rugby, soccer and hockey were the order of the day when the men were at rest and even a rough nine hole golf course was built. Pop's life with the 185th was proving to be very different from that of his fellow Cornishmen in the 251st, just over twenty miles away to the north; the vagaries of war.

Life was relatively quiet during the winter of 1917–1918, with few casualties, and the building of deep dugouts and machine-gun posts continued apace. The tunnellers had never been so well off in terms of food and comfort, with dry and clean clothing always available – a welcome change from the cold and wet conditions Pop had endured with the 251st in 1916. There were few camp duties apart from morning parade, although time was given over to training courses on bridge building. Wood for fires and for the construction of duckboards to avoid the mud was often obtained by demolishing old German dugouts. Canteen food was supplemented by keeping rabbits and growing vegetables, just as it was for the 251st and, one suspects, for many other units.

The additional 500 or 600 infantrymen who were assigned to the 185th and whom they had to accommodate must have found life a welcome change. Such was the comradeship that had now developed between tunneller and infantryman that they inhabited the same billets, all pulling together towards a common cause.

In January 1918, the defences on the Arras–Lens railway were strengthened by making a series of dugouts thirty five feet below ground, each capable of holding a hundred men and each with three or four exits. Machine gun emplacements were also built, some with small surface shelters in banks or hedgerows, others with deep dugout shelters fitted with ladders and fire platforms. The surface shelters were easily made, but the deeper ones took up to four weeks to construct. Each emplacement had to be camouflaged with a hinged frame of wire netting holding strips of coloured cloth that were in keeping with the colours in the local countryside. The infantry were, understandably, still edgy about sounds underground and frequently thought the noise made by the construction work was the enemy tunnelling under their lines. As Captain Graham wrote:

*Besides the work, it fell to our lot as miners to "lay the ghosts" of a host of alleged mining sounds. Some of these sounds were reported near the front line at Arleux, which were investigated and found to be unfounded. They were the usual noises made by men working in trenches or dugouts, but the rumours spread, and we gave much time to discredit the reports. As far back as Farbus and on the upper reaches of the Ridge, some two and a half miles back, reports of mining were coming in. These rumours had their foundation in the discovery of numerous caves which, in that area, had been excavated many years ago for the purpose of mining a hard limestone for building the surrounding villages. Men had reported their discoveries, but had been too timid to carry forward their investigations. The artillery who lived in the neighbourhood instituted their own listening arrangements, with the sure result that they became suspicious of unfamiliar noises, with a consequent "wind up".*

Both sides continued to make trench raids and in late February 1918 the Germans raided the British trenches. Lieutenant Young and a team of sappers were working alongside a Guards battalion at the time and he led a counter-attack to drive the Germans off. Such was his courage that he was awarded the Military Cross, the award being recommended by none other than the colonel commanding the Guards Battalion.

In the spring of 1918 the 185th were working at Arleux and Petit Vimy, with their transport lines in old German dugouts at Nine Elms, near Thélus, modified to make them as comfortable as possible. Many hours were spent underground in these dugouts, with their whitewashed walls and ceilings, lit by electric lamps and with chimneys drilled through to the surface so that the heaters they had 'acquired' could be installed; the drilling for the chimneys being done by using a wombat drill. It was a hard existence, particularly for the infantry, spending so much time in the dugouts; but probably not so for the tunnellers, who were not normally underground in such relative comfort.

*The 'wombat' was a rotary and drill designed by Captain Stanley Hunter of the Australian Mining Corps which was adopted by the British Army. It could be operated by hand or electric motor and could drive 6½ inch holes in any inclination. In some clay areas, the machine was overworked, so alternatives such as the Star, Keystone or Hunter were used. (Picture Courtesy of the Australian War Memorial)*

GUERRE 1914-1917

ARRAS. — *Hôtel de Ville après le bombardement (février 1916).*
*Town-hall after the bombardment (February 1916).*

*This postcard was one of a book bought by Pop as a souvenir. The picture was taken after the bombardment in February 1916 and shows the destruction the Cloth Hall suffered. It is interesting that in the top right hand corner, it refers to the war as 1914–1917.*

All this changed on 21 March when the Germans launched their Spring Offensive, attacking on a front which ran from north of the River Scarpe to the River Oise, a distance of over sixty miles. At the time, the 185th were based at their transport lines, four and a half miles behind the front line, and for the first couple of days only the sound of the booming of the artillery guns told them that an offensive was taking place.

The Germans initially made great progress; the Fifth Army was in retreat everywhere along its front, but the Third Army generally held its ground. If it had not, Arras would have fallen, leaving the possibility of Ludendorff meeting his objective of taking Amiens and Abbeville, and thus splitting two allied armies. This in turn would have put pressure on the First Army, which came under attack itself some two weeks later. Just as at Givenchy, it was crucial that the British held their ground, and the 185th came under pressure to build switch trenches in the forward area to allow men to fall back, if necessary, to new defensive lines being dug furiously by the labour battalions.

In preparation for the enemy advance, the 185th laid explosive charges within their camp and also prepared for the demolition of key culverts, bridges and roads, to slow the German advance. They worked feverishly and were stood to arms several times in the coming days, but this command was always countermanded by the end of the day. It was not so for their counterparts in 176 Tunnelling Company, who not only had to take up battle positions at Maison de la Côte, but also had to abandon their camp after heavy shelling.

The German Army made astonishing advances in the first few days of the offensive, advancing up to thirty eight miles in places and in the process almost destroying the British Fifth Army. But the advance slowed, and despite the Germans deploying some fifteen divisions, the British eventually held their position and on 5 April Ludendorff called off Operation Michael. Although large swathes of ground had been lost, the Germans inability to follow through its advantage resulted in renewed optimism among the Allied forces, as indicated by Captain Plummer of the 185th in one of his letters home:

*...I honestly – and for the first time in the war – believe that hostilities will end this year. The days of settling down to months and months of trench warfare are over.*

Following the failure of Operation Michael, the German offensive moved northwards to an offensive that became The Battle of the Lys, and many infantry battalions were moved to support that sector. To replace them, all units were reorganised and the 185th found itself part of a 3,000 strong composite force that would be called upon in case of attack. This meant that, as well as continuing to rebuild trenches and construct dugouts, they were also drilled like infantrymen, with plans drawn up and preparations made for the positions they would adopt in the case of attack. Exercises were conducted to practise how these measures would be implemented when the time came.

Musketry training now took place for all officers with the intention of passing on their skills to the men upon their return. It is interesting to note that the tunnelling officers were only given fourteen days training in preparation for the necessary examinations at the end of the course, against the infantry's twenty one days. Life became harder for a period when they were encamped in tents on the Scarpe, although fortunately the spring was warm and by May they were back at Écurie Camp. When this was shelled it became a forward camp and the main camp was moved to Mingoval, back under canvas once again.

Based as they were in Mingoval, they were certainly kept very busy in the surrounding areas. On finishing their work constructing dugouts at Quatre Vents on the road between St. Nicholas and Roclincourt, they constructed more dugouts on the high ground overlooking Bailleul and Gavrelle-en-Gohelle, as well as at Fampoux; large dugouts were built into the railway embankment to the east of Arras. Such was the effort put in by the 185th that they created a record at Lance Subway on Reservoir Hill, north of Lens, in driving sixty two feet of subway in just twenty four hours. Another task undertaken by the Company was to examine the caves at Avesnes-le-Comte to see if they could be used to house men; most were unsuitable, but some were recommended and these were used later in the war for that purpose.

Early June saw the army struck by a severe outbreak of influenza, with some units being reduced in strength by 70%. Fortunately, it was a mild strain and the majority were fit again after five or six days. There was a belief at the time that the outbreak might have been exacerbated by the amount of time being spent in dugouts, where men were living in close proximity to one another in damp conditions and with little fresh air circulating, but this was never proven.

By late June, however, spirits were running high, as reserve troops started arriving not only from Britain but also from Italy, Mesopotamia and Salonika. In addition, American troops were coming to the Western Front rapidly now, initially deployed amongst the French and British but very quickly placed under their own command. It was not just the increase in manpower which was improving their spirits; supply ships arrived more frequently, owing to the reduced threat from submarines, following the adoption of the convoy system.

During summer 1918, the 185th left Mingoval because the travelling distances from billet to workplace were now proving too great, and moved to Neuville St. Vaast. From here they worked on the Lens-Avion front, building dugouts, machine gun emplacements and long observation tunnels at Lievin. They must have been very pleased with this move, as they now found they once again had the luxury of being billeted in Nissen huts with electric lighting. Although still under frequent bombardment from German artillery, the late summer was relatively quiet – they even had time to make jam and shoot some partridges to supplement their rations!

Following the successful Second Battle of the Marne, pressure was kept on the Germans by the allies and it was clear that it would not be long before the 185th would be called forward. In preparation for this, training on road making and bridge building was undertaken and special instruction was given to the tunnellers on how to search for and destroy booby traps and concealed mines left by the enemy. All these explosive devices had to be made safe; the usual way of operating was to put scouts forward to identify any suspected trap and then a working party would follow to examine and make safe.

The company was originally under brigade orders, but this became a cumbersome method of operation and was changed to allow the tunnellers to work independently, providing daily reports of the cleared fronts, whilst regular updates on the changing front line were received. As they moved forward, they wore broad red stripes down their sleeves so that their role in mine clearance identified them to the infantry. On 29 September the line moved forward with the tunnellers leading the way, identifying and subsequently clearing potential threats. They met with success from the start but on 2 October the advance was held up for some five days, giving them time to examine their ways of working and modifying them as necessary.

The number of booby traps found and made safe was very high. For example, a return covering just two weeks, from 7 to 21 October 1918, shows that the 185th had made safe or removed: 1,808 land mines, eight delay action mines, 339 enemy demolition charges and 124 other charges, totalling some 44,000 lbs of explosive.

This activity prompted the following letter from Major General Anderson, Chief of Staff First Army, to all units in VIII Corps:

*The Army Commander has a very great satisfaction in circulating for general information the attached return of mines, traps etc. removed by the Tunnelling Companies of the First Army during the past fortnight.*

*The return speaks for itself. Such results could only have been attained by previous instruction and training, combined with skill, gallantry and devotion on the part of Officers, N.C.O's and men.*

*The Army Commander desires to express to the 172nd, 176th, 179th and 185th Tunnelling Companies the highest appreciation of the work so thoroughly performed which has contributed in so marked a degree to the success of our operations.*

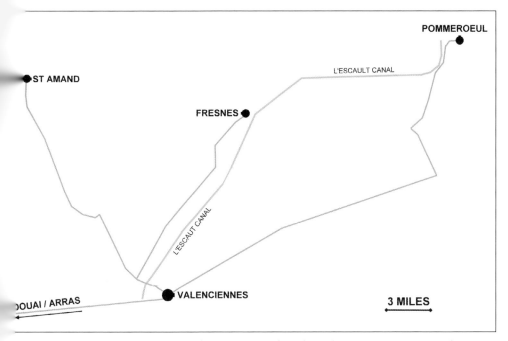

*Map 12. The 185's areas of operations after the Advance to Victory until demobilisation.*

The Advance to Victory was now well under way and by 17 October 1918 the allies had advanced as far as Douai. The tunnellers were sometimes in front of the advance as they were clearing the way for the infantry, and as they approached Douai, the 185th were so far in advance they were actually the first allied troops into the town and had the honour of removing the flag from the German HQ, which had been housed in the Préfecture.

On Armistice Day, Major Tulloch DSO MC, Officer Commanding the 185th was in Valenciennes, but the Company were scattered over a wide area clearing traps, building bridges, filling craters and making roads. After the signing of the Armistice, the Company continued to move through Belgium doing the same sort of work, rebuilding bridges on the Escault Canal that had been destroyed by the Germans, and constructing two eight ton bridges at Pommeroeul.

Mine clearance was conducted in areas marked on maps provided by the Germans under the Armistice agreement, but these mines were often overdue for explosion so there was always the fear that just the vibration from feet could be enough to set the mine off. Obtaining transport for such work was now easier, as a number of German lorries had been handed over after the Armistice. These lorries may have been considered by the men to be uncomfortable but at least they made life easier.

The 185th now moved into billets in St. Amand and demobilisation commenced and, again, the coal miners were the first to leave. Leaving France was always a subdued affair, with no fuss or ceremony, marked only by ships' horns being sounded as they left port. Those left were now moved to Fresnes and remained there until the remnants of the Company were discharged. Pop was finally discharged from the army on 7 March 1919.

*Chapter 14*

# A Land Fit for Heroes?
# The Tin Mines Close

Although mining had been a part of the Cornish heritage for more than 4,000 years and over 600 mines were operational in its heyday, at the end of the nineteenth century the mines in Cornwall were closing with increasing frequency, and would continue to do so towards the end of, and immediately after, the war.

Dolcoath Mine, the 'queen of Cornish mines' as it was known, which had opened in 1720, closed in 1921, along with many others as the demand for tin fell. The development of open cast mining in Malaya, which reduced the cost of extracting tin, so causing prices to drop, made it uneconomic to extract ore from the deep mines of Cornwall. As the mines closed, so too did associated industries such as the National Explosives factory at Hayle, with a loss of another 1800 jobs. As a result many Cornishmen chose to emigrate to other countries where mining industries still flourished and where, with their reputation as highly skilled and productive miners, they would readily find work. The upheaval for families was immense, as they were either parted for many years whilst the head of the household worked abroad, or they moved as a family to such places as the United States, Canada, Mexico, Cuba, South Africa, Australia, Malaya and Chile. In many parts of the world there are Cornish Societies, all created originally by emigrant families wishing to hold on to their Celtic roots; many of these societies are still active today. With no work to come home to, many of those returning from the war joined this exodus. The concept of Cornish miners working in places a long way from home was nothing new, as an extract from *The Western Daily Mercury* dated 7 April 1915 attests:

> *The miners of Cornwall have pioneered in every country of the world where metalliferous mining is done. They have plied pick and gad in the blazing tropics and amid the snows of the Yukon. They faced the dangers and real hardships in the early days of the Rand, in the waterless deserts of Westralia, and in the frozen hills of Alaska.*

Pop's father-in-law, my great-grandfather, Samuel John Rundle, worked abroad for seven years between 1901 and 1908 at the Kennedy Mine in Jackson, California, at that time the deepest gold mine in America, before returning to work at the Dolcoath Mine in Camborne. Pop's own father and grandfather had also spent some time in America in the late 1800s, working in the mines in Crystal Falls, Michigan, from where iron ore was extracted.

As a result of this migration, the decline in the Cornish population between 1911 and 1921 was around 8%, though not as high as in the mining depression in the 1860s, when a third of the population left, but significant all the same when compared to the industrial growth in other parts of the country. For example, Luton in Bedfordshire saw its population grow by 16% during the same period.

Other Cornish mines, such as Wheal Kitty, remained viable and stayed open, until finally closing in 1930. Many of those in 251 Tunnelling Company who came from the St. Agnes area had worked here prior to the war and those men, on their return, may well have found work in Cornwall.

Pop had taken leave in December 1918 to return to Cornwall in order to marry my grandmother, Irene Rundle; and on 9 December, at Camborne Parish Church, they were married. He was formally discharged from the Army on 7 March 1919. It is not known if he found work in the mines on his return to Cornwall after the war, but on 27 October 1920 he travelled to Southampton and stayed at the Cornish (Temperance) Hotel, Queen's Park, Southampton before he sailed, crossed the Atlantic to New York on the RMS *Olympic*, sister ship to the RMS *Titanic*. I feel sure that his mind would have dwelt on his first run down Southampton Water just over five years before, but even for third class passengers this voyage would be more luxurious and far less dangerous.

He left my grandmother and my father, who was born in December 1919, at her parent's home in Camborne. He remained in the States until

*Built by Harland & Wolff in Belfast, at 46,439 tons and 882 feet in length, the triple-screwed RMS* Olympic *was at the time the world's largest ocean liner (after her ill-fated sister ship RMS* Titanic*). She could move her 2,435 passengers and 900 crew at twenty one knots when using all of her twenty nine boilers.*

19 May 1925, when he returned for two months, with the intention of emigrating and taking his wife and son back to the United States with him. He had found life very agreeable in New Jersey, not mining underground but working for the Public Service Railway Company, whilst living in Palisades Park, New Jersey.

However, my grandmother refused to leave Cornwall and so Pop went back to America alone and remained there until returning to

*The Public Service Railway, owned by the Public Service Corporation of New Jersey, operated most of the streetcar lines in New Jersey by the early twentieth century. Public Service lines stretched from north-east New Jersey to Trenton, and then south to Camden and its suburbs. (Pop pictured in the centre).*

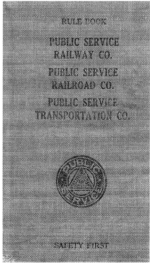

Plymouth on the SS *France* on 20 April 1928, finally coming home to Cornwall to be reunited with his wife and child. In effect, therefore, from the end of the war until he finally returned home from America, he only saw his wife for twenty months and his son for eleven months, in the nine years after his discharge from the Royal Engineers.

Earnings must have been good in America; by the time of his return in 1928 Pop was established enough to buy the old Mine Captain's house in Stray Park, Camborne, from where he ran his haulage and taxi business. This had its own eccentricities in the vehicles he acquired. His lorry, registration number RL 480, was a steam-powered Clayton, similar to the Foden in the photograph below, which had a five ton carrying capacity, with a three way tipper on the back.

The car he bought for his taxi business was equally interesting in that it was a Vauxhall Landaulette, registration number XF 6056, originally

*Although very popular in Britain in the early twentieth century, as a result of the Salter Report an 'axle weight tax' was introduced in 1933 in order to charge commercial motor vehicles more towards the costs of maintaining the road system, and to do away with the perception that the free use of roads was subsidising the competitors of rail freight. The tax was payable by all road hauliers in proportion to the axle load; it was particularly damaging to steam propulsion, as these vehicles were heavier than those driven by the internal combustion engine. (Picture Courtesy of Rob Fish)*

*A Land Fit For Heroes? The Tin Mines Close* 175

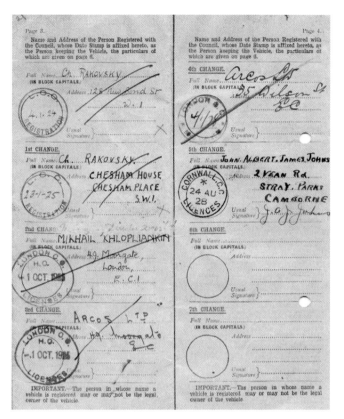

*Log book of XF 6056. Christian Ravovsky was the Russian Ambassador and Mikhail Khopliankin was the Managing Director of Arcos Ltd. He returned to Russia in 1927, where he became Deputy Commisar of Supply.*

purchased by the Russian Embassy and registered in the Ambassador's name. It was subsequently transferred to the 'All Russian Co-Operative Society', or Arcos Ltd, in the name of the managing director. The premises of this organisation were raided by the secret intelligence services (now MI6) in 1927 and the organisation itself was accused of spying and of being implicated in the 1926 general strike. As a result the company was closed when diplomatic relations with Russia were suspended. The vehicle was acquired by my grandfather in 1928, complete with the Russian eagle still mounted on the bonnet. The vehicle must have seemed very grand to those in Camborne who called upon Pop's services.

Pop ran this business until the start of the Second World War. The haulage side of the business met its demise at an earlier date when an overweight load proved to be the final straw on an ascent of Beacon Hill, Camborne; and fuel shortages, together with the directed work scheme, which sent him to the local gas works in Hayle to work for the duration, put paid to the taxi business. Hayle Gas Works was possibly not an ideal place to work for a man whose First World War service had given him pneumonia and long term breathing problems. At the end of the war he retired through ill health and, although it can never be proven, one has to question if the effects of the damage to his lungs sustained during his active service reduced him to this state, since he never worked again. He struggled by with increasing difficulty in breathing until he finally passed away on 28 November 1962.

And so at last the story of the cigarette case is now complete and in what fascinating directions it has led me. The case itself was made in 1918 by Arthur & John Zimmerman of Regent Street, Birmingham, who were founded in 1913, and is 92.5% pure silver. Who did the engraving we will never know, but there were few so adorned and as far as I am aware my grandfather was one of only a few Cornishmen to be presented with one. That is special in itself.

As a postscript to this chapter, the last mine in Cornwall to close was South Crofty, near Camborne. By 1998, when it closed, the extraction of ore was highly mechanised and operated by a much reduced workforce. At the time of writing, there are strong possibilities that this mine might be reopened as the price of tin reaches new levels of some £17,500 per ton and, added to which, rich seams of rare Indium have also been discovered. There is one difficulty to be overcome; the landscape created by Cornwall's defunct mining industry was, ironically, designated as a World Heritage Site in 2006.

*World Heritage Status gives international recognition to Cornwall's mining contribution to the development of our modern industrial society.*
(From World heritage List 13th July 2006)

*Chapter 15*

# Tunnellers: Hearts of Lions, Nerves of Steel

Writing this book has given me a fascinating insight into my grandfather's life; it has also become very clear to me just how dedicated and courageous these Cornish tunnellers and their counterparts in the other tunnelling companies were. That is not to say that any other soldier in this horrific war was not equally as brave, but the cat-and-mouse game of mining and counter-mining, coupled with knowing that if they got it wrong many infantrymen would have died because of their failure, must have put them under a very great pressure.

Lieutenant WJ McBride, 1st Australian Tunnelling Company, wrote a good summing-up of the tunnellers' life:

*Tunnelling was just like a game of chess, one had to anticipate the opponents move. You didn't always know that you were going to get away with it. All the tension, all the time – the strain underground and the darkness. It was terrible. It was not war, it was murder.*

It was clearly stressful for the tunnellers not to know if and when a mine might be blown by the enemy, but despite this they carried on constantly digging and listening, in their underground world, working twenty four hours a day. When the war of offensive and defensive counter-mining came to an end, they constructed communication tunnels, excavated dugouts and subways and, if that were not enough, cleared towns and villages of booby traps, abandoned explosives, and ammunition. Finally, as the enemy withdrew and the allies pushed forwards, they became bridge builders and road makers.

Considering that throughout the war these men were acting as miners, labourers, infantrymen, bridge builders and bomb clearance engineers, according to the demands of their superiors, it must have been more than just luck that so many survived; though, I am sure that luck played a major part too.

This book has focused on the 'Cornish' tunnellers, formed mainly from A Company 10th Battalion DCLI. However, many other Cornishmen took part in the First World War, some with other tunnelling companies on the Western Front, some with other services and some with infantry units, particularly the DCLI, who fought with immense bravery at Mons, Ypres, Arras, Vimy and Passchendaele, as well as in other theatres of the war, such as Salonika, Macedonia, Jerusalem, Palestine and Aden. Without question, these Cornishmen, the majority of whom were miners, recruited initially as pioneers, but who were transferred to work in their natural environment, helped save many thousands of infantrymen's lives, and for that they should not be forgotten.

The following extract from E. Synton's book: *Tunnellers All*, essentially confirms the regard with which these miners were held:

*Everybody damns the Tunneller; GHQ because he invariably has his job finished months before the rest of the Army are ready for the 'Great Push'; Army troops because he invariably upsets all their preconceived notions as to the safety of trenches and dugouts; Divisional troops damn him because he is outside their sphere of influence; Brigade troops because he refuses to move when they do and because he knows by heart that part of the line to which they come as strangers; Brass hats because they dislike his underground habits; Regimental officers because he refuses to allow them to use his deep and snug dugouts; Subalterns because of his superior knowledge; Tommy because he is the direct cause of numerous extra fatigues and – alas that it should be so – because of his extra pay; and last and loudest, the Bosche damn him because of his earnest and unceasing attempts at uplifting and converting them into surprised angels. It is also owing to his success in this noble work of the missionary that the Tunneller is highly respected by all branches of the forces.*

Considering that Field Marshal Haig remarked: *they are the best unit in the Army, there is nothing they cannot do*, it has taken a long time for

*The Tunnellers Memorial is the same size (4 feet x 2 feet 6 inches) as the tunnel in which Sapper Hackett and Private Collins were working when they were killed. The diameter of the base of the memorial is the same width as the Shaftsbury Shaft that they would have entered to gain access to the tunnel, which lay in line with the T on the memorial.*

the work of the tunnellers to be recognised. In the end such recognition came. Overlooking Shaftsbury Shaft in Givenchy-lès-la-Bassée, where Sapper William Hackett VC won this most distinguished and meritorious award, is a memorial to all the tunnellers of the BEF, which was dedicated on 19 June 2010.

The inscription reads:

*This stone commemorates the endeavours*
*of the men of the Tunnelling Companies of*
*Britain, Canada, Australia and New Zealand,*
*who during the Great War lived, fought and*
*died underground in France and Flanders*

*It is erected in special remembrance of*
*Sapper William Hackett VC*
*Of 254th Tunnelling Company RE, and*
*Private Thomas Collins*
*of the 14th Battalion, The Welsh Regiment,*
*who both still lie forty feet beneath the field*
*in front of this memorial.*

*....No record in the world would ever touched the*
*footage, yield per ounce of pluck, endurance*
*and devotion to duty, and no forces endured*
*more. One silent toast to those who memorise*
*a glorious record in their ever silent tunnels.*

*Sir John Norton-Griffiths*

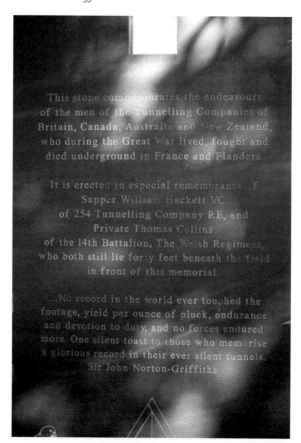

*Inscription on the Tunnellers Memorial at Givenchy-Lès-La-Bassée.*

Tribute should also be paid to the infantrymen who were assigned to the tunnelling companies. To the tin miners at the front, living, working, sleeping and eating underground, by candlelight, sometimes for days at a time, would be difficult, but they were, in some ways, in their home environment. They were used to the dark, to the strange noises, and to the wet and dusty environment that is so damaging to the lungs. Whilst a large number of attached infantrymen were miners before the war, not all were and to those men it must have been a pure nightmare, working in a totally alien and frightening environment, for which they received no extra pay. It has been estimated that over a billion sandbags of spoil were removed from the tunnels during the conflict, and without infantry support the tunnellers would not have been as successful as they were nor would they have been able to work as fast as they did. I would like to think that in many ways this book is as much a tribute to them as it is to the tunnellers. All soldiers who took part in the First World War suffered in some way, mentally if not physically. To all of those who served, we should always remain grateful.

Much of the tunnellers' work was kept secret both during and immediately after the war, so it is now appropriate that we revisit what Field Marshal Sir John French said in a despatch published in *The Times*, when referring to the tunnelling companies as early as November 1915:

> *It is impossible within the limits of a despatch to give any just idea of the work of these units, but it will be found, when their history comes to be written, that it will present a story of danger, of heroism, and of difficulties surmounted worthy of the best traditions of the Royal Engineers, under whose general direction their work is carried out.*

*Appendix 1*

# Officers of
# 251 Tunnelling Company

The following is a list of the Officers Commanding the 251$^{st}$, together with other officers identified during the research for this book. The list is far from complete, so I would very much appreciate hearing of any further information which might be available.

## OFFICERS COMMANDING

### Major FJV Bullen

He was transferred to the 10$^{th}$ DCLI as a lieutenant from the 7$^{th}$ DCLI, and was then transferred again with A Company from the 10$^{th}$ DCLI on the formation of 251 (T) Coy on 29 September 1915 and remained as Commanding Officer until 20 January 1916, when he was replaced by Major Humphrys. He returned to 10$^{th}$ DCLI and fought during the Battle of the Somme, where he was shot twice, once in the head and once in the hand.

### Major HJ Humphrys DSO MC

He transferred, as a lieutenant, from 179 Tunnelling Company on 20 January 1916, when he took over as Commanding Officer from Major Bullen. He had been promoted to temporary Major by 10 April 1916 and left the Company on 22 January 1917 to join the General Staff. He returned as Officer Commanding on 23 March 1917 and remained until transferred to 8$^{th}$ Royal Scots (51$^{st}$ Division) on 5 April 1918 with the rank of temporary lieutenant colonel.

## Captain EC Graham MC

He was made temporary captain on 16 December 1915. Was Officer in Charge of No. 2 Section until 22 January 1917, when he was appointed temporary Officer Commanding, a position he kept until 6 February 1917, when he returned to No. 2 Section. He left on 17 April 1917 to take up an appointment with the Railway Survey Section. He was Mentioned in Despatches on 18 May 1917.

## Captain G Rowan MC

He was transferred from the 7th Black Watch to be Officer Commanding on 6 February 1917; he remained with the Company until 23 March 1917, when he was transferred to 179 Tunnelling Company.

## Major JAH Church DSO MC

He joined the 19th Alberta Dragoons in Canada at the outbreak of war, and was transferred to become Officer in Charge No. 4 Section on 26 October 1915. He was made Commanding Officer on 5 April 1918 and remained in post until the Company was disbanded in February 1919.

## Major DM Brown MC

No mention is made in the War Diary of Major Brown being the Officer Commanding; all dates except for October 1918 are covered, from the formation of the Company to its disbandment. However, he is named on the list of Officers Commanding on the coversheet of the Diaries.

## OTHER OFFICERS

All of the information has been extracted from the War Diary, when they have been mentioned by name. For some it is more complete than for others:

## Major Liddell

He left on 3 March 1916 to become OC 255 Tunnelling Company.

## Captain Auret

He was Officer in Charge of No. 3 Section on 23 July 1917 and was sent with the Northern Detachment to Le Drumez on 8 August 1917. After a period in hospital from 14 August 1917 to 19 December 1917, he rejoined the Company, where he remained until returning to South Africa on 7 September 1918.

### Captain VHM Barratt
He joined the Company on 13 August 1916, was hospitalised from 16 to 20 November and returned to his original battalion (not recorded) on 16 December 1916, only to return to the 251 on 24 May 1917.

### Captain Deacon
He was commissioned into the 10th DCLI and transferred to 251 Tunnelling Company on its formation. He was wounded in an explosion and transferred to hospital in England on 10 April 1916, rejoining the Company on 25 August 1916.

### Captain DI Evans
Joined the Company on 22 February 1916 and was Officer in Charge of No. 2 Section from 19 July 1917. He took temporary command of the Company from 20 to 29 July 1917 when Captain Church took the detachment north to Le Drumez. He left when appointed Assistant Controller of Mines Fifth Army on 29 July 1918.

### Captain Fideo
Joined the Company on 16 November 1916.

### Captain WGC Gundy
Joined the Company on 30 July 1916, but very shortly left, on 3 August 1916.

### Captain OJ Hansen MC
Joined the Company on 5 May 1916 and was Officer in Charge of No. 1 Section.

### Captain RW Hislop
Joined on 1 May 1916 and was Officer In Charge of No. 3 Section. He was Mentioned in Despatches on 18 May 1917. He was gassed on 22 July 1917 when the Germans broke into a British mine and blew a charge. He is buried in Cambrin Military Cemetery.

**Captain BD MacGregor**
Joined the Company on 21 December 1916.

**Captain NB Paddon**
Joined the Company on 8 February 1918 and left on 28 February 1918, when he transferred to 253 Tunnelling Company.

**Captain TW Walker MC and Bar**
Joined on 5 July 1916 and was made Officer in Charge No. 1 Section on 1 February 1918, subsequently being moved to Officer in Charge No. 3 Section on 14 February 1918.

**Captain TC Woods MC**
Joined the Company on 7 July 1916 and was made Officer in Charge of the Portuguese detachment on 1 February 1918.

**Lieutenant Amy**
Joined the Company on 19 August 1916.

**Lieutenant WM Anderson**
It is not known when he joined the Company but he rejoined from hospital on 11 November 1916 and moved to 176 Tunnelling Company on 21 May 1917.

**Lieutenant FJV Bullen MC and bar**
Older brother of Frank Bullen, the first Officer Commanding of 251. Was commissioned directly into the Royal Engineers and posted to 251 Tunnelling Company. He remained with the unit until it was disbanded.

**Lieutenant RW Balmenno**
Joined the Company on 7 November 1918.

**Lieutenant GA Cock**
Other than his name being mentioned, no other information was obtained from the War Diary.

**Lieutenant OL Gibbon**
Joined the Company on 29 July 1916. Was hospitalised on 1 March 1917 and rejoined the Company twelve months later, on 30 March 1918.

**Lieutenant CT Landrey**
Joined the Company on 30 July 1916 and was killed during the Battle of the Lys on 21 April 1918. He is buried at Lapugnoy Military Cemetery.

**Lieutenant FW Markham**
Joined the Company on 23 August 1917.

**Lieutenant H Mein**
Joined the Company on 5 August 1918.

**Lieutenant WO Reid**
Joined the Company on 4 May 1916.

**Lieutenant E Ritchie**
Other than his name being mentioned, no other information was obtained from the War Diary.

**Lieutenant CA Roe**
Joined the Company on 8 May 1918.

**Lieutenant FA Schneider MC**
Posted to 251 Tunnelling Company from the Royal Engineers and was one of the first officers to join the Company. He went to hospital on 18 April 1916, rejoining the Company on 28 April 1916. He had a further spell in hospital when he was wounded on 5 August 1916 and did not rejoin the Company until 23 February 1917.

**Lieutenant R Smart MC**
Joined the Company on 14 August 1917.

**Lieutenant Townsend**
Joined the Company on 3 August 1916 as a replacement for Captain Gundy.

**Lieutenant Turner I**
Joined the Company on 14 May 1917.

**Lieutenant Turner II**
Joined the Company on 21 September 1916 and was transferred to 254 on 24 May 1917.

**Second Lieutenant Allan**
Other than his name being mentioned, no other information was obtained from the War Diary.

**Second Lieutenant J Barker**
Joined the Company on 10 May 1917 and was wounded on 14 April 1918, rejoining the unit on 10 May 1918.

**Second Lieutenant GC Barnard**
Other than his name being mentioned, no other information was obtained from the War Diary.

**Second Lieutenant Bendall**
Joined the Company on 22 July 1917 and was transferred to 256 Tunnelling Company on 21 December 1917.

**Second Lieutenant AF Campbell**
Joined the Company on 30 July 1918.

**Second Lieutenant CH Cameron**
He was transferred to 173 Tunnelling Company on 2 February 1916.

**Second Lieutenant JK Forrester**
He arrived in France with 3 Australian Tunnelling Company. He joined 251 Tunnelling Company on 28 August 1918 and returned to 3rd Australian on 25 February 1919.

**Second Lieutenant C Garner**
Joined the Company on 9 November 1918, just two days before the Armistice.

**Second Lieutenant EC Gwylym**
Joined the Company on 3 September 1918.

### Second Lieutenant P Hunter
Joined the Company on 7 March 1916, and was killed during a raid on 17 April 1916. He is buried in Cambrin Military Cemetery.

### Second Lieutenant T Marsland
Joined the Company on 23 August 1917.

### Second Lieutenant THE Morgan MC
Joined the Company on 24 February 1916. He was hospitalised on 25 February 1917. After rejoining on 1 February 1918, he was hospitalised again on 17 June 1918, coming back five weeks later, on 27 July 1918.

### Second Lieutenant RV Morris
Joined the Company on 18 May 1916; he was transferred to 257 Tunnelling Company on 7 July 1916.

### Second Lieutenant RA Perkins
Other than his name being mentioned, no other information was obtained from the War Diary.

### Second Lieutenant WV Pettit
On the formation of 251 Tunnelling Company he was transferred from the Borders Regiment. Was transferred again to 173 Tunnelling Company where on 29 June 1916 he was killed aged 42. He is buried in Noux les Mines.

### Second Lieutenant MA Phillimore
He was with the Essex Regiment and was attached to the 251. He was killed on 25 June 1916. He is buried in Cambrin Military Cemetery.

### Second Lieutenant JC Prag
He was transferred to 255 Tunnelling Company on 2 April 1916.

### Second Lieutenant Prisk
Other than his name being mentioned, no other information was obtained from the War Diary.

### Second Lieutenant HS Redmond, Australian Imperial Forces
He was attached to the Company on 31 August 1918.

**Second Lieutenant BE Rees MC**
Joined the Company on 21 December 1916.

**Second Lieutenant FR Richards**
Other than knowing that he was one of the first officers appointed on the formation of the 251 Tunnelling Company, no other information has been obtained.

**Second Lieutenant TC Sharpe**
Joined the Company on 4 July 1918.

**Second Lieutenant Spencer**
He transferred into the Company on 12 December 1916.

**Second Lieutenant P Starley**
Joined the Company on 7 July 1916.

**Second Lieutenant Walters**
Joined the Company on 26 April 1916.

**Second Lieutenant PHS Watson**
He was hospitalised between 29 February 1916 and 8 March 1916. He was transferred to 253 Tunnelling Company on 21 December 1917.

**Second Lieutenant JC Watson**
Other than his name being mentioned, no other information was obtained from the War Diary.

**Second Lieutenant PN Whitehead**
Other than knowing that he was one of the first officers appointed to 251 Tunnelling Company on its formation, no other information has been obtained.

# Appendix 2

# List of Cornishmen in the Tunnelling Companies

The following were all from the 10th DCLI, and part of the 251st when it was formed.

| Rank | Ser No | Surname | Christian Names | Award | Born | Died | Town | Comment |
|------|--------|---------|-----------------|-------|------|------|------|---------|
| Sapper | 132168 | Abrahams | William John | | 1878 | | Redruth | |
| Sapper | 132400 | Angove | Bertie | | 1892 | | Redruth | |
| Sapper | 132315 | Bartle | Edward John | | 1888 | | Camborne | |
| Sapper | 132310 | Bawden | Elijah | | 1887 | | Redruth | |
| Sapper | 132303 | Bennett | John | | 1888 | | Praze | to 175th and 179th |
| Sapper | 132167 | Bickford | Leonard | | 1896 | | St. Day | |
| Sapper | 132297 | Bowden | George Henry | | 1895 | | Flushing | to 173rd |
| Sapper | 132225 | Bray | Walter | | 1885 | | Redruth | |
| Sapper | 132250 | Bray | Lewis | | 1877 | | Redruth | |
| Sapper | 132353 | Bray | John Arthur | | 1895 | | Redruth | |
| Sapper | 132357 | Bray | William | | 1878 | | Illogan | |
| Sapper | 132224 | Broadley | Edwin John | | 1893 | | Redruth | to 252nd |
| Sapper | 132222 | Brown | Richard John | | 1895 | 02/07/1916 | Scorrier | |
| Sapper | 132228 | Butler | William James | | 1889 | | Portreath | to 171st |
| Sapper | 132233 | Butler | Alfred John | | 1894 | | Portreath | |
| Sapper | 132351 | Carne | Frederick | | 1896 | | St. Agnes | |
| Sapper | 132314 | Carter | Henry | | 1884 | | Redruth | to 253rd |
| Sapper | 132241 | Collins | Albert | | 1886 | | Harrowbarrow | |
| Sapper | 132294 | Collins | Arthur Samuel | | 1890 | | Carn Brea | to 175th |
| Sapper | 132157 | Colwill | Cyril Claud | | 1884 | | Redruth | |
| Sapper | 132278 | Curry | William Henry | | 1890 | | Carn Brea | to 254th |
| Sapper | 132197 | Curtis | Edward James | | 1890 | | Lanner | |
| Sergeant | 132201 | Daddow | William John | | 1892 | | Illogan | |
| Sapper | 132226 | Davey | Charles | | 1895 | | Illogan | |
| Sapper | 132305 | Davey | Stanley | | 1895 | | Mount Hawke | |
| Sapper | 132274 | Duff | William Charles | | 1883 | | Lanner | |
| Sapper | 132359 | Dunn | George Alfred | | 1891 | | Redruth | to 182nd, 176th & 179 |
| Sergeant | 132176 | Dunstan | William Ogarth | | 1894 | | Stithians | |
| Sapper | 132210 | Dunstan | Fred | | 1895 | | Redruth | to 254th |
| Sapper | 132365 | Dunstan | William Henry | | 1894 | | St. Agnes | |
| Sapper | 132279 | Ellery | John James | | 1889 | | Camborne | |
| Sapper | 132286 | Eva | Ernest | | 1893 | | Brea | |

| Rank | Number | Surname | Forename | | Born | Died | Place | Notes |
|---|---|---|---|---|---|---|---|---|
| ...pper | 132360 | Evans | Thomas Lockwood | | 1877 | | St. Agnes | to 179th |
| ...pper | 132363 | Finch | Alfred George | | 1894 | | St. Agnes | |
| ...Cpl | 132260 | Francis | Joseph James | | 1894 | 20/07/1918 | Redruth | to 180th |
| ...pper | 132187 | Geach | William James | | 1894 | 31/01/1916 | Lanner | |
| ...apper | 132248 | Geach | Joseph Henry | | 1893 | | Lanner | |
| ...apper | 132204 | George | William John | | 1896 | | Redruth | |
| ...apper | 132304 | George | Reginald | | 1891 | | Redruth | |
| ...apper | 132281 | Gibbings | Arthur | | 1879 | | Fowey | |
| ...apper | 132165 | Gibson | William | | 1880 | | Illogan | |
| ...apper | 132257 | Gilbert | Garfield | | 1893 | | Redruth | |
| ...apper | 132163 | Gill | Ernest Charles | | 1883 | | Redruth | |
| ...apper | 132199 | Glasson | John Thomas | | 1888 | 10/12/1915 | Lanner | |
| ...orporal | 132266 | Glasson | James Thomas | | 1885 | | Hayle | |
| ...apper | 132291 | Glasson | Harry | | 1896 | | Praze | to 256th and 255th |
| ...apper | 132191 | Gleed | James | | 1888 | 31/01/1916 | Carharrack | |
| ...apper | 132174 | Goldsworthy | John Davey | | 1893 | | Redruth | to 175th |
| ...apper | 132259 | Graham | Frederick Robert | | 1882 | | Frogpool | to 184th |
| ...apper | 132362 | Greet | Wallace | | 1893 | | St. Agnes | |
| ...apper | 132177 | Gunn | William | | 1876 | | St. Agnes | |
| Sergeant | 132321 | Hancock | John Parkyn | | 1881 | | Illogan | |
| Sergeant | 132319 | Harris | William Horace | | 1895 | | Redruth | |
| Sapper | 132338 | Harris | William Henry | | 1892 | 02/09/1916 | Helston | |
| Sapper | 132364 | Harris | Edgar | | 1889 | | St. Agnes | |
| Sapper | 132344 | Hicks | Richard | | 1881 | 05/10/1914 | Fowey | Died before sailing |
| Sapper | 132235 | Hitchins | George | | 1895 | | Carharrack | |
| Sapper | 132236 | Hitchins | William | | 1894 | 28/10/1917 | Carharrack | |
| L/Cpl | 132368 | Hoare | Frederick | | 1895 | | Scorrier | |
| L/Cpl | 132323 | Hocking | Wilfred | | 1895 | | St. Day | |
| Sapper | 132334 | Holmes | Ernest | | 1894 | 09/11/1915 | Summercourt | |
| Sapper | 132372 | Honeychurch | Richard | | 1895 | | Redruth | |
| Sapper | 132256 | Hosking | Nicholas Sidney | MM | 1891 | | Redruth | |
| Corporal | 132292 | James | Albert | | 1885 | | Carn Brea | |
| Sapper | 132251 | Jenkin | Alfred | | 1878 | | Redruth | |
| Sapper | 132309 | Jenkin | Albert | | 1891 | | Penzance | |
| Sapper | 132218 | Jewell | Samuel Charles | | 1896 | | Redruth | |
| Corporal | 132205 | Jewell | Wilbert | | 1894 | | St. Day | |
| Corporal | 132280 | Johns | Thomas Reed | | 1879 | | Four Lanes | |
| Sapper | 132290 | Johns | John Albert James | | 1895 | | Praze | to 185th |
| Sapper | 132332 | Johns | Alfred | MM | 1887 | | Redruth | |
| Corporal | 132169 | Johnson | Sidney James | MM | 1886 | | Newlyn East | |
| Sapper | 132216 | Keast | Thomas James | | 1893 | | Redruth | to 176th and 174th |
| Corporal | 132214 | Kent | John | | 1874 | | Illogan | |
| Sapper | 132374 | Kessell | Charles | | 1888 | | Four Lanes | to 185th |
| Sapper | 132200 | Kistle | William | | 1889 | | Penzance | |
| Sapper | 132371 | Knight | Alfred | | 1892 | | Scorrier | |
| Sapper | 132244 | Knott | Archibald | | 1895 | | Harrowbarrow | |
| Corporal | 132238 | Knowles | William Harold | | 1894 | 18/04/1918 | St. Day | |
| Corporal | 132213 | Laity | Percy | | 1892 | | Redruth | |
| Sapper | 132316 | Laity | William | | 1887 | | Camborne | |

| | | | | | | | |
|---|---|---|---|---|---|---|---|
| Sapper | 132254 | Maddern | Thomas | | 1890 | | St. Just | |
| Sapper | 132277 | Maddern | Thomas | | 1878 | | Redruth | |
| Sapper | 132198 | Martin | Albert Eric | | 1894 | | Carharrack | |
| Sapper | 132245 | Martin | Wesley | | 1876 | | Callington | |
| Sapper | 132246 | Martin | William | | 1895 | | Callington | |
| Sapper | 132271 | Martin | William H | | 1893 | | Falmouth | |
| Sapper | 132269 | Matthews | William T | | 1871 | | Summercourt | |
| Sapper | 132287 | Mayne | Charles | | 1887 | | Camborne | |
| Sergeant | 132221 | Menadue | Simeon John | DCM,MM | 1896 | | St. Day | |
| Sapper | 132181 | Michell | James Frederick | | 1893 | | Carharrack | |
| Sapper | 132313 | Millett | Thomas John | MM | 1896 | | Redruth | |
| Sapper | 132164 | Mottley | Robert Edward | | 1880 | | St. Day | |
| Sapper | 132220 | Moyle | William Francis | | 1896 | | Redruth | |
| Sapper | 132217 | Nancarrow | Francis | | 1881 | | Redruth | |
| L/Cpl | 132361 | Nankivell | Henry | | 1882 | 20/02/1916 | St. Agnes | |
| Sapper | 132325 | Ninnes | John Paynter | | 1895 | | Manaccan | |
| Sapper | 132275 | Oates | Edward | | 1886 | | Carn Brea | |
| Sapper | 132175 | Oliver | William G | | 1894 | | Carharrack | |
| Sapper | 132261 | Osmond | Thomas | | 1887 | 29/01/1916 | Helston | |
| CQMS | 132158 | Parker | George Leslie Hamley | | 1890 | | Redruth | |
| Sapper | 132366 | Parkin | John | | 1892 | 17/06/1916 | St. Agnes | |
| Sapper | 132247 | Paull | John | | 1892 | | Illogan | |
| Sapper | 132166 | Peters | William Henry | | 1884 | | Redruth | |
| Sapper | 132172 | Pett | Arthur Francis | | 1890 | | Redruth | |
| Sapper | 132333 | Phillips | William Thomas | | 1894 | | Newlyn East | |
| Sapper | 132227 | Polkinghorne | Charles | | 1893 | 14/04/1918 | Redruth | to 254th |
| Sapper | 132182 | Pooley | Frederick Gordon | | 1891 | | Redruth | to 252nd |
| Sergeant | 132196 | Pooley | Albert Seymour | DCM | 1894 | | Redruth | |
| Sapper | 132283 | Pooley | Edwin John | | 1881 | | Illogan | |
| Sapper | 132193 | Reynolds | William | | 1895 | | Four Lanes | to 176th |
| Sapper | 132296 | Reynolds | Joseph Thomas | | 1896 | | Manaccan | |
| Sapper | 132270 | Rickard | William Henry | | 1875 | | Grampound Road | |
| Sapper | 132311 | Roberts | Richard | | 1890 | 25/09/1917 | Camborne | to 170th |
| Sapper | 132215 | Rolling | Richard John | | 1899 | 23/03/1916 | Redruth | |
| Corporal | 132192 | Salmon | Wilfred | | 1889 | 15/10/1916 | Carn Brea | to 258th |
| Sapper | 132206 | Salmon | Thomas John | | 1876 | | Redruth | |
| Sapper | 132345 | Salmon | Charles | | 1895 | 10/12/1915 | Truro | |
| Sapper | 132178 | Scoble | Charles | | 1878 | | Redruth | |
| Sapper | 132202 | Sedgemore | Richard | | 1889 | | Illogan | to 183rd |
| Sapper | 132288 | Semmens | Albert | | 1885 | | Camborne | |
| Sergeant | 132155 | Sherman | William | MSM | 1880 | | Redruth | |
| Sergeant | 132265 | Siddall | John | | 1874 | | Menheniot | |
| Sapper | 132188 | Sinkins | Frederick E | | 1879 | | Redruth | |
| Sapper | 132173 | Sleeman | William Thomas | | 1887 | | Illogan | |
| Sergeant | 132262 | Sloman | John Henry | | 1879 | | St. Dennis | |
| Sapper | 132328 | Smith | Frederick Charles Thomas | | 1890 | | Redruth | |
| Sapper | 132180 | Stephens | Garfield | | 1895 | | Redruth | |
| Corporal | 132267 | Stephens | Richard Henry | | 1888 | | Helston | |
| Sapper | 132335 | Stephens | Ernest John | | 1885 | | Helston | to 253rd and I |
| Sapper | 132336 | Stephens | William James | | 1890 | | Helston | |
| Sapper | 132349 | Stephens | Richard John | | 1886 | | Illogan | |
| Sapper | 132306 | Stevens | Jowel | | 1884 | | Troon | |

| | | | | | | | |
|---|---|---|---|---|---|---|---|
| pper | 132237 | Symons | Robert Henry | 1882 | | Redruth | |
| pper | 132330 | Tamblyn | Howard | 1891 | | Newlyn East | |
| Cpl | 132284 | Temby | William Charles | 1896 | | Troon | to 177th |
| pper | 132352 | Thomas | Henry Wilson | 1895 | 25/12/1917 | St. Agnes | |
| pper | 132370 | Tonkin | William James | 1885 | | Redruth | |
| orporal | 132186 | Tregidgo | John James | 1880 | | Carharrack | |
| pper | 132369 | Treglown | Alfred | 1883 | | St. Agnes | |
| Cpl | 132317 | Treloar | Samuel John | 1889 | | Redruth | |
| orporal | 132234 | Triggs | John Andrew | 1886 | | Redruth | |
| apper | 132231 | Triniman | Norman | 1895 | | Redruth | |
| apper | 132299 | Tucker | James Henry | 1880 | | St. Agnes | to 256th |
| apper | 132312 | Uren | William Edward Harvey | 1898 | | Penzance | |
| orporal | 132329 | Verran | James Henry | 1890 | | Redruth | to 177th |
| apper | 132308 | Waller | William | 1866 | 09/04/1916 | Chacewater | |
| Sapper | 132358 | Waters | Joseph Stewart | 1896 | 10/12/1915 | Illogan | |
| Sapper | 132249 | Webb | John | 1874 | | Truro | |
| Sapper | 132179 | Webber | John | 1890 | | Redruth | |
| Sapper | 132354 | Whitford | William Charles | 1894 | | Carn Brea | |
| Sapper | 132373 | Wilcock | John | 1892 | 06/07/1917 | Scorrier | to 254th |
| Sapper | 132209 | Wilkinson | Harry | 1891 | 09/04/1916 | Redruth | |
| Sapper | 132272 | Williams | Earnest Charles Theodore | 1870 | | Gweek | |
| Sapper | 132289 | Williams | Mark | 1877 | | Camborne | to 3 Prov |
| Sapper | 132295 | Williams | Orlando | 1887 | | St. Columb Minor | to 179th |
| Sapper | 132229 | Wills | William | 1881 | | Redruth | |

The following soldiers were almost certainly amongst the 221 who were recruited from the 10th DCLI. Their serial numbers are part of those issued by Chatham and they all transferred to France on the same day as the 251st, however the relevant records are currently missing.

| Rank | Ser No | Surname | Christian Names | Award | Born | Died | Town | Comment |
|---|---|---|---|---|---|---|---|---|
| Sapper | 132230 | Ash | Erastus | | 1895 | | Carharrack | |
| Sapper | 132302 | Bale | William Charles | | 1894 | | Newlyn | |
| Sapper | 132276 | Barnard | James Palmer | | 1892 | | Camborne | To 174th |
| Sapper | 132346 | Barrett | Walter | | 1885 | | St. Columb Minor | |
| Sapper | 132327 | Bawden | Samuel | | 1895 | | St. Day | |
| CSM | 132159 | Buckingham | William G | | nk | | nk | |
| Sapper | 132341 | Congdon | Francis Cecil | | 1885 | | Four Lanes | |
| Sapper | 132211 | Corrick | Edward | | 1885 | | Penzance | |
| Corporal | 132156 | Crawford | Sidney William | | 1896 | 11/10/1917 | Redruth | |
| Sapper | 132243 | Gerry | Noah | | 1886 | | Calstock | |
| Sapper | 132301 | Hall | Richard John | | 1893 | | Penzance | |
| Sapper | 132252 | Hosking | William Thomas Henry | | 1892 | | Camborne | |
| Sapper | 132350 | Jenkin | Richard | | nk | | nk | |
| Sapper | 132331 | Middleton | William | | 1876 | | St. Day | |
| Sapper | 132258 | Nancarrow | Henry | | 1866 | | Gwinear | |
| Sapper | 132273 | Nicholls | Norman Emmanuel | | 1881 | | St. Keverne | |
| Sapper | 132190 | Oliver | Brenchley Thomas | | 1892 | | Truro | |
| Sapper | 132326 | Renfree | Thomas Henry | MID | 1896 | | Penzance | |
| Sapper | 132298 | Thomas | John H | | nk | | nk | |
| Sergeant | 132171 | Toy | William Thomas | | nk | | nk | Commissioned into Somerset LI |

| Rank | Number | Surname | Christian Names | Born | Date of Entry | Died | Town | Comment |
|---|---|---|---|---|---|---|---|---|
| Sapper | 132307 | Toy | Alfred | nk | | | nk | |
| Sapper | 132189 | Tregellas | Richard Hocking | 1893 | | | Redruth | |
| Sapper | 132324 | Treglown | Howard | 1891 | | 04/09/1916 | Carn Brea Village | With 7 DCLI when killed |
| Sapper | 132208 | Tremellen | Henry | nk | | | nk | |
| Corporal | 132348 | Wetherelt | Sydney Albert | 1892 | | | Redruth | |

The following have regimental numbers that reconcile with the numbers allocated for the recruitment of the 221 men to the 251st but, as there are no surviving Army Records, it cannot be stated with any proof that they were part of the 251st.

| Rank | Number | Surname | Christian Names | Born | Date of Entry | Died | Town | Comment |
|---|---|---|---|---|---|---|---|---|
| Sapper | 132194 | Bryant | Leonard | 1894 | 10/10/1915 | | Redruth | |
| Sergeant | 132184 | Carpenter | Richard James | 1883 | 10/10/1915 | | Perranporth | |
| Sapper | 132375 | Dwyer | William | 1880 | 10/10/1915 | | Penzance | |
| Sapper | 132170 | Francis | Walter Henry | 1884 | 10/10/1915 | | Redruth | |
| Sapper | 132320 | Goff | Henry | 1887 | 10/10/1915 | | Redruth | |
| Sapper | 132282 | Hayward | Sidney Montague R | 1884 | 10/10/1915 | | Penzance | |
| Sergeant | 132322 | Knuckey | William T | 1875 | 10/10/1915 | | Stithians | |
| Sapper | 132367 | Lawrence | John | 1890 | 10/10/1915 | | Scorrier | |
| Sergeant | 132318 | Murley | Thomas | 1897 | 10/10/1915 | 04/09/1916 | St. Just | |
| Sapper | 132337 | Palmer | Joseph Henry | 1887 | 12/12/1915 | | Chacewater | |
| Sapper | 132268 | Pitwood | Herman William | nk | 10/10/1915 | | nk | |
| Sapper | 132355 | Ray | Albertus | 1887 | 10/10/1915 | | Camborne | |
| Sergeant | 132255 | Stephens | William | nk | 10/10/1915 | | nk | |
| Sapper | 132347 | Tonkin | John F C | 1887 | 10/10/1915 | | St. Just | |
| Sergeant | 132240 | Vincent | Theophilus | 1889 | 10/10/1915 | | Linkinhorne | |
| Sapper | 132160 | Weatherhead | William John | 1887 | 10/10/1915 | | Camborne | |
| Sapper | 132195 | Webb | Wiiliam Henry | 1894 | 10/10/1915 | | Scorrier | |
| Sergeant | 132185 | Webb | George Walter | nk | 10/10/1915 | | nk | Commissioned in Notts & Derby |
| Sapper | 132223 | Wills | Joseph | | | | | |
| Sapper | 132285 | Woods | William John | 1871 | 10/10/1915 | | Camborne | |

The following joined 251Tunnelling Company either directly on entry to France, or from other Tunnelling Companies.

| Rank | Ser No | Surname | Christian Names | Born | Died | Town | Comment |
|---|---|---|---|---|---|---|---|
| Corporal | 104937 | Berryman | William Henry Coles | 1880 | | Goldsithney | from 170th |
| Sapper | 104981 | Eva | Frederick | 1884 | | Redruth | from 170th |
| Sapper | 112521 | Glasson | John Thomas | 1888 | 22/09/1916 | Ludgvan | |
| Sapper | 104912 | Glasson | Robert Henry | 1878 | | Praze | from 170th |
| Sapper | 132056 | Gribben | Arthur James | 1893 | | Redruth | to 179th |
| Sapper | 112533 | Hodge | Harry | 1887 | | Camborne | from 183rd |
| Sapper | 132043 | Jeffree | William Herbert | 1886 | | Camborne | |
| Sapper | 104911 | Jenkins | Richard John Keverne | 1891 | | Camborne | from 170th |
| L/Cpl | 144971 | Jose | William | 1888 | | Scorrier | |
| Sapper | 104929 | Laity | Edward | 1896 | 10/03/1918 | Beacon | from 170th |

| | | | | | | | |
|---|---|---|---|---|---|---|---|
| pper | 144974 | Lawry | Edward Thomas | 1893 | 28/12/1917 | St. Just | |
| pper | 132054 | Lean | Frederick | 1893 | | Redruth | |
| pper | 104983 | Parsons | Edward Charles | 1876 | | Mount Hawke | from 170th |
| pper | 104940 | Rascoe | William Martin | 1872 | | Praze | from 170th |
| pper | 132055 | Paull | James | 1890 | | Redruth | |
| pper | 132034 | Rule | John | 1890 | 10/12/1915 | Camborne | |
| pper | 104928 | Semmens | Charles Arthur | 1882 | | Gwinear | |
| orporal | 132293 | Solomon | William John | 1895 | 16/09/1916 | St. Austell | to 6th DCLI |
| ergeant | 132239 | Venton | Frederick Horton | 1890 | | Four Lanes | Commissioned in 2 DCLI |
| ergeant | 132212 | Walker | Henry | | | | |

The following men were part of the 10th DCLI but were transferred to other Tunnelling Companies.

| ank | Ser No | Surname | Christian Names | Born | Town | Comment |
|---|---|---|---|---|---|---|
| apper | 132242 | Barber | Richard | 1877 | Truro | to 3rd Prov |
| apper | 112751 | Cundy | Thomas | 1884 | Camborne | to 177th and 250th |
| apper | 112754 | Davies | Ernest Howard | 1895 | Camborne | to 175th and 3rd Prov |
| apper | 132263 | Oates | James Henry | 1881 | St. Just | to 183rd |
| Sapper | 132162 | Pascoe | William Curtis | 1884 | Redruth | to 3rd Prov and 174th |
| Sapper | 132253 | Peters | William James | 1890 | Redruth | to 175th and 171st |
| Sapper | 132203 | Phillips | James | 1888 | Redruth | to 250th |
| Sapper | 132183 | Richards | William Henry | 1876 | Redruth | to 3rd Prov |
| Sapper | 132264 | Semmens | Thomas | 1896 | Pendeen | to 176th and 254th |
| Sapper | 132343 | Stevens | Charles | 1879 | Helston | Discharged |
| Sapper | 132300 | Vigus | Frederick Hedley | 1890 | Gwinear | to 3rd Prov |
| Sapper | 132207 | Williams | John | 1879 | Redruth | to M Coy and 3rd Prov |
| Sapper | 132342 | Wilton | William Henry | 1889 | Illogan | to 175th and 256th |

*Appendix 3*

# In Remembrance

The following pages remember those men of 251 Tunnelling Company who were Cornish by birth, and those who, whilst born elsewhere, lived in and joined up in Cornwall at the outbreak of war. Some were with the 251ˢᵗ throughout their service, whilst others started with the 251ˢᵗ but were transferred, for whatever reason, to other tunnelling companies. Beneath each picture is their age, date of death and the location of the grave or remembrance panel.

**The Arras Memorial**

26 September 1917
Age 26
Bay 1

Sapper Richard Roberts (132311) was born in 1891 and came from Camborne. He was a tin miner, single and lived with his mother, Mrs EM Roberts. He originally joined the 251st but was transferred to 170 Tunnelling Company on 20 August 1916. He was reported missing and declared, in a letter from the War Office dated 17 June 1918, to have died on or before 25 September 1917.

## Béthune Town Cemetery

9 November 1915
Age 21
IV.F.86

Sapper Ernest Holmes (132334) was born in Kettering in 1895 but was living at Summercourt when he joined the 251st. He was single and was the son of Mr Robert Holmes and his late wife Anne. He had two brothers and four sisters. He was gassed in a mine on the Cambrin sector and died at the 5th Field Ambulance in Béthune.

10 December 1915
Age 20
IV.G.31

Sapper Joseph Stewart Waters (132358), a single man and a tin miner, was born in 1895 and was the only son of Joseph and June Waters of Illogan, near Redruth. He had two sisters. He was injured when a mine was blown, which killed three of his fellow sappers. He was transferred to the 33rd Casualty Clearing Station at Béthune but died of his wounds the same day.

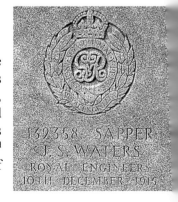

31 January 1916
Age 21
IV.H.81

Sapper William James Geach (132187), born in 1895 and single, came from Lanner, near Redruth, where he lived with his father and mother, William and Margaret Geach; he had an older brother, Joseph, and a younger sister, Millie. He died of wounds, possibly received from a mine blast on 29 January 1916, at the 33rd Casualty Clearing Station at Béthune.

25 December 1917
Age 23
VI.H.65

Sapper Henry Wilson Thomas (132352) was born in 1895. A single man who was a tin miner, he lived with his mother, Jane Thomas, in St Agnes. Although the records show no casualties occurring around Christmas Day 1917, he died of wounds that day at the 33rd Casualty Clearing Station in Béthune.

**Cambrin Military Cemetery**

10 December 1915
Age 26
E.5

Sapper John Thomas Glasson (132199) was born in Gwennap, near Redruth, in 1889. He was a single man and lived in Lanner with his mother, Mary Glasson. A tin miner, he was working in a mine when the Germans blew a gallery and was one of four miners and six Argyll & Sutherland Highlanders killed in that explosion.

10 December 1915
Age 25
E.5

Sapper John Rule (132034) came from Tuckingmill, near Camborne. He was a tin miner; although only twenty five years of age he had already served three years with the DCLI. He left behind his wife Mary Annie Rule, and three children. The youngest, James, was born twelve days after his father was killed. He was not part of the 10th DCLI but did sail with them on 9 October 1915 and was posted to the 251st on arrival in France.

10 December 1915
Age 19
E.5

Sapper Charles Salmon (132345) was born in 1896 and lived in Truro with his father and mother, Richard and Lottie Salmon. He had a younger brother, Richard and an older sister, Louise. His occupation was a storekeeper but he was made a tunnellers mate and, like both his fellow soldiers above, was killed when the Germans blew a mine on 10 December 1915.

29 January 1916
Age 30
E.2

Sapper Thomas Osmond (132261) had served with the 4th DCLI although he was a miner. He was born in 1887 in Helston, where he lived with his wife, Henrietta Osmond, and children, Annie Jane, who was just under three, and Thomas John, who was just under two when he died. It is not known how he died but a German mine was blown on the Cambrin sector the day before he died.

31 January 1916
Age 28
E.4

Sapper James Gleed (132191), born in 1888, used to work in a tin smelting works. He lived in Carharrack, near Redruth. He was married to Elizabeth and was the father of two children, Maurice and Hazel. It is not known how he died, but two German mines were blown on 28 and 29 January 1916 and so his death may have been related to these events.

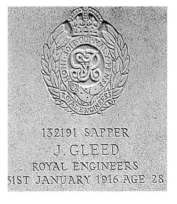

20 February 1916
Age 32
F.5A

Lance Corporal Henry Nankivell (132361) was born in 1882 and was a tin miner. Before the outbreak of war he already had done over five years of military service. He lived in St Agnes with his wife Annie and three children, James, George and Kathleen. He was killed in the Cuinchy sector along with three other miners on 20 February 1916 when the Germans blew a mine in one of the British galleries.

23 March 1916
Age 17
F.25

Sapper Richard John Rolling (132215) was a tin miner, born in Falmouth in 1899, so was only sixteen when he signed his attestation papers in April 1915, declaring himself to be nineteen years of age. He was single and lived with his Grandmother in Redruth. He had two older sisters, Lilian and Blanche, and a younger brother, William, aged sixteen, who was a member of 124 Company RDC in London.

9 April 1916
Age 24
F.39

Sapper Harry Wilkinson (132209), a single man and tin miner, died of consumption aged 24. He came from Redruth, where he lived with his mother, Elizabeth and his sister, also called Elizabeth. His father was working in British Columbia in Canada, his older brother Thomas, in London and his younger brother, James, in Delhi.

2 September 1916
Age 23
G.31

Sapper William Henry Harris (132338) lived at Helston with his father and mother, Thomas John and Charlotte Ann Harris. He had two younger brothers, Edward J, and Frederick Charles, as well as an elder sister, Elizabeth Mary. He was a labourer who had already seen service with the 4th Battalion DCLI. It is believed he died from wounds inflicted when the Germans blew a mine at the RWF Craters on 1 September 1916. His brother, Frederick Charles, fell on 31 May 1918 at the age of eighteen whilst serving with the 2nd Devonshires.

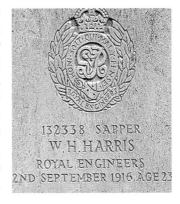

22 September 1916
Age 40
G.32

Sapper John Thomas Glasson (112521) was born in 1876 at Ludgvan, near Penzance. He was married to Mary and had three children, Joseph, Harold and Elsie. He was a labourer in a tin mine. At the age of 39 he enlisted in London and was sent to the 251st. No military records could be found for him and it is not known how he died.

10 March 1918
Age 21
N.12

Sapper Edward Laity (104929) was born in Porthleven, a single man who lived with his father, also Edward Laity, in Beacon, near Camborne. He was born in 1896, a tin miner who joined the Royal Engineers in London, but was sent to the 251st, having initially served three months with 170 Tunnelling Company.

**Franvillers Communal Cemetery Extension**

20 July 1918
Age 24
II.A.7

Lance Corporal Joseph James Francis (132260) was born in 1894, a tin miner who lived in Lanner, near Redruth. He was single at the start of the war but married Rosamund Ellen King at the beginning of 1918, just a few months before he was killed in action. He was originally with the 251<sup>st</sup>, but subsequently was transferred to 180 Tunnelling Company.

## Lapugnoy Military Cemetery

21 April 1916
Age 39
VI.E.10

Lieutenant Cecil Thorpe Landrey was born in Bodmin in 1882 to Joseph and Emily Landrey. He had a brother, Cyril Bertram, a sergeant, who was killed in 1916 whilst serving with the 11th Battalion Royal Fusiliers. A Civil Engineer, he married Eleanor in 1906 and they moved to Newcastle-on-Tyne. He was killed by a rifle grenade at Givenchy at 6 pm on 21 April 1916.

**The Loos Memorial**

9 April 1916
Age 49
Panels 4&5

Sapper William Waller (132308) was born in Haywards Heath, where his mother, Elizabeth lived. He was single and forty nine years of age when he was killed in action on 9 April 1916, although the date of birth on his attestation papers made him forty five years of age. A road foreman, living in Chacewater, he had already served with 3rd Battalion Rifle Brigade before the outbreak of war, when he joined 251 Tunnelling Company.

17 June 1916
Age 23
Panels 4&5

Sapper John Parkin (132366) was born in 1893 and, as a single man, lived with his father and mother, John and Susan, at St Agnes. He had two younger brothers, Mathew and Thomas, and a younger sister, Olive. A tin miner, he was killed on 17 June 1916 along with three other miners when the Germans blew a mine at Jerusalem Hill, near Cuinchy.

2 July 1916
Age 20
Panels 4&5

Sapper Richard John Brown (132222) was born in 1896. He was a single man who had two sisters, Alice and Gwendoline. He lived with his widowed mother, Edith, in St Day, near Redruth, where he was a tin miner. He was killed on 2 July 1916 alongside one of his fellow sappers, with four others injured, when the Germans blew a mine at Jerusalem Hill, Cuinchy.

15 October 1916
Age 27
Panels 4&5

Corporal Wilfred Salmon (132192) was born at Perranuthnoe in 1889 but lived with his wife Beatrice, his daughter and four sons in Portreath. A tin miner, he had two brothers and three sisters, and had transferred from 251 to 258 on 3 August 1916. His father and mother, John and Charlotte Salmon were to suffer an additional loss when his brother was killed with the Monmouthshire Regiment in 1918.

**Namps-Au-Val Military Cemetery**

14 April 1918
Age 25
II.C.35

Sapper Charles Polkinghorne (132227) was born in 1893, a carpenter by trade, who lived with his widowed mother, Ameila, in Redruth. He had two brothers, William and Andrew and two sisters, Ada and May. He was transferred to 254 on 13 March 1916 and was wounded in the 1918 German Spring Offensive. He was transferred to a Casualty Clearing Station where he died of his wounds.

**The Ploegsteert Memorial**

18 April 1918
Age 23
Panel 1

Corporal William Harold Knowles (132238) was born at Gwennap in 1895. He had five brothers and three sisters and lived at St Day, where he worked as a tin miner. He was single at the start of the war but married Ellen Millicent Harrison on 15 February 1918. He was killed on 18 April 1918 in action with the infantry during the German Spring Offensive, just two months after his wedding.

## Poperinghe New Military Cemetery

6 July 1917
Age 24
II.B.25

Sapper John Wilcock (132373) was a single man, a farm labourer aged twenty four, who lived in St Agnes. His father and mother, Francis and Mary Wilcock, lived at St Allen, near Truro, and he had three brothers and two sisters. He served with the 251st until transferred to 254 Tunnelling Company just five weeks before he was killed.

## The Thiepval Memorial

4 September 1916
Age 19
Pier & Face 6B

Sergeant Thomas Murley (132318) was nineteen years of age and came from St. Just; he was the son of Mrs T Oates, also of St. Just. He joined the 251st from 10th Battalion DCLI, but transferred to 1 Battalion DCLI whilst in France. He died with the DCLI on 4 September 1916 during the Battle of the Somme.

4 September 1916
Age 25
Pier & Face 6B

Private Howard Treglown (132324) joined 10th Battalion DCLI and was transferred to 251 Tunnelling Company on its formation. Twenty five years of age, he came from Carn Brea, Camborne and was the son of Mrs Eliza Treglown, who lived in Torquay. He had transferred whilst in France to 7th Battalion DCLI and was also killed on 4 September 1916 during the Battle of the Somme.

**The Tyne Cot Memorial**

11 October 1917
Age 21
Panel 80 to 82
and 163A

Corporal Sidney William Crawford from Redruth (132156) was twenty one when he died on 11 October 1917 during the Battle of Passchendaele. He was the son of Mrs Harriet Crawford, a widow from Redruth. He joined the 251st from 10th DCLI but transferred whilst in France to 1st Battalion DCLI.

# Other Cornish Miners on the Western Front

During the research into this book it was found that a number of Cornish miners became tunnellers on the Western Front, working for companies other than the 251st. So far it has been established that Cornishmen were in twenty of these units, as well as two of the Canadian Tunnelling Companies. The following notes give a very brief account of when the companies were formed and the sectors in which they operated. At the end of the appendix is a list of the Cornishmen who served with these companies.

**170 Tunnelling Company**
The Company was the first formed, in February 1915, and had at its core Norton-Griffith's clay kickers, some of whom were from his workforce working on a contract he held for a sewer system in Manchester. Thirteen Cornishmen joined the 170th around August 1915, all no doubt, as the direct result of a recruiting drive that promised those who joined up as tunnellers more pay than a man could earn working in the mines of Cornwall. Of those original twelve, seven were transferred to the 251st shortly after its formation; two went to the 252nd and another to the 179th; and three remained with the 170th. Two further Cornishmen joined when one was transferred from the 175th and one from the 182nd.

They were initially sent to the area around Givenchy, Cambrin and Cuinchy to counter mine against the growing German mining system that existed there. Following a move to Noeux-les-Mines, where they took over a sector from the French, they transferred again to the Hohenzollern Redoubt sector, where they are credited with blowing the two mines that heralded the start of the Battle of Loos.

By 1918 the 170th were in the Béthune area; the town and surrounding area was heavily bombarded during the German Spring Offensive, which caused many fires to break out. Fires that occurred in dugouts had given the tunnellers a lot of experience in fire-fighting, and these skills were put to good use in extinguishing more than twelve fires that were burning as a result of the bombardment in various parts of the city.

One of the Cornishmen who remained with the 170th, Sapper William Gliddon from Chacewater, went missing on or after 18 March 1916 and he was later declared to have died on this date, as the following extract from his records shows:

*Form DP*
*War Office London SW*
*9th March 1917*

*The Army Council has decided that the following soldier is to be regarded for official purposes, as having died on or since the date quoted against his name.*

*The next-of-kin should be notified accordingly on Army form B.104.82A, and the usual papers prepared, if this has not already been done.*

*Signed*

| Regtl. No | Rank & Name | Coy | Died on or since | Ref No |
|---|---|---|---|---|
| 104913 | Spr. Gliddon W.H. | 170th | 18.3.16 | E/322483/1 |

Sapper Gliddon is remembered on the Ploegsteert Memorial.

## 171 Tunnelling Company

The Company was formed under Captain Wellesley with a small number of specially enlisted miners and troops selected from the 1st and 3rd Battalions Monmouthshire Siege Company RE. Six Cornish miners served with this Company, four being posted to it directly upon enlistment, one transferring from the 251st and one from the 175th.

Although earlier the Dehra Dun Brigade of the Indian Corps had attempted, unsuccessfully, to attack a German trench using a 45 lb charge of guncotton placed at the end of a shallow tunnel, in March 1915 171

Tunnelling Company had the honour of firing the first British mine of the war, when they were operating in the Ypres area, at the Bluff and Hill 60.

After some time at Ploegsteert they moved to the Spanbroekmolen sector, facing Messines Ridge. Here they sunk two shafts from which they tunnelled two mines, driving one 150 yards and the other 320 yards, tunnelling at a rate of ten yards per shift, a remarkable feat; 20,000 and 40,000 lbs of ammonal were placed in the chambers ready for detonation as part of the assault on the Messines Ridge.

In a striking similarity to what happened with the 251st, Major HM Hudspeth MC DSO was appointed as Officer Commanding and remained with the unit until January 1919. Like Major Humphrys of the 251st, he had been in the Mine Inspectorate, being a junior Inspector of Mines in Yorkshire and the North Midlands prior to the war; and became HM Inspector of Mines for the Scottish Division after the war.

## 172nd Tunnelling Company

The 172nd was formed in early 1915 by Captain W Johnstone VC, a regular RE soldier who had won his Victoria Cross in September 1914 for his bravery in ferrying men and equipment across the bullet swept River Aisne. He handed over command of the Company to Captain C Hepburn, who had been a colliery manager prior to the war, shortly after its formation.

Only two Cornishman were with the 172nd, Sapper Courtenay who transferred from the 182nd and Sapper J Williams from Ludgvan, near Penzance, who was killed in action on 23 June 1916, and is buried at Ecoivres Miltary Cemetery, Mont-St.Eloi.

The Company started work after its formation at the Mound, near St. Eloi, where German mining activity had been intense and where they had blown up several British trenches, inflicting a large number of casualties. The 172nd were set to work with urgency to counter the devastating effect the German mines were having on the morale of the British infantry. They then moved headquarters to Berles, south of Vimy, with a forward base at Au Rietz, where they dug the Grange subway. Owing to the urgency with which this work had to be completed, the Company strength was increased to well over four figures by the number of infantrymen attached to the unit, this being quite usual on the Vimy sector for much of 1916 and early 1917.

During the Battle of Arras in 1917 they took the Schwaben and Volker subways from the Germans, cutting through the detonation wires to the explosives with which the subways had been booby trapped and, in the course of the action, taking many Germans prisoner. During the German Spring Offensive they, like so many other tunnellers, were stood to arms, fighting alongside the 12th Notts and Derbys at Villecholes, to the northwest of St. Quentin.

## 173 Tunnelling Company

The Company was formed under the command of Major G Williams and was based in the Fauquissart area. In January 1916, when 255 Tunnelling Company was formed, some of the officers and men from the 173rd were transferred to this new company.

Three Cornishman were in the 173rd, one joining directly, whilst the other miners were transferred from the 251st and the 183rd. In addition, there was one Cornish officer, Major TM Lowry from Camborne. He had studied at the Camborne School of Mines and worked at Dolcoath Mine prior to becoming a Mine Inspector in Nigeria. He returned to England at the outbreak of war and joined 3rd DCLI; suffering from frostbite, he was invalided back to England where he trained the newly formed 10th DCLI, subsequently being transferred from the DCLI to 174 Tunnelling Company. On 8 October 1915 he distinguished himself trying to rescue a fellow Cornishman, Lieutenant John Paynter, a school friend who also attended the CSM with him. He was awarded the Military Cross and, on 1 January 1916, was made up to temporary major and became Officer Commanding 173 Tunnelling Company. In June 1918 he was awarded the Distinguished Service Order, was mentioned in despatches twice, and after the war was awarded the Italian Order of the Crown.

The 173rd were moved to Hulluch, before moving again to Boesinge in the Yser Canal sector where, apart from their mining and defensive work, they built storage chambers into both sides of the canal bank in which bridge building equipment was stored, with the intention of it being ready for the commencement of bridge work immediately after an offensive against the Germans.

During the German Spring Offensive they were working on the Fifth Army's 'Green Line' near Wiencourt and the Company played an important role in destroying the bridges over the Somme at Frise, Cerisy and Sailly-Lorette in an attempt to slow the enemy advance. They also blew up bridges over the Rivers Arve and Luce and an ammunition dump, before being 'stood to arms' and acting in an infantry capacity. During the offensive they were combined with other RE troops in XIX

Corps into a composite force and became the 2nd Battalion RE, their OC, Major Lowry, taking command of the new battalion.

As a postscript to this précis about the 173rd, it is interesting to note that Captain D Richards MC, 173 Tunnelling Company, was the last tunneller to leave France.

## 174 Tunnelling Company

Upon its formation, under the command of Major B Danford, the Company was based in the Houplines area. Three Cornishmen joined this company directly, two sappers and one officer, Lieutenant John Paynter from St. Ives. Lieutenant Paynter, a Cornishman, had been a student at the Camborne School of Mines and was a mining engineer working in Rhodesia when war commenced. He was killed in action on 8 October 1915 when the enemy blew a camouflet whilst he was on listening duty; he is buried at Point 110 Old Military Cemetery, Fricourt. One further Cornishman was transferred from the 176th.

At Houplines mine shafts had to be sunk through waterlogged sand beds to the blue clay below; an innovative design by Lieutenant Nicol for a wooden caisson to sink through the sand was one of the Company's greatest contributions to military mining. Following their success with this procedure, they moved to Carnoy, Fricourt, Maricourt and La Boisselle, where they took over the work on no less than sixty six shafts from the French army.

Having moved to the Mametz sector for a year, they then went to Bullecourt where, during the German Spring Offensive of March 1918, the 174th, who were employed constructing machine-gun emplacements, lost two officers and thirty seven other ranks whilst fighting as infantry.

One of their finest achievements was when they were working on a long section of trench near Monchy-au-Bois, where they dug and wired over 9,000 yards of trench within the space of a week.

## 175 Tunnelling Company

The 175th were formed at Terdeghem under Major Cowan in April 1915 but did not move into action immediately and several of the men were attached to other companies to gain experience. Thirteen Cornishman joined the 175th, four sappers being transferred from 251 Tunnelling Company, whilst the others joined directly, but some being transferred from the 10th DCLI. One officer, Lieutenant Frank Thomas from St. Just, also joined directly. He had previously been the agent of the Levant

Mine in Cornwall before moving to the Gold Coast of Africa, where he contracted malaria. On his return to England at the outbreak of war he joined the 175th.

They were first assigned to the Railway Wood–Hooge–Armagh Wood area of the Ypres Salient where, with the Company being very short of officers, one officer, Lieutenant Cassels, set a record by having to spend six weeks in his dugout, virtually on duty twenty four hours a day.

Following a transfer to Hill 60, they then moved to Spanbroekmolen before being moved again to the Cambrai sector. Here their demolition skills came to the fore. As the Germans advanced during the Spring Offensive they destroyed the entrance inclines to the Hermies Catacombs to prevent them falling into enemy hands; these caves had been used by both the allies and the Germans before them as shelters to house several thousand men.

Three Cornishmen died whilst serving with the 175th: Lieutenant Thomas died on 1 October 1915 and is buried in Larch Wood (Railway Cutting) Cemetery; Sapper John Collins was killed on 2 July 1916 and Sapper Robert Glasson on 27 September 1916; both are buried at Ecoivres Military Cemetery, Mont St Eloi.

## 176 Tunnelling Company

This Company was formed in April 1915 at Lestrem by Captain Momber, who had previously been a civil engineer. He was injured in an explosion and on his return to active service he was promoted to major and made officer commanding of 177 Tunnelling Company; during his wartime career he was awarded the Military Cross and Distinguished Service Order. Like 175 Tunnelling Company, the 176th did not move into action immediately; but, in a similar fashion, several men were attached to other companies to gain experience. Four Cornishman joined the 176th, three directly upon enlistment and one transferred from the 251st; of the four, two were eventually transferred to other tunnelling companies.

The 176th were initially based at Bois du Biez, near Neuve Chappelle, before moving to Givenchy and then to Neuville St Vaast and Vimy. Here they were responsible for the construction of the Souchez, Gobron and Coburg subways and prepared mines for the attack on Vimy Ridge. Later, they returned to the Loos area, taking over the construction of the Hythe Tunnel, before joining in the pursuit to Mons during the Advance to Victory.

The tactics used by the 251$^{st}$ in encouraging the Germans to occupy craters before firing a mine beneath them was obviously a common strategy used by tunnelling companies, as the following citation in the *London Gazette* demonstrates:

*Captain Edward Marie Felix Momber. 176th Tunnelling Company RE.*

*For consistent good service and resource on several occasions, notably on Nov 25th 1915, near Givenchy, when, by firing a small charge, he induced the enemy to occupy the crater in considerable force. Two large charges were at once fired, by which about 50 of the enemy are believed to have been killed, and much damage done to the German parapet and galleries.*

Major Momber was killed on 20 June 1917 and has two craters named in his memory, one at Vimy from his time with the 176$^{th}$, and one at Railway Wood, where he was with the 177$^{th}$. He is buried in Lijssenthoek Military Cemetry.

## 177 Tunnelling Company

Captain Bliss formed the Company, the last of the eight original tunnelling companies authorised, at Terdeghem in June 1915. The 177$^{th}$ had quite a strong Cornish contingent, with twenty two men who joined in August 1915 following a recruitment drive in Cornwall; and two men were transferred in from 251 Tunnelling Company.

Two weeks after being formed, they were moved into an area facing Wytschaete, where they stayed until moving to Railway Wood, where they remained for the next two years. Railway Wood Cemetery is arguably the smallest cemetery maintained by the Commonwealth War Graves Commission and contains just twelve graves. These are for the eight tunnellers and four attached infantry of 177 Tunnelling Company who died underground during the defence of Ypres between November 1915 and August 1917.

March 1918 saw the Company working on the construction of the Fifth Army's 'Green Line' near Templeux-Le-Guérard, building machine-gun posts and dugouts, prior to the Advance to Victory which saw them move through Albert, Cambrai and on to Sambre. On one occasion they were constructing a bridge over the River Phonelle when they came under attack. Dropping tools and picking up rifles, the tunnellers successfully repulsed the attack and then continued with the repair of the bridge.

Sapper James Aubrey Jones from Camborne was awarded the Military Medal on 11 May 1917, and although an entry appears in the *London Gazette* on 9 July 1917, there is no citation, as was frequently the case by this time of the war. The only other reference to his medal is in his Service Record, which notes that it was awarded for *Bravery in the Field*.

One Cornishman, Sapper William Nancarrow from Wendron, died on 22 August 1917 and is commemorated on the Tyne Cot Memorial.

## 179 Tunnelling Company

The Company was formed in Rouen in October 1915 under Captain Alabaster and commenced work at La Boiselle under the direction of Captain Piraud, a French mining engineer. Twelve Cornishmen were in the 179th, three transferring in from the 251st, one from the 170th, two from the 177th, one from the 3rd DCLI, and five were posted direct.

The 179th covered a large front of some seven miles, from Beaumont Hamel to south of La Boisselle. During the Battle of the Somme, on 1 July 1916 at 07.28 am, Captain Young of the 179th blew what is claimed to be the largest ever man made crater, the Lochnagar Crater, which was over 300 feet wide and seventy feet deep. Cecil Lewis, piloting an observation aircraft, reported debris rising as high as 4,000 feet, whilst the 60,000 lbs of ammonal explosive destroyed some 300–400 feet of dugouts in a German stronghold known as the Schwaben Höhe.

The 179th remained in this area during the Spring Offensive and saved a significant amount of time and labour when working with the 2nd Australian Tunnelling Company by placing mines in old dugouts and mine galleries with which they were familiar, having mined the sector since 1916. As a measure designed to slow the German advance, the mines were detonated, blocking the road in three separate places and thus a difficult task had been executed with efficiency.

Three Cornishmen who served with the 179th died during the course of the war.

Sapper Elliott was killed in action on 14 September 1915, less than one month after joining the 179th on the 19 August 1915.

Sapper Webb, who had served with the 3rd DCLI for eighteen months before transferring to the Royal Engineers, was killed in action 18 July 1916 and is buried in Albert Communal Cemetery Extension.

Sapper Watters, who was conscripted on 14 September 1916, when eighteen and a half years of age, died from gas poisoning on 13 July 1917 and is buried in Lijssenthoek Military Cemetery.

## 180 Tunnelling Company
The Company was formed at Labuissière in the autumn of 1915 under Captain WE Buckingham. Four Cornishmen joined the 180th directly and one was transferred from the 251st; Captain Matthew Roach MC, one of those who joined the 180th from the outset, was transferred to the 255th on 6 January 1916, and a further one to the 252nd on 8 August 1917.

The 180th were sent to the Loos sector, where the infantry urgently required the support of the tunnellers to build saps and communication trenches as quickly as possible in preparation for the Battle of Loos of September 1915. During the battle itself, they provided further support by bringing up supplies of bombs, ammunition and other essential equipment. They subsequently moved to the Givenchy area; and then showed great courage during the 1918 Spring Offensive, fighting alongside the infantry and holding their own line between St. Emilie and Ronssoy. After being relieved they withdrew to Hamelet and, on the evacuation of Péronne and Sailly Laurette, went on to destroy a total of twenty one bridges, two camps, a large RE ammunition dump and many billets, thus slowing the advance and preventing the Germans taking possession of these assets.

The Company were in Albert during the Advance to Victory of 1918 when, operating under difficult circumstances, they cleared thirty two unexploded charges and over one hundred land mines. They were under constant attack from machine guns and high explosive shells, whilst the operation was made even more difficult by the need to wear gas masks because of the enemy's use of gas shells.

The Armistice on 11 November brought no respite for the Company, however, as on 15 November 1918, four days after the Armistice and the cessation of hostilities, one officer and seven other ranks were killed when clearing mines and booby traps in Epéhy.

Captain George James Cunnack MC, who came from Helston, was also with the 180th. He had studied at the CSM before the war and won a Military Cross when, with another officer and a sapper, he rushed a sentry at a dugout; after knocking out an officer he drew his pistol and captured two officers and 201 other men. He died on 17 October 1918 and is buried at Serain Community Extension at Aisne.

Two further Cornishmen who served with the 180th also died in action. Sapper Peters was killed on 6 January 1918 and is buried at Epéhy Wood Farm Cemetery; whilst Lance Corporal Francis was killed on 20 July 1918 and is buried in Franvillers Communal Cemetery Extension.

## 181 Tunnelling Company

The Company was formed at Steenwerck in the autumn of 1915 under Captain JN Cash. Two Cornish miners served with the 181st, Sapper Collins, who joined directly, and Sapper Tresidder was transferred to the Company on 14 October 1917 on returning to France after a period in hospital when wounded whilst serving with the 183rd. His service with the 181st was short lived, though, as on 20 November 1917 he was wounded again and, following his return to hospital in England, was discharged on 15 June 1918.

The 181st were based in Cordonnerie, north of Neuve Chapelle, and then moved south to Vimy Ridge, establishing their headquarters in Berles, where they worked very quickly to curtail German offensive mining. At one stage, whilst extending one of their galleries, they broke through into an enemy gallery where, although no Germans were to be found, they could be heard working close by. A listening officer was stationed for two days in a three foot by two foot sap from where he listened to the conversations taking place in the German mine, gleaning much useful information. When it was decided that further listening would be of little use the decision was taken to blow the mine.

By the spring of 1917 they were in Ronville, a small commune just south of Arras, working alongside the New Zealand Tunnelling Company in the caves and tunnels in that area. These caves provided infantry billets for up to 24,000 men and, by linking the caves with tunnels, they also provided shelters for headquarters and signals. The 181st moved forward during the Advance to Victory through Bapaume and Caudry.

## 182 Tunnelling Company

Five Cornishmen joined the 182nd, one from the 253rd, one from the 4th DCLI, one joining directly on attestation, one joining directly on conscription, and Sapper Dunn transferred from the 251st. He was only to remain with the Company for just under two months, as he was transferred to 176 Tunnelling Company on 20 March 1917. He was discharged on 11 March 1919 and died three years later on 3 November 1922. He was diagnosed with fibrosis of the left lung, which was deemed attributable to his war service.

The 182nd worked near Bailleul, then took over the newly begun Kruisstraat deep mines near Wytschaete before being moved to Armentières, followed by yet another move to the Berthonval sector, where they constructed subways in Zouave Valley.

Assigned to the Canadian Corps, they took part in the action on the Scarpe and at Hill 70. By the time of the German Spring Offensive, the 182nd were in the very southern part of the area occupied by the Fifth Army and were scattered over a wide area around St Quentin. They were ordered to Fargniers, where they were used as emergency infantry in the defence of both No. 1 and No. 2 Keeps, before taking part in a fighting withdrawal to Baboeuf, where the Company dug a new line of defences.

During the Advance to Victory they were involved in the capture of the Bellicourt Canal Tunnel. At Landrecies an interesting incident occurred when the infantry halted to allow the 182nd to continue towards a road bridge to check for booby traps. The Germans blew the bridge as the 182nd approached but the tunnellers rushed forward over the lock bridge and, although outnumbered two to one, secured the lock, taking fourteen German prisoners and capturing one machine gun. After rapidly removing ten charges, they swiftly rebuilt a road bridge to allow the infantry and tanks to cross, thus enabling the British advance to continue.

**183 Tunnelling Company**
This Company was formed in Rouen in October 1915 under Captain HCB Hickling, where thirty one Cornishmen joined the Company directly, mainly as a result of Norton Griffith's recruitment drive, with two others being transferred in, one from the 251st and one from the 177th.

They were sent to Fontaine-le-Capp where they took over from the 2nd Wessex Field Company and were, in fact, the first tunnelling company to be based south of the River Somme. From there they moved to Carnoy-Maricourt to prepare mines and saps and flame thrower and machine gun emplacements for the Fourth Army attack on the Somme on 1 July 1916.

A move up into Belgium brought with it a change of work. The village of Poelcapelle was almost flattened in the action that took place in the days and weeks leading up to the Battle of Poelcapelle on 9 October 1917. The allies deployed twelve tanks during this battle but unfortunately all were lost, with four taking a direct hit and eight becoming bogged down in the mud. The area around Poelcapelle became known as a tank graveyard and 183 Tunnelling Company was charged with the dismantling and clearing of the wrecked tanks.

After moving to Boeschepe, which came under attack during the Spring Offensive, the 183$^{rd}$ joined six other tunnelling companies in digging an urgently needed defensive line from Reninghelst to St. Omer. For a period these seven Tunnelling Companies were the only troops holding this rear defensive line, until relieved by the French.

December 1915 brought some of the worst days for any of the tunnelling companies when eight men and one officer of this Company, all Cornishman, were killed when the Germans detonated a mine near Fricourt. The dead were Lance Corporal F Eddy and Sappers J Eva, WG Jenkin, and CL Matthews, who are buried in Citadel New Military Cemetery, Fricourt. Sappers S Davey, S James and J Higgins are commemorated on the Thiepval Memorial and Sapper R Thomas is on the Ploegsteert Memorial. Lieutenant HL Twite, a mining engineer of some repute, who came from St. Agnes, and who had travelled to mining areas in South America before the war, was also killed in the explosion and is buried in Citadel New Military Cemetery, Fricourt.

Another Cornishman, Sapper L Kent, was gassed on 2 December 1916, and is also buried in Citadel New Military Cemetery, Fricourt; whilst Sapper James Higgins from Camborne was killed on 13 December 1915 and is remembered on the Thiepval Memorial.

On 31 May 1916 Sapper Richard Wills was discharged with bronchitis, aggravated by active service and climate (damp). He died the following year on 26 December 1917 and is buried at St. Day Church.

On 17 July 1916 Lance Corporal Tresidder was discharged with TB brought about by an explosion. He died just over five months later on 3 February 1917 and is buried in Redruth Cemetery.

## 184 Tunnelling Company

The Company was formed in Rouen in October 1915 under Captain J Gwyther and immediately proceeded to Suzanne on the Somme to work at Maricourt. Four Cornishmen were with the 184th, three who joined directly and one who was transferred from the 251st.

From the Somme they moved to Vimy where, in the lead up to the attack at Arras in April 1917, they became actively engaged on Fish Avenue Tunnel, helping to construct emplacements for heavy trench mortars. They also worked with the New Zealand Tunnelling Company on the cave systems in Arras, which were used as deep shelters, making exits and entrances and connecting the caves with tunnels. Later, in June 1917, they were transferred to Nieuport, where they constructed underground shelters and dugouts along the coast to La Panne, a task made more difficult by having to tunnel through sand.

On the move again, they were sent to the Ypres–Brielen sector, where they were attached to the Tank Corps, building tank crossings over the Ypres Canal and rough causeways across Kemmelbeke and Lambardtbeke. This work, at times, had to be done under fire from enemy artillery; the enemy's use of gas shells made their work even more difficult because of the need to wear gas masks when working.

One Cornishman, Sapper Penwarden, was killed in action just eleven days before the Armistice on 30 October 1918. He is buried in Kezelberg Military Cemetery.

## 250 Tunnelling Company

The 250th was formed in Rouen in October 1915 under Captain C Cropper. Four Cornishman were in the 250th; Second Lieutenant George Jewell Roberts, Sapper Thomas Cundy, who was transferred from the 177th on 12 February 1916 and Sapper James Phillips. Sapper Phillips was one of the 221 men transferred to the RE from the 10th DCLI; he sailed from England on the same day as the rest of the men but was sent to the 250th, not the 251st. Sergeant Beare joined directly on his return home from the Sudan, whence he returned after the war.

They were sent to La Clytte in the Ypres sector, where they commenced digging an offensive mining system, working on some 300 yards of the front. Following their move to Bois Carré, they became custodians of 3000 yards of tunnels, which were difficult to work given the very wet nature of the ground.

At Petit Bois they experimented with the use of a mechanical excavator, a smaller version of that which was used to dig the London Underground. Although early results were good, with it cutting through the clay at a rate of two feet per hour, it had a tendency to 'dive' and eventually the experiment was abandoned. The excavator was left behind and to this day lies buried under eighty feet of Flanders soil.

They remained in this sector to undertake what was perhaps the hardest work of the whole Messines offensive scheme. At Maedelstede, the 250th drove a tunnel over 533 yards in length, which they completed just one day before the Messines Ridge mines were blown on 7 June 1917.

The success of this operation was to turn sour when, on 10 June, the Germans fired two large mines, causing the main gallery to collapse, and as a result twelve men were trapped inside. Such is the comradeship between miners that their colleagues dug for six days to get to the trapped men. Having cleared the clay, they found eleven bodies and one man, Sapper Bedson, who was miraculously still alive, his only complaint being that he was thirsty and that it had been a long shift.

Six days later, on 17 June 1916, Second Lieutenant Roberts from Perranporth, another CSM engineer, was killed; he is buried in Bailleul Community Extension.

### 252 Tunnelling Company

The Company was formed in Rouen under Captain Trower in 1915 and just a week later was moved to Toutencourt (Somme) to begin work at the Redan. Six Cornishmen were in the 252nd, one joining directly, whilst five were transferred into the 252nd; two from the 251st, one from the 170th, one from the 180th and one from the 175th. All survived the war with the exception of Sapper McCarthy, who was accidentally killed when a gun was discharged in his billets on 24 November 1915. He is buried in Varennes Military Cemetery.

During the preparations for the opening of the Battle of the Somme they, with the support of 1900 attached infantry, constructed nine mines opposite Serre and opened 3,400 yards of galleries, which accommodated some 1,900 infantry troops. All of this work took them just seven months; a significant achievement.

On 1 July 1916, at the start of the Battle of the Somme, at 7.20 am, they blew the first mine at Hawthorn Ridge. The mine chamber was some one hundred foot deep and contained 40,600 lbs of ammonal. It created a crater some forty feet deep and 300 feet across, destroyed a German redoubt and deep dugouts, and killed many German infantry.

The 252nd operated in this area throughout the battle; after one attack took prisoner fifty five German soldiers and three officers from a deep dugout. After the battle they continued working in the same sector, clearing and repairing captured German dugouts, as well as conducting salvage operations, road making and building further dugouts for the infantry and signallers.

Eventually they moved to Boursies, where they were engaged in defensive operations during the German Spring Offensive, placing mines on the Albert to Bapaume road, which when detonated would severely slow German progress.

## 253 Tunnelling Company

Many sources state that 253 Tunnelling Company was formed under Major EB Currie in January 1916. This date, however, produces a conundrum, as the service records of Sapper William Henry Dumble, a Cornishman, show that he transferred to the 253rd from the 8th DCLI on 2 November 1915 and was re-mustered as a tunneller on 7 January 1916.

Ten other Cornishmen joined the Company, six joining directly, whilst two transferred from the 251st, one from the 179th, and one from the 8th DCLI.

The 253rd moved to Sailly-Labourse and the northern front line areas of the old Loos battlefield, to the north of the Vermelles to Hulluch road, where they commenced mining with urgency. Before their arrival in the area two enemy mines had already been fired and shortly after they started work two more were fired, all of them under the British front line.

On moving to the La Bassée Canal to Souchez River sector, they were, along with other tunnelling companies, urgently constructing subways to protect the infantry from German trench mortar attacks. Following this, sections of the Company were assigned to an RE tramway companies to help in the laying and maintaining of tramways and light railways running from the lorry parks to the battery positions of the Fifth Army.

They were in Wiencourt when the 1918 German Offensive commenced and, in a bizarre incident, they were stood to arms with orders to halt a panic retreat by French troops on the Guillaucourt to Marcelcave road, which they did by placing trucks across the road to halt the stampede.

They were subsequently absorbed into Major General Grant's Force as part of a composite battalion and dug in as infantry in front of Marcelcave, whilst at the same time they were still actively engaged in building a number of defensive posts. After a confused defensive battle and suffering ten killed and more than ninety wounded, the Company was scattered and the men attached themselves to any infantry unit in the vicinity. The Company was later reformed at Boves, near Amiens. One Cornishman, Sapper William Parkyn from Wadebridge, was killed on 9 November 1917. He is buried in Mendinghem Military Cemetery.

## 254 Tunnelling Company

254 Tunnelling Company was formed in England under Major HW Laws and went to Gallipoli in December 1915, where it was merged with XVIII Corps' Mining Company; Major Laws was awarded a DSO whilst in Gallipoli.

In spring 1916 the Company was sent to France and went to the Givenchy area to work. The 254th were billeted in Béthune, on the opposite side of the La Bassée Canal to the 251st, and they worked very closely together, which might explain why seven Cornishmen were transferred from other companies into the 254th. One sapper, John French from Redruth, joined them after returning from Arizona in 1915, where he had been working in the mines with his brother, Harold. He was awarded the Military Medal and was commissioned on 22 February 1918. Lieutenant French was awarded the Military Cross 'for conspicuous bravery' in 1919 whilst serving with the 178th; after the war he returned to the USA, to Detroit.

Part of the 254th was sent to assist with the digging of mines under the Messines Ridge. Sergeant Gerald Minear was killed on 3 July 1917 whilst Sapper John Wilcock was killed in action on 6 July 1917, a month after the ridge was blown. They both lie buried in Poperinghe New Military Cemetery.

The Company then moved south and worked in the Arras area. Sapper Charles Polkinghorne died of his wounds at a Casualty Clearing Station on 14 April 1918 and lies buried in Namps au Val British Cemetery.

One incident in the 254th, which perhaps above all others typifies the comradeship amongst miners during the war, and which resulted in a posthumous award of the Victoria Cross, took place in 1916:

*On the morning of 22 June 1916, Sapper
William Hackett and four other miners of 254
Tunnelling Company were driving a tunnel
towards the enemy lines below the cratered
surface of the Givenchy sector of northern
France. At about one-quarter of the way
towards the German trenches at a depth of
about 35 feet, the timbered gallery 4' 3" high by
2' 6" wide was still in the early stages of
development; it was served by a single shaft –
the Shaftesbury Shaft. At 2.50am the explosion
of a heavy German mine (the Red Dragon)
blew in 25 feet of the tunnel, cutting the five
men off from the shaft and safety. On the
surface, a rescue party was immediately*

*Sapper William Hackett
VC – 254th Tunnelling
Company RE. His VC is
proudly displayed at the
Royal Engineers Museum at
Chatham. (Picture courtesy
of the Tunnellers Memorial)*

*organised. After two days of digging an escape hole was formed
through the fallen earth and broken timbers, and the tunnellers
contacted. William Hackett helped three men to safety. However,
with sanctuary beckoning, and although himself apparently
unhurt, he refused to leave until the last man, seriously injured
22 year-old Thomas Collins of the Swansea Pals (14th Battalion,
the Welsh Regiment), was rescued. His words were said to be, "I
am a tunneller, I must look after the others first". The rescuers
worked on, but were frequently immobilized by German shelling
and mortaring of the shaft-head. Conditions above and below
ground became more treacherous by the minute. Eventually the
gallery collapsed again, entombing the two men. Both still lie
beneath the fields of Givenchy today.
(From www.tunnellersmemorial.com)*

## 255 Tunnelling Company

The Company was formed in January 1916, with some of the officers
and men transferring from 173 Company. Three Cornishmen served with
the 255th; Sapper Lewis Russell Miners, who went to France on 24 July
1915, Sapper Harry Glasson, who transferred from the 251st to the 256th,
then joining the 255th on 18 August 1918, and Captain M Roach MC,
who initially joined 180 Tunnelling Company and was transferred to the
255th on 6 January 1916. Captain Roach was a remarkable officer who,
in 1916, was awarded the Military Cross for carrying a charge with a

lighted fuse into a gallery and placing it in position. After the mine was blown, he descended to ascertain the results and although overcome by fumes refused to leave before the ordinary relief.

On 3 March 1916 a new Officer Commanding, Major Liddell, was appointed, transferred from 251 Tunnelling Company.

The Company moved into the Red Lamp–Neuve Chapelle sector to work before transferring to the Somme, where they were engaged in the digging of subways. An interesting task was given to them when in the Calonne Souchez area on the Vimy front. They constructed two 50,000 gallon underground water reservoirs, which were to supply the forward troops during the attack on Vimy Ridge in April 1917.

Sapper Miners was killed in action on 14 March 1916 and is remembered on the Loos Memorial. Captain Roach MC was killed on 2 July 1916 when a trench mortar landed on the shaft entrance where he was helping to rescue miners who had been overcome by gas; he is commemorated on the Arras Memorial.

## 256 Tunnelling Company

The 256th, formed in July 1916 under Captain WT Wilson, was the last tunnelling company to be formed. Three Cornishmen, all from the 251st, were transferred to the 256th on 8 November 1916, 6 April 1917 and 31 October 1917 respectively.

The Company was initially sent to Vimy before transferring to Nieuport, where it had the difficult task of constructing shelters in the dunes; these were to house the infantry whose job it was to protect the crossings on the Yser. This sector was crucial, as the support line ran to the east of the Yser; there were only three temporary bridges and all stores and materials had to cross these.

During the Advance to Victory, the 256th were responsible for the repair and maintenance of the railway line from Trônes Wood to Ytres and Fins and in due course removed six tons of explosive from the track. On moving forward, they found, at Bellenglise, what must have been one of the largest shelters constructed by the Germans, as it extended to Magny la Fosse, almost one mile away. It contained thirty five living chambers, two magazines for explosives and an engine room with two lighting sets. It was suspected that the shelters had been booby trapped and so it was decided that captured German engineers should assist in making it safe.

## 258 Tunnelling Company

The Company was formed at Rouen in April 1916 under Captain AW Pope and was sent to Noeux-les-Mines. Four Cornish sappers served with this Company, one transferring from the 251st, one from the 176th, one from the 258th; and one entered directly.

During the German Spring Offensive, the tunnellers were stood to arms under Captain Gilchrist, entering the line in front of Rosières-en-Santerre; after constructing 500 yards of fire trench they effectively managed to hold off an enemy advance with rifle fire alone. After several days of fighting, they successfully fought a dogged rearguard action near Vrély, before withdrawing to Moreuil, and then reforming on 31 March 1918.

Corporal Salmon was killed in action on 15 October 1916, just two months after joining the Company. He is commemorated on the Loos Memorial.

## Canadian 2nd Tunnelling Company

The Company was formed from recruits in Alberta and British Columbia under Major RW Coulthard and, on arrival in France, was sent to the Ypres sector to work alongside 171 and 250 Tunnelling Companies RE. For most of the war they worked in the Reninghelst sector, where they were building shelters for battle headquarters, underground dressing stations, subways, troop shelters and trenches for cables.

Some Cornishmen working in Canada at the outbreak of war signed up with the Canadian tunnelling companies. Sapper William Michael Tucker from Caerhayes was one such soldier who joined the 2nd Canadian Company; he was killed in action on 5 June 1917 and is buried in Lijssenthoek Military Cemetery.

## Canadian 3rd Tunnelling Company

The 3rd Canadian Tunnelling Company was formed under Captain AW Davis, formerly of 177 Tunnelling Company RE, at St. Marie Cappel in January 1916. It consisted of the original mining sections of the 1st and 2nd Canadian Divisions who were withdrawn from their positions south of Ypres and transferred into this new company.

The 3rd took over the front line at Spanbroekmolen, facing Messines Ridge, and then moved to Hill 60.

Two Cornishmen who had been living overseas joined this Company. Sapper William Worth, originally from Bude but living in Canada, joined the 3rd Canadian in August 1915; he was killed in action on 19 October 1916 and is buried in Lijssenthoek Military Cemetery. Sapper Frank Reynolds, originally from Liskeard, was living with his wife in Los Angeles in 1917. He attested on 18 September 1917 and was killed in action just three days before the Armistice, on 8 November 1918. He is buried in St. André Communal Cemetery, near Lille.

| Rank | Ser No | Surname | Christian Names | Award | Born | Died | Town | Comment |
|------|--------|---------|-----------------|-------|------|------|------|---------|
| 170th Tunnelling Company | | | | | | | | |
| Sapper | 104914 | Butler | Charles Henry | | 1890 | | Camborne | to 252nd |
| Sapper | 102961 | Gilbert | Charles Henry | | 1877 | | Camborne | |
| Sapper | 104913 | Gliddon | William Henry | | 1877 | 18/03/1916 | Chacewater | |
| Sapper | 120781 | Jenkin | Frank | | 1893 | | Carn Brea | |
| Sapper | 102964 | Langman | Thomas | | 1877 | | Camborne | to 252nd |
| Sapper | 104931 | Uren | Herbert Stanley | | 1892 | | Camborne | |
| Sapper | 104930 | Richards | Thomas | MM | 1888 | | Hayle | to 179th |
| 171st Tunnelling Company | | | | | | | | |
| Sapper | 104944 | Ashcroft | William | | | | Truro | to 257th and 173rd |
| Sapper | 102490 | Green | Charles | | 1883 | | Penzance | to 173rd |
| Sapper | 104979 | Martin | Samuel John | | 1870 | | Constantine | |
| Sapper | 216560 | Parkin | Foster | | 1895 | | Illogan | |
| 172nd Tunnelling Company | | | | | | | | |
| Sapper | 112716 | Williams | James Henry | | 1889 | 23/06/1916 | Penzance | |
| 173rd Tunnelling Company | | | | | | | | |
| Sapper | 58923 | Roberts | William Thomas | | 1894 | | Saltash | |
| 174th Tunnelling Company | | | | | | | | |
| Major | | Lowry | TM | MC | 1875 | | Camborne | to 173rd |
| Sapper | 211704 | Michell | Stanley | | 1898 | | Redruth | |
| Lt | | Paynter | John | | 1885 | 08/10/1915 | St. Ives | |
| 175th Tunnelling Company | | | | | | | | |
| Sapper | 112750 | Collins | John | | 1892 | 02/07/1916 | Redruth | |
| Sapper | 104938 | Glasson | Robert | | 1880 | 27/09/1916 | Long Rock | |
| Sapper | 132441 | Manuell | Joseph Telfer | | 1893 | | Redruth | to 185th |
| Sapper | 104892 | Mundy | Edwin | | 1869 | | Camborne | to 176th |
| Sapper | 132443 | Nicholls | William Henry | | 1876 | | Mount Hawke | to 170th |
| Sapper | 102995 | Osborne | Samuel John | | 1888 | | Camborne | to 252nd |
| Lt | | Thomas | Frank | | 1884 | 01/10/1915 | St. Just | |
| 176th Tunnelling Company | | | | | | | | |
| Sapper | 211837 | Aver | Samuel | | 1887 | | St. Agnes | |
| Sapper | 203508 | Hosking | William John | | 1888 | | Troon | |
| Sapper | 132437 | Tonkin | William | | 1895 | | St. Just | to 258th |

### 77th Tunnelling Company

| | | | | | | | | |
|---|---|---|---|---|---|---|---|---|
| Sapper | 104908 | Bishop | Charles | | 1879 | | Penzance | |
| Sapper | 104997 | Burgoyne | John Michael | | 1880 | | Camborne | to 174th |
| Sapper | 104903 | Carlyon | William Thomas Walter | | 1879 | | Camborne | |
| Sapper | 104896 | Carter | William | | 1873 | | Praze | |
| Sapper | 104898 | Gilbert | William John | | 1896 | | Camborne | |
| Sapper | 112886 | Gray | James Harold | | 1885 | | Redruth | |
| Sapper | 104905 | Griffin | John | | 1894 | | Carn Brea | |
| L/Cpl | 104890 | Hocking | John Leslie | | 1893 | | Camborne | |
| Sapper | 104891 | Johns | Samuel Garfield | | 1891 | | Camborne | |
| Sapper | 104901 | Jones | James Aubrey | MM | 1892 | | Camborne | |
| Sapper | 112753 | Nancarrow | William Josiah | | 1888 | 22/08/1917 | Wendron | |
| Sapper | 102993 | Pearce | William Joel | | 1891 | | Camborne | |
| Sapper | 104904 | Peters | Francis Henry | | 1895 | | Camborne | |
| Sapper | 102988 | Peters | Richard James | | 1890 | | Camborne | |
| Sapper | 104897 | Phillips | William Henry | | 1896 | | Camborne | to 179th |
| Sapper | 104902 | Roach | Jacob | | 1885 | | Camborne | to 179th |
| Sapper | 104907 | Salmon | Theo Jefferson | | 1886 | | Camborne | |
| Sapper | 102999 | Smitherham | Samuel James | | 1892 | | Camborne | |
| Sapper | 102990 | Swan | Albert Charles | | 1894 | | Camborne | |
| Sapper | 104893 | Wills | Norman | | 1891 | | Camborne | to 183rd |

### 179th Tunnelling Company

| | | | | | | |
|---|---|---|---|---|---|---|
| Sapper | 148532 | Davey | Joseph | 1891 | | Redruth | |
| Sapper | 112537 | Davies | William Blair | 1884 | | Camborne | to 3 Prov |
| Sapper | 102822 | Elliott | William | 1875 | 14/09/1915 | Camborne | |
| Sapper | 216561 | Foss | Robert John | 1888 | | Redruth | |
| Sapper | 211887 | Watters | Sidney | 1898 | 13/07/1917 | Praze | |
| Sapper | 155779 | Webb | Frederick | 1878 | 18/07/1916 | Ponsanooth | |
| Corporal | 52306 | Yates | Francis John | 1882 | | Liskeard | |

### 180th Tunnelling Company

| | | | | | | | |
|---|---|---|---|---|---|---|---|
| Sapper | 90509 | Peters | Thomas John | | 1895 | 06/01/1918 | Callington | |
| Captain | | Roach | Mathew | MC | 1888 | 02/07/1916 | Paul | to 255th |
| Sapper | 146531 | Roberts | James | | 1886 | | Perranporth | to 252nd |
| Sapper | 132442 | Venner | Clifton | | 1892 | | Redruth | |

### 181st Tunnelling Company

| | | | | | | |
|---|---|---|---|---|---|---|
| Sapper | 91904 | Collins | Thomas John | 1897 | | Redruth |

### 182nd Tunnelling Company

| | | | | | | |
|---|---|---|---|---|---|---|
| Sapper | 211791 | Courtenay | William Ewart | 1890 | | St. Just | to 172nd |
| Sapper | 211989 | Honeychurch | James | 1888 | | Redruth | |
| Sapper | 211836 | Paull | Harry | 1895 | | Chacewater | to 170th |

### 183rd Tunnelling Company

| | | | | | | |
|---|---|---|---|---|---|---|
| Sapper | 102991 | Brokenshire | Llewellyn | 1896 | | Camborne | to 3 Prov |
| Sapper | 104939 | Bryant | Frank | 1881 | | Penzance | |
| Sapper | 121844 | Davey | Stephen | 1873 | 01/12/1915 | St. Agnes | |

| Rank | Number | Surname | Forename | | Year | Date | Place | Transfer |
|---|---|---|---|---|---|---|---|---|
| L/Cpl | 121843 | Eddy | Frederick | | 1876 | 01/12/1915 | Linkinhorne | |
| Sapper | 112535 | Eva | John | | 1895 | 01/12/1915 | Camborne | |
| Sapper | 112756 | Higgins | James | | 1883 | 01/12/1915 | Camborne | |
| Sapper | 112748 | James | Stanley | | 1893 | 01/12/1915 | Illogan | |
| Sapper | 112529 | Jenkin | William Gendall | | 1896 | 01/12/1915 | Camborne | |
| Sapper | 112600 | Jenkin | Abertrall William | | 1877 | 20/10/1917 | Camborne | |
| Sapper | 144924 | Jenkin | Albert | | 1879 | | St. Hiliary | to 254th |
| Sapper | 112641 | Kent | Lambert | | 1894 | 02/12/1915 | Camborne | |
| Sapper | 144926 | Lanyon | James H | | 1890 | | St. Mabyn | |
| Sapper | 121802 | Lemin | Edward | | 1879 | | Goldsithney | to 173rd and 1 |
| Sapper | 104895 | Lovelock | William John | | 1886 | | Troon | |
| Sapper | 104899 | Matthews | Charles Leonard | | 1895 | 01/12/1915 | Camborne | |
| Sapper | 132263 | Oates | James Henry | | 1881 | | St. Just | |
| Sapper | 104936 | Thomas | Richard | | 1889 | 01/12/1915 | Penzance | |
| Sapper | 104932 | Tonkin | William Henry | | 1884 | | Camborne | |
| L/Cpl | 121875 | Tresidder | John | | 1876 | 03/02/1917 | Redruth | to 3 Prov |
| Sapper | 144927 | Tresidder | Peter | | 1893 | | St. Day | to 181st |
| Lt | | Twite | Harold Llewellyn | | 1879 | 01/12/1915 | St. Agnes | |
| Sapper | 112644 | Verran | Percival | | 1895 | | Camborne | |
| Sapper | 121650 | Webber | Joseph | | 1886 | | Redruth | |
| Sapper | 121649 | Wills | Richard | | 1869 | 26/12/1917 | St.. Day | to 252nd |

**184th Tunnelling Company**

| Rank | Number | Surname | Forename | | Year | Date | Place | Transfer |
|---|---|---|---|---|---|---|---|---|
| Sapper | 121834 | Campbell | Harry | | 1879 | | Bude | |
| Sapper | 102994 | Eslick | James | | 1885 | | Camborne | |
| Sapper | 146642 | Goldsworthy | Foster Jackson | | 1893 | | Camborne | to 258th |
| Sapper | 193344 | Penwarden | Samuel | | 1890 | 30/10/1918 | Camborne | |

**250th Tunnelling Company**

| Rank | Number | Surname | Forename | | Year | Date | Place |
|---|---|---|---|---|---|---|---|
| Sergeant | 146569 | Beare | Leonard Rumming | | 1890 | | Penzance |

**252nd Tunnelling Company**

| Rank | Number | Surname | Forename | | Year | Date | Place |
|---|---|---|---|---|---|---|---|
| Sapper | 132519 | McCarthy | James | | 1878 | 24/11/1915 | Camborne |

**253rd Tunnelling Company**

| Rank | Number | Surname | Forename | | Year | Date | Place | Transfer |
|---|---|---|---|---|---|---|---|---|
| Sergeant | 132125 | Courts | James | | 1875 | | Truro | |
| Sapper | 151313 | Dumble | William Henry | | 1890 | | St. Austell | |
| L/Cpl | 151491 | Dunstan | John Thomas | | 1893 | | Camborne | |
| Sergeant | 151297 | Minear | Gerald Clair | | 1895 | 01/07/1917 | St. Columb Major | to 182nd |
| Sapper | 132124 | Nicholls | Joseph | | 1886 | | Mount Hawke | to 250th |
| Sapper | 151354 | Parkyn | William | | 1893 | 09/11/1917 | Wadebridge | |
| Sapper | 151530 | Solomon | Harold | | 1896 | | Newquay | |
| Sapper | 102996 | Wills | Thomas Henry | | 1890 | | Camborne | to 179th |

**254th Tunnelling Company**

| Rank | Number | Surname | Forename | | | Year | Date | Place |
|---|---|---|---|---|---|---|---|---|
| Lieut | 144962 | French | John Thomas | MC MM | | 1892 | | Redruth |

**255th Tunnelling Company**

| Rank | Number | Surname | Forename | | Year | Date | Place |
|---|---|---|---|---|---|---|---|
| Sapper | 147812 | Miners | Lewis Russell | | 1895 | 14/03/1916 | Grampound Road |

| | | | | | | | |
|---|---|---|---|---|---|---|---|
| h Tunneling Company | | | | | | | |
| er | 158434 | Tregunna | Clifford | | | St. Austell | to 185th |
| h Tunnelling Company | | | | | | | |
| per | 363047 | Hendy | Reginald | 1896 | | Bugle | |
| adian 2nd Tunnelling Company | | | | | | | |
| per | | Tucker | Michael Williams | 1889 | 05/06/1917 | Caerhayes | |
| adian 3rd Tunnelling Company | | | | | | | |
| per | | Reynolds | Frank | 1890 | 08/11/1918 | Pensylva | |
| per | | Worth | William | 1890 | 19/10/1916 | Bude | |

Whilst writing this book many people have provided me with information regarding the Cornish miners who served on the Western Front with the tunnelling companies. I would like to build on this knowledge and would welcome any information the reader might have, however trivial it may seem. Small pieces of information all help to complete the jigsaw. Any additional data would be very much appreciated, so if you have anything that you believe may add to this book, please contact me through my publishers, or through my web-site, www.robertkjohns.co.uk

Many thanks,
Robert K Johns

# Bibliography

**Books and Articles:**

Aiken, A., *Courage Past: A Duty Done: Glasgow Highlanders at High Wood, July 1916,* A.Aiken 1971

Anon. Diary of a Nursing Sister on the Western Front 1914-1915, 1915 Gutenberg Project

The Atlanta Constitution, 8 March 1912, p. 29.

Barrie, A., *War Underground: The Tunnellers of the Great War.* Spellmount, Kent, 2000.

Beckett, I., *Haig's Generals.* Pen & Sword, London, 2006.

Blackwell, H.C., *From a Dark Stream: The story of Cornwall's Amazing People and Their Impact on the World.* Dyllansow Truran, Truro, 1986.

Blades, G.D., The Battle of the Lys: The British Army on the Defensive in April 1918. M. Phil. thesis, King's College, London.

Bridgland, T. & Morgan, A., *Tunnel-Master and Arsonist of the Great War: The Norton-Griffiths Story.* Pen & Sword 2003.

Brittain, F., *Arthur Quiller Couch: A Biographical Study of Q.* Cambridge University Press, Cambridge, 1947.

Brown, F. *Audio Recordings of Tunneller, 256302 Sapper Fred Brown, 251 Tunnelling Company RE.* At http://jeremybanning.co.uk/2013/04/03/audio-recordings-of-tunneller-256302-sapper-fred-brown-251-tunnelling-company-re/, accessed January 2014.

Carter, C., *Cornish Engineering: 1801–2002: Holman, Two Centuries of Industrial Excellence in Camborne.* Trevithick Society, Camborne, 2001.

Cave, N and Robinson, P., *The Underground War:Vimy Ridge to Arras.* Pen & Sword, Barnsley, 2011.

Commonwealth War Graves Commission

Cornwall Family History Society

Cunnife, R., *The Militia Regiments of Alberta 1901 to 1939.* Riveredge Foundation, Calgary, 1971.

Dale-Logan, Lieutenant Colonel. D., 'The difficulties and dangers of mine rescue work on the western front; and mining operations carried out by men wearing recue apparatus.' *Transactions of the Institute of Mining Engineers* 1918-19 Vol LVII, pp197-222.

Davies, A., *Tunnelling Reminiscences: Mining on the Western Front.* Canadian Institute of Mining, 1919.

Davies, W., *Underneath Hill 60.* Random House, London, 2011.

De Groot, G., *Douglas Haig 1861–1928.* Unwin Hyman, London, 1988.

Doig, J.F., *A Life Worthwhile: Major James A.H. Church.* Mailman Publishing, Lawrencetown, NS, 1990.

DCLI Museum, Bodmin

Durham Mining Museum

Finch, H., *The Goodchilds of Grundisburgh: Four Brothers in the First World War.* Privately printed, 2008.

Finlayson, D., *Crumps and Camouflets: Australian Tunnelling Companies on the Western Front.* Big Sky, Newport, NSW, 2010.

Fletcher, M. 'Lethal relics from World War One are still emerging.' *Telegraph* online, 12th July 2013. At http://www.telegraph.co.uk/history/britain-at-war/10172232/Lethal-relics-from-WW1-are-still-emerging.html, accessed January 2014.

Glasgow Highlanders Association, Newsletter, 2nd Special Edition, Feb 2011

Graham, H.W., *The Life of a Tunnelling Company.* Catherall, Hexham, 1927.

Grieve, W. & Newman, B., *Tunnellers: The Story of the Tunnelling Companies, Royal Engineers, during the World War.* Navy & Military, reprint of 1936 original.

Hampson, T., *A Medical Officer's Diary and Narrative of the First World War.* At http://myweb.tiscali.co.uk/philsnet/

Hay, S., *Historic Lucknow.* Asian Educational Services, India, 1939 edition (15 Feb 2007)

Anon, History of the Royal Engineers, Chatham, 1932

Hodge, A., *Notes from Charles Kenyon, Descendant of Major Humphrys.* 1983. Private Papers

Institute of the Royal Engineers Chatham, *Work of the RE in the European War 1914-19, Geological Work on the Western Front,* Chatham, W. J. Mackay & Co Ltd, 1922

Jones, S. Extracts from Humphrys Diaries

Jones, S. Extracts from the Diary of WE Buckingham, Royal Engineers, Chatham

Jones, S., *Underground Warfare 1914–1918,* Pen & Sword, London, 2010

La Boisselle Project

Memorial Museum Passchendaele, Zonnebeke

Morrison, TA, *Cornwall's Central Mines: The Southern District 1810-1895*. Alison Hodge, Penzance, 1983.

National Archives, Kew

Office of National Statistics

Payne, D., 'The British clay kickers and moles of the Western Front.' *Journal of the Western Front Association*, 30th December 2008.

Payne, D., 'The far from anonymous Major Sir John (Jack) Norton-Griffiths on the Western Front.' *Journal of the Western Front Association*, 30th December 2008.

Payton, P., *The Cornish Overseas: A History of Cornwall's 'great Emigration',* Cornwall Editions Limited; Revised and updated edition (10 Feb 2005)

Poldark Mine Museum

Royal Engineers, *Register of Tunnelling Company Officers: Roll of Honour, France, Flanders and Gallipoli 1915–1918*. RE War Records Office, Chatham, *1925.*

Royal Engineers, *251ˢᵗ Tunnelling Company War Diary,* RE War Records, Chatham

Skinner, R., *Kitchener's Camp at Seaford; A First World War Landscape on Aerial Photographs*. English Heritage, London, 2011.

Stirling, J., *The Territorial Divisions 1914–1918*. JM Dent & Sons, London, 1922.

Synton, E, *Tunnellers All*, 1918. Unknown

TES Connect, 'The issue – school leaving age', *TES* newspaper, 10th September, 2010.

Tomaselli, P., *The Battle of the Lys 1918: Givenchy and the River Lawe.* Pen & Sword, London, 2011.

The Trevithick Society, Camborne, Cornwall

Warner, P., *The Battle of Loos*. Wordsworth, Ware, 1976.

White, H., *One and All: The History of the Duke of Cornwall's Light Infantry.* Tabb House, Padstow, 2006.

Wyrall, E., *The History of the Duke of Cornwall's Light Infantry 1914-1919*, Methuen & Co London, 1932, reprinted by Naval & Military Press

**Periodicals:**
*The Cornishman*
*Liverpool Echo*
*London Gazette*
*Manchester Evening News*
*The Northern Mine Newspaper, Australia*
*The Straits Times, Singapore*
*Western Times*
*Western Daily Mercury*

**Online sources:**
All accessed January 2014.
http://www.1914-1918.invisionzone.com
http://www.1914-1918.net/haigs_michael_despatch.html
http://www.1914-1918.net/oob.htm
http://www.1914-1918.net/tunnelcoyre.htm
Above 4 sites, with courtesy of Chris Baker's site The Long, Long
   Trail
http://www.awm.gov.au/collection/records/awm4/16/4/awm4-16-4-
   1.pdf
http://www.clydesite.co.uk/clydebuilt/viewship.asp?id=2276
http://www.collectionscanada.gc.ca
http://www.cornish-mining.org.uk
http://www.cornwall-calling.co.uk/
http://www.csmassociation.com/downloads/140508-CSM-WW1-
   records-draft-1-cr.pdf
http://www.engineering-
   timelines.com/scripts/engineeringItem.asp?id=1190
http://www.firstworldwar.com/bio/nortongriffiths.htm
http://www.greatwar.co.uk/french-flanders-artois/museum-wellington-
   quarry.htm
http://www.greatwar.co.uk/research/maps/british-army-ww1-trench-
   maps.htm
http://www.gutenberg.org/cache/epub/17369/pg17369.txt
http://www.gwpda.org/medical/liceand.htm
http://www.hampsthwaite.org.uk/595
http://www.haynes.co.uk/wcsstore/SuttonPublishing/images/PDFs/S3
   6908spread3.pdf
http://www.hut-six.co.uk

http://lib.militaryarchive.co.uk/library/Corps-
    Histories/library/Corporals-All-With-the-Special-Brigade-1915-191
    9/files/assets/basic-html/page2.html

http://www.raoc.websitetoolbox.com (forum)

http://www.reubique.com

http://www.rhf.org.uk/gh/GH_News_SE2.pdf

http://www.slsa.sa.gov.au

http://www.tallfaily.co.uk/susan/dudleywhite.html

http://www.tes.co.uk/article.aspx?storycode=6057675, accessed
    January 2014.

http://www.themanchesters.org/wd191712.html

http://www.truroschool.com/wp-content/uploads/sites/2/2013/07/100-
    WW1-stories.pdf

http://www.tunnellers.net/corps_history/british_tunnellers_war_diary.
    doc

http://www.tunnellersmemorial.com

http://www.ucis.pitt.edu/nceeer/1986-623-3-Getty.pdf, career patterns
    in the soviet democracy

http://www.webmatters.net/txtpat/?id=454

*  *  *

## Measures Cross Reference

*Metric to Imperial*

| | |
|---|---|
| 1 metre | 3.28 feet |
| 1 metre | 1.09 yards |
| 1 kilometre | 0.62 miles |
| 1 kilogram | 2.21 lbs |

*Imperial to Metric*

| | |
|---|---|
| 1 foot | 0.31 metres |
| 1 yard | 0.91 metres |
| 1 mile | 1.61 kilometres |
| 1 lb | 0.46 kilograms |
| 1 cwt | 50 kilograms |
| 1 ton | 1000 kilograms |

# Index